A Boone and Crockett Club Field Guide to

Measuring and Judging Big Game

A BOONE AND CROCKETT CLUB FIELD GUIDE TO MEASURING AND JUDGING BIG GAME

First Edition 2003

Library of Congress Catalog Card Number: 2003104875
ISBN Number: 0-940864-44-4
Published July 2003

Published in the United States of America
by the
Boone and Crockett Club
250 Station Drive
Missoula, MT 59801
406/542-1888
406/542-0784 (fax)
www.booneandcrockettclub.com

A Boone and Crockett Club Field Guide to Measuring and Judging Big Game

By Philip L. Wright and William H. Nesbitt

Edited by Eldon L. "Buck" Buckner and Jack Reneau

Illustrated by DeWayne Williams and Larry Jensen

Layout and design by Julie T. Houk

Sponsored by Leupold and Stevens

LEUPOLD
MADE RIGHT, MADE HERE?

BOONE AND CROCKETT CLUB®
Missoula, Montana
2003

FOREWORD
Third Generation... Once Removed

Eldon "Buck" Buckner

The Boone and Crockett Club's trophy scoring system is relatively new, copyrighted in 1950 after 12 years of development. It was readily accepted in both the United States and Europe as the standard by which North American big game species is judged. A history of records keeping is included as a separate chapter in this guide for those interested.

Grancel Fitz of New York was a major developer of the B&C scoring system, as well as the first sportsmen to take trophy heads of all North American big game species. One of Grancel's ambitions was to publish an inexpensive guide for the average sportsman that would explain the scoring system for the various big game species. In 1963, Grancel's soft cover *How to Measure and Score Big Game Trophies* was published by *Outdoor Life*, with a foreword by both B&C Records Committee chairman Samuel Webb and Grancel's friend and famous gun writer, Jack O'Connor. Unfortunately, Grancel died as the book was being published.

I am very familiar with Grancel's guide, as it was the only thing available on measuring in 1969 when I organized the first measuring seminars for Arizona's records program. Already out of print, I was finally able to acquire three dozen copies from Grancel's widow, Betty. Boone and Crockett measurers began being trained in a similar fashion some six years later, which led to the next publication on measuring technique.

This guide may be considered a third generation distant relative of Grancel's little book, directly descended from Wm. Harold Nesbitt and Philip L. Wright's *Measuring and Scoring North American Big Game Trophies* published by the Boone and Crockett Club in 1985, and later updated and revised in 1997 and 2000. These editions, originally developed in response to the glaring need for a comprehensive instruction manual for training new official measurers, mentioned earlier, continue to be revised and published for that purpose.

As the interest in selective hunting and big game trophies continues to increase and new generations become involved, there is an increasing demand for more information on the subject. This publication is intended to answer questions about how to score big game trophies, with numerous illustrations,

Eldon "Buck" Buckner is the current Chairman of the Boone and Crockett Club's Records of North American Big Game Committee. First appointed an Official Measurer in 1968 while serving as a U.S. Forest Service range conservationist in Arizona. He has served as Judges Panel Chairman, Consultant and Judge for Boone and Crockett Club Awards Programs since 1990. Buck is a past board member of the Arizona Desert Bighorn Sheep Society and Oregon's Bighorn Sheep Restoration Project, and presently serves on Oregon Wildlife Department Access and Habitat Council and Oregon State Shooting Association. He is a NRA certified rifle and pistol instructor with state championship titles won in Arizona and Oregon. He is an international hunter with many years of guiding experience in the West.

as well as to give helpful pointers on field judging trophy quality in the field on the hoof. It also provides answers to many common questions about distribution of species categories and trophy entry procedures. Too, I think most hunters will find the comparison photos of World's Record heads and those barely meeting minium scores both interesting and helpful in evaluating what they see in the field.

Hunting is a special outdoor pursuit that has many different facets for each of us. Some of us take it much more seriously than others. However, we should all remember that it is meant primarily as outdoor recreation, although a recreation that involves the eternal natural cycle of life and death and thus should be engaged with only the utmost respect for the animals pursued. If the information on the following pages helps you achieve greater appreciation, satisfaction, or enjoyment from your all-too-few days afield, then its objective will have been met. ■

TABLE OF CONTENTS
A Boone and Crockett Club Field Guide to
Measuring and Judging North American Big Game

TABLE OF CONTENTS
Continued

RECORDS KEEPING
A Brief History

William H. Nesbitt

1

The Boone and Crockett Club was founded in 1887 by Theodore Roosevelt and a group of his close friends. The Club was established because of their mutual love of hunting and the native big game animals of North America. At that time, there were no closed hunting seasons or other regulations on the taking of game. But even this early, the Club and its members were foresighted and well ahead of current need. The concept of "Fair Chase" was introduced in the bylaws of the Club. Early on, the publications of the Club spelled-out certain acts, such as burning animals from their dens or "crusting" (running down deer and other animals on deep snow), as being against the Club's philosophy. The significance of this declaration is fully understood only when you realize that these acts were neither illegal nor unethical to the general public in those days.

During the days of his presidency, Theodore Roosevelt would gain well-justified recognition as our "Conservation President." His contributions were legion. Under his administration, the following were created: 21 reclamation projects, 150 national forests, 51 federal bird reservations, four national game preserves, five national parks and 18 national monuments. A number of conservation conferences and commissions were also established. His reign in office set a firm foundation for today's conservation and wildlife management in the United States.

The actual coining of the word conservation was by Gifford Pinchot, the far-sighted forester and Club member who was the first head of the U.S. Forest Service. Pinchot developed the word conservation to define the whole complex of actions necessary to properly manage our natural resources in good stewardship. As he defined it, it meant in the most simple

James L. Clark, former vice director of exhibits at the American Museum of Natural History, New York City, was photographed at the end of a successful grizzly bear hunt in British Columbia in 1925. Jimmy was a member of the committee that created the Club's universally recognized scoring system for native North American big game.

terms, "wise use". Conservation today should therefore mean full rational use of renewable resources (such as forests and wildlife) and the lowest rational usage of non-renewable resources (such as minerals, coal, and oil).

By the end of Roosevelt's presidency, things were indeed looking bleak for many of the native big-game animals. Bison were reduced to a few hundred head, and whitetails and other big game were largely eliminated from the states east of the Mississippi. Many folks believed there could be no other final result of civilization's push West than the extinction of all big game. Even several prominent Club members such as William T. Hornaday and Madison Grant agreed with this dismal forecast. During the years of 1906-1922, Hornaday worked industriously to establish the National Collection of Heads and Horns at the Bronx Zoo in New York City. Opened in a large building in 1922, the collection was dedicated to "...the vanishing big-game animals of the world." Today, the collection is the property of the Boone and Crockett Club and is on display at the Buffalo Bill Historical Center, Cody, Wyoming. It includes many fine specimens such as the L.S. Chadwick Stone's sheep, acclaimed by many as the finest specimen of North American big game ever taken. It is an outstanding collection that will give much enjoyment to the hunter and other serious students of our native North American big game. More importantly, today it represents the outstanding success stories of modern game management and conservation that have restored our game populations to healthy levels that can be utilized in consumptive uses such as hunting, as well as just the plain enjoyment of watching these magnificent creatures in the wild.

The presence of the National Collection and the beginning of conservation in the 1920s spurred interest in the recording of measurements of our big game animals. In 1932, Prentiss N. Gray, a long-time Club member, authored the first big-game records book of the Club titled, Records of North American Big Game. It was published with the cooperation of the National Collection of Heads and Horns. The measurements were quite simple, the length of skull, or the longer antler or horn, plus a basal circumference. This volume was followed in 1939 by a second edition called North American Big Game. Again, simple measurements were used to rank the trophies listed. This edition is especially notable for several fine chapters on subjects related to measurement and big game. Grancel Fitz had a lengthy chapter on his idea of a complex system of measurements that would, as a result

Grancel Fitz measuring the main beam circumference on the A.S. Reed Alaska-Yukon moose (240-7/8 points) that is currently in the Boone and Crockett Club's National Collection of Heads and Horns. Not only was Grancel on the committee that developed the Club's copyrighted scoring system, but he and his wife Betty coordinated the day to day records-keeping activities of the Club for many years from their New York City apartment.

of the numeric score total, rank trophies naturally. This chapter furnished an excellent counterpoint to the rival system being used by Dr. James L. Clark, a noted taxidermist and long-time Club member, for his Big Game Competitions. Fitz's system was a bit more objective, while Clark's was more imaginative in its measurements. Both systems had serious flaws but were superior to the single measurement ranking used in the 1932 and 1939 records books of the Club.

The Second World War years occupied all of America fully. Following the war, as things began to return to normal, interest was renewed in the Boone and Crockett Club in big-game records keeping. In 1947, the Club began annual Big Game Competitions, with the winners being chosen by a Judges' Panel. But, while these proved popular, they also pointed out the subjective nature of awards based entirely upon the opinions of a group of judges, no matter how well qualified. There was an obvious need for an objective system that could be applied by sportsmen to their own best trophies.

In 1949, Samuel B. Webb, well-known to major Club members and a close friend of both Grancel Fitz and Dr. James L. Clark, was chosen to chair a special committee of the Club to devise an equitable, objective measurement system for the big game of North America. In addition to Webb, Fitz and Clark, the committee members included Dr. Harold E. Anthony, Milford Baker and Frederick K. Barbour. All were experienced big game hunters with strong interest in giving recognition to exceptional big game trophies. The committee worked during the year to arrive at the system adopted by the Boone and Crockett Club in 1950. Prior to publication, the system was circulated to 250 sportsmen, biologists, and other interested parties for their comments. Once adopted, the system quickly became established as the universally accepted standard for measuring native North American big game.

That the committee was able to evolve a comprehensive system meshing the best points of both Fitz's and Clark's systems is a distinct tribute to the committee chair, Samuel B. Webb. Fitz and Clark were both very intelligent and accomplished men with full confidence that their own system was the best. Drawing on his friendships with both, Webb was able to focus the committee to arrive at the resulting system that combined the stronger points of both systems into a system so objective and fair that it continues today in essentially the same form as originally formulated.

The scoring system depends upon carefully taken measurements of the enduring trophy characteristics to arrive at a numerical final score that provides instant ranking for all trophies of a category. By measuring only enduring characters (such as antlers, horns, and skulls) rather than skin length or carcass weight, the measurements may be repeated at any later date to verify both the measurements and the resulting ranking in each category. Anyone doubting the correctness of a particular trophy's ranking can readily prove or disprove his own contentions by a simple replication of the measurements.

The system places heavy emphasis on symmetry, penalizing those portions of the measured material that are non-symmetrical. This results in even, well-matched trophies scoring better and placing higher in the rankings than equally developed but mismatched trophies, a result that most people readily agree with and accept. For those antlered trophies with unusual amounts of abnormal antler material, non-typical categories were developed to give them recognition as they would be unduly penalized in the typical categories.

With the newly established system in place, the Club set about rescoring those trophies previously recognized in the 1932 and 1939 records books. The results, along with other trophies qualifying under the new system, were published in 1952 in **Records of North American Big Game**. This is then the "first" records book that used the Club's copyrighted scoring system adopted in 1950. It was followed by editions in 1958, 1964, 1971, 1977, 1981, 1988, 1993 and 1999. The

North American Big Game Awards Programs Summary

Year	Chairman	Program	Location
1947	Samuel B. Webb	1st Competition	Am. Mus. of Natural History, New York, NY
1948	Samuel B. Webb	2nd Competition	Am. Mus. of Natural History, New York, NY
1949	Grancel Fitz	3rd Competition	Am. Mus. of Natural History, New York, NY
1950	Grancel Fitz	4th Competition	Am. Mus. of Natural History, New York, NY
1951	Milford Baker	5th Competition	Am. Mus. of Natural History, New York, NY
1954	Milford Baker	6th Competition	Am. Mus. of Natural History, New York, NY
1956	Donald S. Hopkins	7th Competition	Am. Mus. of Natural History, New York, NY
1958	George Browne	8th Competition	Am. Mus. of Natural History, New York, NY
1960	Arthur C. Popham	9th Competition	Am. Mus. of Natural History, New York, NY
1962	Elmer Rusten	10th Competition	Am. Mus. of Natural History, New York, NY
1964	Elmer Rusten	11th Competition	Carnegie Museum, Pittsburgh, PA
1966	John E. Hammet	12th Competition	Carnegie Museum, Pittsburgh, PA
1968	George E. Norris	13th Competition	Carnegie Museum, Pittsburgh, PA
1971	Frank Cook	14th Competition	Carnegie Museum, Pittsburgh, PA
1974	Bernard Fashingbauer	15th Awards	Marriott Motor Hotel, Atlanta, GA
1977	Philip L. Wright	16th Awards	Denver Mus. of Natural History, Denver, CO
1980	Glenn St. Charles	17th Awards	Radisson-Muehlebach Hotel, Columbia, MO
1983	Dean Murphy	18th Awards	Dallas Mus. of Natural History, Dallas, TX
1986	George Tsukamoto	19th Awards	Nevada State Museum and Historical Society, Las Vegas, NV
1989	C. Randall Byers	20th Awards	New Mexico Mus. of Natural History, Albuquerque, NM
1992	Eldon L. Buckner	21st Awards	Milwaukee Public Museum, Milwaukee, WI
1995	Jack Graham	22nd Awards	Dallas Mus. of Natural History, Dallas, TX
1998	Glenn E. Hisey	23rd Awards	Wilbur D. May Museum, Reno, NV
2001	Frederick J. King	24th Awards	Bass Pros Shops, Springfield, MO

Table A

1977 edition was notable because it was the only edition ever published in cooperation with another organization. It was published in cooperation with the National Rifle Association, the co-sponsor of the records-keeping during 1973-1980. The next edition of the records book will be published in 2005.

In 1984, the special 18th Awards Program records book titled, *Boone and Crockett Club's 18th Big Game Awards*, was published. Its listings were limited to the 950 trophies accepted during the 18th Awards Program entry period of 1980-1982. Awards Program records books have been subsequently published every three years, the year following the close of each Awards Program. Thus, there is an all-time records book every six years and an Awards Program records book every three years. The two differ in important ways. The all-time records book includes all trophies over current all-time minimum entry scores and meets other stated requirements that have been entered since the beginning of the system. The Awards Program records book includes only those trophies of the stated three-year Awards Program, as based on the lower entry minimums applicable for many categories. Thus, a good many trophies get recognition in the Awards Program records book that cannot qualify for listing in the all-time records book. The inclusion of the hunting stories and photos of the trophies receiving awards makes the Awards Program records book a uniquely enjoyable book for the trophy hunter, while the all-time records book provides the definitive answers to questions regarding statistics for native North American big game.

The original annual competitions of the Club that were begun in 1947 were changed to a biennial basis in 1952 and to a triennial basis in 1968. In the early 1970s, the word competition was changed to awards to better identify the basic concept of recognition of fine trophies taken under conditions of Fair Chase rather than "competition" of such trophies. The three-year basis of trophy entry continues today **(see Table A)**.

Following the close of each Awards Program entry period, the finest few trophies of each category are invited to a central location for Final Judging. Trophies remeasured by the Judges' Panel and subsequently certified by the Panel for awards are eligible to receive the Boone and Crockett Club Big Game Medal and/or Certificate. Trophies receiving awards are featured with photos and their hunting stories in the Awards Program records book, (e.g. ***Boone and Crockett Club's 24th Big Game Awards***) published the year following the close of an Awards Program entry period. Entries accepted during two Awards Program entry periods that do score over stated minimums for the all-time records book and meet other stated requirements will be added to the listings of the last all-time records book to comprise the next edition of the all-time records book ***Records of North American Big Game***. Of course, only trophies never before entered and/or published in a Boone and Crockett Club records book can be accepted as entries.

As noted, some categories do require lower minimum scores for entry into the Awards Program entry period and Awards records book than for the all-time records book. The current list of minimum entry scores for both the Awards Program entry period and the all-time records book is located in the reference section of this book. For specific requirements of trophy entry beyond minimum score and geographic location for certain categories (see chapter 2 for complete explanation of geographic boundaries), refer to chapters 18 and 19, General Procedures and General Policies. ∎

CATEGORY BOUNDARIES
For North American Big Game

2

The Boone and Crockett Club's big-game records keeping deals only with certain native North American big game animals. For such purposes, the southern boundary is defined as the south boundary of Mexico. Only cougar, jaguar and whitetail deer of the recognized trophy categories range south of this boundary, and only the first two reach recordable size south of Mexico. The northern limit for trophies such as polar bear and walrus is the limit of the continent and associated waters held by the United States, Canada or Greenland. Continental limits and held waters define east and west boundaries for all categories.

A number of species show geographical variation so that there are smaller varieties inhabiting some parts of the continent and larger ones elsewhere. For example, mature moose from Wyoming, Montana, Idaho, etc., of the Shiras' variety, although they may grow large and beautiful racks, are unable to compete with the monstrous moose from the Alaska-Yukon region. So it has been necessary to break up the total ranges of some of the species into various categories in order to provide proper recognition.

The Records Committee has, over the years, gradually defined the areas from which trophies may be entered and has modified these boundaries in some cases when more thorough knowledge of the distribution of the animals in question has become known. The Committee creates new categories from time to time. Other new trophy categories have been proposed, but the Committee maintains a conservative stance in reviewing such proposals. New categories are considered only when the following conditions are met:

1) there are extensive geographical areas where the proposed animals occur;
2) the animals occur in good numbers;
3) there are suitable boundaries that can be drawn;
4) the game department(s) managing the proposed class are in favor of setting up such a new category.

The following material will review the categories for which there are geographically defined boundaries. Obviously these boundaries must be observed in the taking of a trophy in order for it to be considered for that category. As a general rule, the categories are set so there is virtually no chance of a larger category specimen (or a cross-bred animal) being taken within the boundary for the smaller category. While this may exclude some deserving specimens of the smaller category that are resident in the larger category's range, it is a price that must be paid to keep the smaller categories pure.

Brown, Grizzly and Polar Bears

The big brown bears are found on Kodiak and Afognak Islands, the Alaska Peninsula, and eastward and

southeastward along the coast of Alaska. The smaller interior grizzly is found in the remaining parts of the continent. The boundary between the two was first defined as an imaginary line extending 75 miles inland from the coast of Alaska. Later this boundary was more precisely defined **(figure 2-A)** with the current definition as follows:

FIGURE 2-A
THE BOUNDARY SEPARATING GRIZZLY BEAR (WHITE) AND ALASKA BROWN BEAR (SHADED)

A line of separation between the larger growing coastal brown bear and the smaller interior grizzly has been developed such that west and south of this line (to and including Unimak Island) bear trophies are recorded as Alaska brown bear. North and east of this line, bear trophies are recorded as grizzly bear. The boundary line description is as follows: Starting at Pearse Canal and following the Canadian-Alaskan boundary northwesterly to Mt. St. Elias on the 141 degree meridian; thence north along the Canadian-Alaskan boundary to Mt. Natazhat; thence west northwest along the divide of the Wrangell Range to Mt. Jarvis at the western end of the Wrangell Range; thence north along the divide of the Mentasta Range to Mentasta Pass; thence in a general westerly direction along the divide of the Alaska Range to Houston Pass; thence westerly following the 62nd parallel of latitude to the Bering Sea.

Polar bear must be taken in either United States or Canadian-held water and/or land mass in order to be eligible. This definition is necessary because of the wide range of polar bears in the far northern hemisphere.

American, Roosevelt's and Tule Elk

The Roosevelt's elk category was established in 1980. Roosevelt's elk trophies have thicker, shorter antlers, and many of the largest trophies develop crown points, a very distinctive feature.

Roosevelt's elk are acceptable from Del Norte, Humboldt and Trinity Counties, California, as well as that portion of Siskiyou County west of I-5 in northern California; from west of Highway I-5 in Oregon and Washington; from Vancouver Island, B.C.; and from Afognak and Raspberry Islands of Alaska. The Alaskan animals are the result of a successful transplant from the Olympic Peninsula of Washington. To date no trophies from Alaska have been entered that reach the current all-time records book minimum score of 290. Most of the entered trophies to date have come from coastal Oregon and Washington, with a smaller number from Vancouver Island.

The tule elk category was established in 1998 by the Records Committee after several years of careful and detailed review. The geographical boundary **(figure 2-B)** for tule elk is as follows: That portion of California within a line beginning at the junction of the Pacific Ocean and the Ventura-Santa Barbara County line; north along the Ventura-Santa Barbara County line to the Kern County line; east along the Kern County line to Interstate Highway 5; north along Interstate Highway 5 to the Kern County line; east along the Kern County line to the San Bernardino County line; east along the San Bernardino County line to the California-Nevada state line; northwest along the California-Nevada state line to Interstate Highway 50; west along Interstate Highway 50 to Interstate Highway 5 in Sacramento County; north along Interstate Highway 5 to the Tehama County line; west along the Tehama County line to the Mendocino County line; north and then west along the Mendocino County line to US Highway 101; south along US Highway 101 to State Route 156 in Monterey County; south-

FIGURE 2-B
TULE ELK BOUNDARY (SHADED)

west along State Route 156 to State Route 1 in Monterey County; south along State Route 1 to San Jose Creek in Monterey County; south along San Jose Creek to the crest of the Santa Lucia Range in Monterey County; southeast along the crest of the Santa Lucia Range to State Route 41 in San Luis Obispo County; southwest along State Route 41 to Morro Creek in San Luis Obispo County; southwest along Morro Creek to the Pacific Ocean; south along the Pacific Ocean to the point of beginning.

All other elk varieties, primarily from the Rocky Mountains, are now referred to as either typical or non-typical American elk.

FIGURE 2-C
COLUMBIA AND SITKA BLACKTAIL DEER RANGE (SHADED)

Mule Deer, Columbia and Sitka Blacktail Deer

The problem of properly defining the boundary between the large antlered mule deer, which ranges widely over most of the western third of the United States and western Canada, and its smaller relatives, the Columbia and Sitka blacktails of the West Coast, has been difficult from the beginning of the records keeping. The three varieties belong to the same species and thus are able to interbreed readily where their ranges meet. The intent of the Club in drawing suitable boundary lines is to exclude intergrades from each of the three categories. These boundaries have been redrawn as necessary, as more details have become known about the precise ranges of these animals.

The current boundary **(figure 2-C)** for mule and Columbia blacktail deer is as follows:

British Columbia — Starting at the Washington-British Columbia border, blacktail deer range runs west of the height of land between the Skagit and the Chilliwack Ranges, intersecting the Fraser River opposite the mouth of Ruby Creek, then west to and up Harrison Lake to and up Tipella Creek to the height of land in Garibaldi Park and northwesterly along this divide past Alta Lake, Mt. Dalgleish and Mt. Waddington, thence north to Bella Coola. From Bella Coola, the boundary continues north to the head of Dean Channel, Gardner Canal and Douglas Channel to the town of Anyox, then due west to the Alaska-British Columbia border, which is then followed south to open water. This boundary excludes the area west of the Klesilkwa River and the west side of the Lillooet River.

Washington — Beginning at the Washington-British Columbia border, the boundary line runs south along the west boundary of North Cascades National Park to the range line between R10E and R11E, Willamette Meridian, which is then followed directly south to its intersection with the township line between T18N and T17N, which is then followed westward until it connects with the north border of Mt. Rainier National Park, then along the north, west and south park boundaries until it intersects with the range line between R9E and R10E, Willamette Meridian, which is then followed directly south to the Columbia River near Cook.

Oregon — Beginning at Multnomah Falls on the Columbia River, the boundary runs south along the western boundary of the National Forest to Tiller in Douglas County, then south along Highway 227 to Highway 62 at Trail, then south following Highway 62 to Medford, from which the boundary follows the range line between R1W and R2W, Willamette Meridian, to the California border.

California — Beginning in Siskiyou County at the Oregon-California border, the boundary lies between townships R8W and R9W M.D.M., extending south to and along the Klamath River to Hamburg, then south along the road to Scott Bar, continuing south and then east on the unimproved road from Scott Bar to its intersection with the paved road to Mugginsville, then south through Mugginsville to State Highway 3, which is then followed to Douglas City in Trinity County, from which the line runs east on State Highway 299 to Interstate 5. The line follows Interstate 5 south to the area of Anderson, where the Sacramento River moves east of Interstate 5, following the Sacramento River until it joins with the San Joaquin River, which is followed to the south border of Stanislaus County. The line then runs west along this border to the east border of Santa Clara County. The east and south borders of Santa Clara County are then followed to the south border of Santa Cruz County, which is then followed to the edge of Monterey Bay.

On the Queen Charlotte Islands of British Columbia and along the coast of Alaska ranges another subspecies of mule deer, the Sitka blacktail. Accordingly, after a compilation of scores of the largest Sitka blacktail deer trophies from southern Alaska (including those from Kodiak Island where they have been transplanted), a separate trophy category was established for Sitka blacktail deer in 1984 with a minimum all-time records book entry score of 108.

Sitka blacktails have been transplanted to the Queen Charlotte Islands and are abundant there. Thus, the acceptable area for this category includes southeastern Alaska and the Queen Charlotte Islands of British Columbia.

Whitetail and Coues' Deer

Whitetail deer range widely over North America, with recordable trophies known from almost all of this range. The largest specimens are more common from the northern states and southern Canada. Although there is some sentiment for subdividing the range of whitetails into more than two categories, with lower minimums for the southern states, there are no natural boundaries to use in such an effort. But, the tiny Coues' whitetail of the southwest is a different story. It has been recognized in a separate trophy category since the start of the Club's big game records keeping in 1932. The acceptable area for Coues' whitetail deer entries is defined as central and southern Arizona and the Mexican states of Sonora and Chihuahua. In New Mexico the Coues' whitetail deer boundary is defined as: the Arizona border to the west, the New Mexico border to the south, the Rio Grande River to the east and Interstate Highway 40 to the north.

Canada, Alaska-Yukon, and Wyoming Moose

The boundaries for the three classes of moose have remained essentially unchanged since the beginning of the records keeping. But, hunting opportunities for moose have increased in recent years so that moose are now hunted in the Mackenzie Mountains of Northwest Territories, northern Utah, northeastern Washington, northern Minnesota, Maine, New Hampshire and Vermont.

The Alaska-Yukon moose category includes moose from Alaska, Yukon Territory and Northwest Territories.

The Canada moose category includes moose from all of the remaining provinces of Canada, plus Maine, Minnesota, New Hampshire, North Dakota and Vermont.

The Wyoming (or Shiras') moose category has the Canadian border as its northern boundary. Its range includes all of the Rocky Mountain region south of Canada and west to the Pacific Ocean, including the following states: Colorado, Idaho, Montana, Utah, Washington and Wyoming.

Barren Ground, Mountain, Woodland, Quebec-Labrador and Central Canada Barren Ground Caribou

The various varieties of caribou, which vary widely in size and antler configuration, have required subdivision of the species into five different trophy categories: mountain, woodland, barren ground, Central Canada barren ground, and Quebec-Labrador. Prior to 1960, the classification of the different species and subspecies of the world was in disarray. At that time, Frank Banfield (a Canadian wildlife biologist) reviewed all of the available museum specimens of the world's caribou and reduced the number of valid subspecies. Among his conclusions were that the new world caribou and the old world reindeer should all be classified as one species, but that northern barren ground caribou differ from the more southerly distributed woodland caribou, both in Eurasia and in North America.

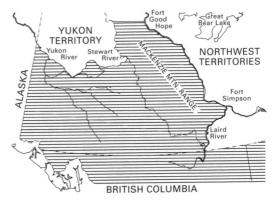

FIGURE 2-D
NORTHERN BOUNDARY FOR MOUNTAIN CARIBOU (SHADED)

The largest antlered caribou from North America are the Grant's variety from Alaska and northern Yukon Territory. These caribou, called barren ground caribou for records-keeping purposes, have long, rounded main beams with very long top points. They also have the highest all-time records book minimum entry score of 400 points. (*See below also for description of boundary between barren ground caribou and mountain caribou in Yukon Territory.*)

The so-called mountain caribou, now regarded as a variety of woodland caribou, is found in British Columbia, Alberta, southern Yukon Territory, and the Mackenzie Mountains of Northwest Territories. In Yukon Territory, the boundary (**figure 2-D**) begins at the intersection of the Yukon River with the boundary between Yukon Territory and the state of Alaska.

The boundary runs southeasterly following the Yukon River upstream to Dawson; then easterly and southerly along the Klondike Highway to Stewart Crossing; then easterly following the road to Mayo; then northeasterly following the road to McQuesten Lake; then easterly following the south shore of McQuesten Lake and then upstream following the main drainage to the divide leading to Scougale Creek to its confluence with the Beaver River; then south following the Beaver River downstream to its confluence with the Rackla River; then southeasterly following the Rackla River downstream to its confluence with the Stewart River; then northeasterly following the Stewart River upstream to its confluence with the North Stewart River to the boundary between Yukon Territory and Northwest Territories. North of this line caribou are classified as **barren ground caribou** for records-keeping purposes, while those specimens taken south of this line are considered **mountain caribou**.

Central Canada barren ground caribou occur on Baffin Island and the mainland of Northwest Territories, as well as in northern Manitoba. The geographic boundaries in the mainland of Northwest Territories are: the Mackenzie River to the west; the north edge of the continent to the north (excluding any islands except Baffin Island); Hudson's Bay to the east; and the southern boundary of Northwest Territories to the south.

The boundary **(figure 2-E)** for Central Canada barren ground caribou in Manitoba begins at the point of intersection of the south limit of township 87 with the provincial boundary between the provinces of Manitoba and Saskatchewan. The boundary then follows this township line east to the point of confluence with Waskaiowka Lake. From there it proceeds in a northeasterly direction along the high-water mark of the north shore of the aforementioned lake following the sinuosities of the shoreline to the point of intersection with the water connection to Hale Lake. From this point, the high-water mark of the north shoreline is followed to the point of intersection with the Little Churchill River. Henceforth, it follows the high-water mark of the north or westerly shore of the Little Churchill River including expansions of the river into lakes to the point of confluence with the Churchill River. From there the boundary crosses the mouth of the Little Churchill River and follows the high-wa-

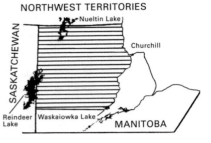

ter mark on the south or easterly shore of the Churchill River to the community of Churchill located on Hudson Bay.

Caribou taken in Manitoba north of the above described boundary are now classified as Central Canada barren ground caribou.

The Quebec-Labrador caribou category was established in 1968. This large woodland caribou has very wide, long-beamed antlers with almost universally palmated bez formations. To have left these animals in competition with the woodland caribou of Newfoundland would have resulted in a complete swamping of the smaller-antlered woodland caribou from Newfoundland. Boundaries for Quebec-Labrador caribou are just as the name implies, Quebec and Labrador.

FIGURE 2-E
CENTRAL CANADA BARREN GROUND CARIBOU BOUNDARY IN MANITOBA (SHADED)

Woodland caribou are eligible for entry from Nova Scotia, Newfoundland and New Brunswick. Woodland caribou occur sparingly all the way across Canada to southern British Columbia. Although there may be some open seasons in these provinces, they are not taken in large numbers anywhere. It would seem inappropriate to place such animals in competition with those from Newfoundland where they have been regularly hunted for more than 100 years.

Bighorn, Desert, Dall's and Stone's Sheep
The wild sheep of North America belong in only two species, the thin-horned sheep of northern British Columbia northward (Ovis dalli), and the bighorn sheep ranging from central B.C. southward to Baja, California (Ovis canadensis).

Dall's (or white) sheep range over much of Alaska, most of Yukon Territory, and the Mackenzie Mountains of Northwest Territories. Stone's sheep occur primarily in northern British Columbia. Where the ranges of these two subspecies meet, the intergrade animals may range through a variety of dark gray shades to almost white. This intergrade was, at one time, regarded as a separate subspecies (Fannin's sheep), but this form cannot really be defined and the idea of a separate category for such animals was rejected many years ago. After consultation with guides, knowledgeable biologists and hunters, the decision was made that any thin-horned sheep that shows any black hairs on the body is classified as a Stone's sheep, unless only the tail is black. In the case of a black tail only, the trophy would be considered a Dall's sheep. The area from which Fannin-type trophies are known is primarily the Pelly Mountains of the southern Yukon. But, they might be recorded from extreme northern British Columbia, and perhaps other localities in the southern Yukon.

The bighorn sheep are separable into Rocky Mountain bighorn and desert bighorn. Desert sheep are found in Nevada and southward into and including Mexico, and eastward into Arizona and southern New Mexico into extreme western Texas. Rocky Mountain bighorns are found in the main Rocky Mountains northward into western Alberta and southeastern British Columbia. Numerous bighorn sheep transplants have been made in the Western states, some of which have been spectacularly successful in restoring sheep to ancestral ranges. In some cases, extremely high scoring trophies have come from these transplanted animals or their progeny.

These transplants have resulted in problems for trophy recordation in the case of the restoration of the so-called California bighorn, which has flourished in natural populations only from central and southcentral British Columbia. This subspecies originally ranged from extreme northeastern California through eastern Oregon, into eastern and central Washington, extreme southwestern Idaho, and northward into central British Columbia. Successful transplants from British Columbia have now been made into North Dakota (where the now extinct Audubon's sheep originally occurred), as well as many other areas within the original range of the subspecies. Currently, a few California bighorns are recorded in the listing for Rocky Mountain bighorns, and these specimens are largely from native animals taken in British Columbia. Since it appears that California bighorns do not have as large horns as those from the Rocky Mountains, there have naturally been requests to establish a new trophy category for such animals. For now, they are considered as Rocky Mountain bighorns for the records keeping.

Several years ago the Club started receiving Rocky Mountain bighorn sheep from Greenlee County, Arizona, where specimens of this category of sheep were transplanted a number of years ago. More recently, the Club received a desert sheep from Mesa County, Colorado, where specimens of this category were transplanted some years ago.

Atlantic and Pacific Walrus

To be eligible for entry, walrus trophies must be taken within U.S., Canadian or Greenland waters and/or land areas. The geographical boundary for Pacific walrus is: That portion of the Bering Sea east of the International Dateline; south along coastal Alaska, including the Pribilof Islands and Bristol Bay; extending eastward into Canada to the southwest coasts of Banks and Victoria Islands and the mouth of Bathurst Inlet in Nunavut Province (formerly known as Northwest Territories).

The geographical boundary for Atlantic walrus is basically the Arctic and Atlantic coasts south to Massachusetts. More specifically the Atlantic walrus boundary in Canada extends westward to Mould Bay of Prince Patrick Island, to just east of Cape George Richards of Melville Island and to Taloyoak, Nunavut Province (formerly known as Spence Bay, Northwest Territories); and eastward to include trophies taken in Greenland.

Bison

Essentially, bison exist as wild, free-ranging herds in their original setting in very few places. Accordingly, only trophies from Alaska and Canada are fully eligible for consideration for possible awards as well as publication in the records books. Over most of the lower 48 states, existing bison herds are semi-domesticated and are regulated as domestic livestock. Since 1977, hunter-taken trophies from the lower 48 states are acceptable only for the records books (both Awards and all-time), not for consideration of the usual place awards, and only if they were taken in a state that recognizes bison as wild and free-ranging and which requires a hunting license and/or big-game tag for hunting bison.

Muskox

Beginning with the 8th (1981) edition of the all-time records book, the two previously recognized categories of muskox (Greenland and barren ground) were combined into a single category. Muskox from Alaska, Canada and Greenland are all eligible for entry into the single category recognized today.

Jaguar

Jaguar must be taken north of the south boundary of Mexico (the southern boundary of North America for big-game records keeping purposes) in order to be eligible. ∎

A BOONE AND CROCKETT CLUB FIELD GUIDE TO MEASURING AND JUDGING BIG GAME

MEASURING TECHNIQUES
For North American Big Game

The chapters that follow present a description of the methods used to measure the various species of North American big game animals that are displayed in the Boone and Crockett Club's book, *Records of North American Big Game*. A summary list of the minimum score requirements for the 38 entry categories for the Club's records books is included at the back of this manual. Certain commonalities exist in the measuring of trophies and are presented here as an introduction to the measuring process. Some of these are directly referenced in later chapters as well. The measurer should be aware of these general procedures as he or she begins the process of measuring a trophy animal and should, from time to time, again familiarize himself or herself with these techniques and rules.

With a minor investment in equipment, almost anyone can make a reasonably accurate measurement of his or her big game trophies. In fact, it is likely that you already have some of the equipment needed to perform accurate measurements.

Without a doubt, the single most useful piece of measuring equipment is a 1/4-inch wide, flexible steel measuring tape, graduated in sixteenths of an inch. It can be used to take all length and circumference measurements required by the scoring system. Such tapes come equipped with either a "ring-end" or a "clip-end." The ring-end tape, equipped with a blank space before the zero mark, is the most useful since it can be used to take all circumference measurements, as well as all length measurements. With the ring-end tape, the circumferences can be read at the zero point; with a clip-end tape, you must read your measurements at some increment (e.g. 10-inch mark) greater than zero, and then subtract the increment to arrive at the correct measurement.

The use of a round, flexible steel cable (such as a bicycle brake cable) for taking point and main beam length measurements is described in the appropriate sections of this manual.

Another useful piece of equipment is a system for taking greatest spread measurements. A very accurate setup consists of two carpenter's levels with c-clamps affixed to one

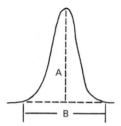

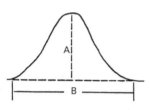

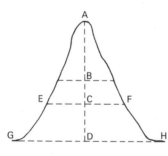

end to serve as bases so the levels are freestanding. The right angles formed by the upright levels (final positioning by the bubbles) form the boundaries for the measurement line, which is read with a steel tape or folding carpenter's rule. This same setup is excellent for taking the length and width measurements of cat and bear skulls.

A folding carpenter's rule with a brass slide as depicted below is indispensable for taking inside spreads. As necessary, the rule is unfolded and the extension is used to accurately determine spread measurements.

Calipers are required for the boss and horn width measurements of muskox and in the hands of an experienced user, they can also be used for skull measurements of cats and bears.

Finally, but certainly not least, copies of the *current* copyrighted score charts are needed to perform accurate measurements. Reproductions of each of the 17 score charts are scattered throughout this manual in the appropriate chapters. Score charts can also be downloaded in PDF format from the Club's official web site (www.boone-crockett.org). Copies to fill-out for scoring trophies can be obtained at nominal cost from the Club's office, and the specially made Boone and Crockett Club Official Big-Game Measuring Tape (ring-end) and cables can also be ordered directly from the Club.

Prior to January 1989 the definition of a point was open to more than one possible interpretation. The definition was then rewritten to clarify the approach and to have wording that is clearly stated and open to only a single interpretation. The definition of a point is as follows: To be counted a point, the projection must be at least one inch long, with the length exceeding width at one inch or more of length. Once it is established that a projection is a point, its length is then taken from the tip to the base line of the point. The only exception to this rule is for caribou for which the point must be at least one-half inch long and longer than wide at length one-half inch or more. **Figure 3-A** provides illustrations of applications of this definition.

In some cases the length of a point may exceed 1" and

the width of the base is greater than the overall length of the point. This may still be a point as long as the measurer can come down one inch or more from the tip and find a location where length exceeds the width at that location. Once it is determined that a projection qualifies as a point, it is measured from its tip to its naturally occurring baseline. **Figure 3-B** illustrates this situation.

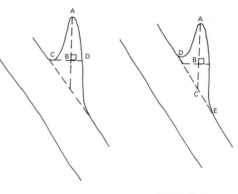

FIGURE 3-C
Left illustration:
This is a point.
AB = 1"
CD = 6/8"

Right illustration:
This is NOT a point.
AB = 1"
AC = 1-1/8"
DE = 1-2/8"

Several questions have arisen in the past concerning the determination of whether a projection was a point or not. Some measurers were taking the width of a point at an angle other than 90 degrees when ascertaining whether or not a projection was a qualifying point. This is an appropriate procedure when measuring along the point's natural base but not at other times. In 1998 the Records Committee approved the following clarification for point determination. *Unless taken at the point's natural baseline, the width must be taken perpendicular to the length when determining whether or not a projection qualifies as a point.* See **figure 3-C.**

When measuring a point or beam, or when taking a circumference, the measurement does not always fall exactly on an eighth-inch mark. The measurer should round the value to the nearest eighth inch, and if the measurement falls exactly on a sixteenth-inch mark, the measurer should round to the next higher eighth-inch mark. In the case of

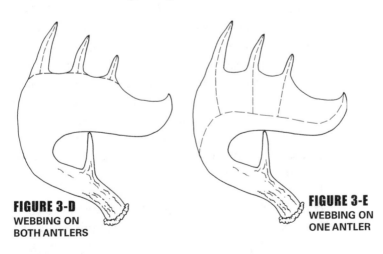

FIGURE 3-D
WEBBING ON
BOTH ANTLERS

FIGURE 3-E
WEBBING ON
ONE ANTLER

FIGURE 3-F
COMMON BASE
POINTS

FIGURE 3-G
NOT COMMON
BASE POINTS

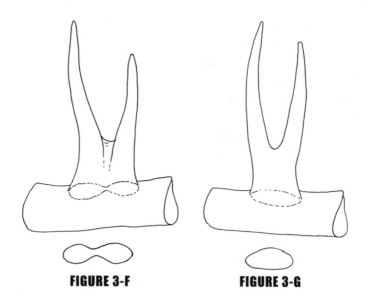

FIGURE 3-F   **FIGURE 3-G**

skull measurements, the measurer rounds to the nearest six-teenth of an inch. If a measurement falls exactly between sixteenths, the measurement is again rounded up. One situation where the round-up rule does not apply is in the case of point length determination. Here the projection must be at least one-inch long. Thus a 31/32-inch long projection cannot be a point as it is not at least one inch long.

Occasionally, "palmation" or "webbing" may occur on one or both antlers so that there is a noticeable "filling-in" between individual points. If both antlers are palmated, establish the individual point base lines on the top edge of the palmation, then measure points and circumferences in the usual manner **(figure 3-D)**. The trophy will receive credit for the symmetry of web-bing on both antlers via the increased circumference measurements. If only one antler is palmated, draw the individual point base lines along the main beam where it would be if there were no palmation and then mea-sure the individual points to this line **(figure 3-E)**. In this case, the lack of symmetry caused by the webbing will be penalized by the circumference measurement dif-ferences, justifying the allowance for point length "hidden" in the webbing.

Common base points present certain issues that need to be addressed when measuring a trophy. Simply stated com-mon base points are points that are joined at their bases and share some degree of webbing between them. Frequently, it is difficult to determine if two points are sharing a common base, or if one is a branch of the other. In order to be treated as common base points, and not as a point with a branch, the cross section of the bases of both points must be a figure eight shape, as **figure 3-F** demonstrates, if both points were cut off at their bases. *This cross section must be **clearly** a figure eight.* Two points **(figure 3-G)** with an oval-shaped base or with a base that is half oval and the remainder figure-eight shaped must be treated as a single point with an abnormal branch point.

Common base and webbed points differ. Webbing is the filling-in with antler material of two clearly separate points that are not joined together except by the webbing. Common base points are two separate points joined together at the base that, as they merge together, share common point material. While they are not the same, the measuring technique is similar. If the common base points are found only on one antler, the point lengths are measured from their tips to the main beam **(figure 3-H)**. If the condition occurs at or before G-4 and involves normal points, the corresponding circumference measurement will be inflated. This increase is compensated for by the corresponding increase in the difference column associated with the measurement of the opposite side circumference.

If both sides of the antlers display common base normal points that occur at or prior to G-4, it would be

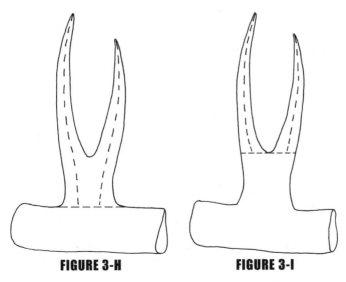

FIGURE 3-H

FIGURE 3-I

FIGURE 3-H
COMMON BASE
POINTS
ON ONE SIDE

FIGURE 3-I
MATCHING
COMMON BASE
POINTS
ON BOTH SIDES

FIGURE 3-J

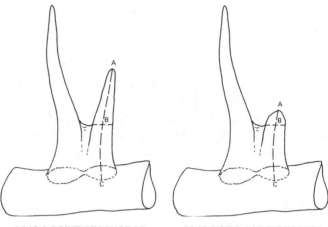

AC IS A POINT BECAUSE AB
QUALIFIES AS A POINT BY
ITSELF

AC IS NOT A POINT BECAUSE
AB DOES NOT QUALIFY AS A
POINT BY ITSELF

inappropriate to measure both points to the beam and then to also record the inflated circumference measurement brought about by the shared point material. As both sides now display the shared webbing, no compensating deduction in the difference column would occur. Thus, if matched pair, common base points occur on both antlers, the base line for these points is established by moving it parallel to the main beam upwards through the lowest part of the gap between the common base points **(figure 3-I)**. The points are then measured from their tips to their centers on this adjusted base line.

Often the question of whether a point is one, two or more points arises when a point that forks into several tips occurs. Such cases are most common on brow tines but also are present on abnormal point clusters. Some of these clustered points display common base type structures; others are simply a point with possible forks. The proper interpretation in such cases is that each projection, when measured from its tip to the bottom of the gap between them, must separately meet the definition of a point which is any projection at least one inch long and longer than wide at some location at least one inch from the tip of the projection is a point. Thus, for example, if a point that splits into two tips arose from the beam, each tip when measured from its tip down to the bottom of the gap between the tips would individually have to qualify as a point for this structure to be treated as having two separate points. Otherwise, it would simply be measured as one point. **Figure 3-J** illustrates this procedure. While **figure 3-J** demonstrates the proper techniques to use when the projections in question share a common base, the same principle holds when one of the projections is a branch off the other. In **figure 3-K** A-B and D-E are not two separate points themselves because neither projection qualifies as a point above the webbing. However, the whole structure could be classified as a single point only as long as it, measured from either tip to the base, qualifies as a point. This structure is then measured only from A-C or D-F, whichever is longer. **Figure 3-K** illustrates a situation where the length of DF is longer than AC.

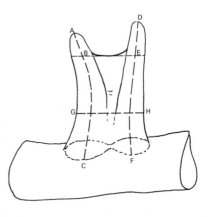

FIGURE 3-K
AB and DE are less than 1", hence, not two separate points. DF qualifies as a point since DH is longer than 1" and greater IN LENGTH than GH width.

Burr points are those points that develop directly as part of the burr material. In order for these projections to qualify as a point, the definition of a point is once again applied. A key step in determining whether or not a burr projection is a qualifying point is the establishment of the proper base line. Since the burr itself is part of the main beam, the measurer must treat the natural burr shape as beam and allow for it when establishing the base line. **Figure 3-M** demonstrates the proper procedure for establishing a base line for a burr point. Essentially the line is drawn from burr edge to burr edge across the point, not to the inside edge of the burr. If the trophy is not mounted, the measurer can often find the base of the burr by looking on the underside of the burr to determine the end of burr material.

One other procedure to note concerns the measurement of abnormal points or crown points that project from the juncture of two points. These points are often joined in a web that reflects antler material not yet measured. If one simply draws a base line from edge to edge across the point, one is shorting the point some of its true length. Thus, the measurer should project the natural curve of the antler as if the webbing were not present for the base line for the length measurement in this situation. **Figure 3-L** provides an il-

FIGURE 3-L
BURR POINTS

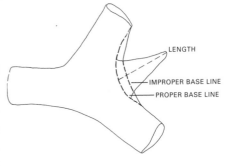

LENGTH
IMPROPER BASE LINE
PROPER BASE LINE

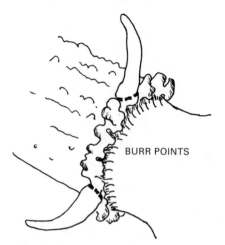

BURR POINTS

FIGURE 3-M

lustration of this procedure. Often the measurer can determine a visual reference for this base line by comparing it to the other antler.

Though the previous discussions and illustrations deal with unusual point structures that occur on whitetail deer, similar scoring procedures would be used on elk and mule deer when the occasion arises, especially so on Roosevelt's and tule elk crown points.

Official measurements cannot be taken until the antlers, horns, skulls or tusks have air dried at normal room temperature for least 60 days after the animal was killed. If the trophy has been frozen prior to cleaning, as is often the case with skulls, the 60-day drying period begins once the cleaning process is complete. The drying process for trophies that have been boiled or freeze-dried starts the day they are removed from the boiling pot or freeze-drier, respectively.

In the case of picked up trophies, the 60-day drying period also applies. If it is clear from the condition of the antlers, horns, skulls or tusks that the trophy has dried for more than 60 days, one does not have to wait another 60 days from when it was found to measure it. However, it is necessary to enter the approximate date the animal died on the line provided for the date of kill on the score chart. Trophy owners may be asked to provide a brief history for "picked up" trophies or trophies of unknown origin to substantiate the approximate date of death.

Many other commonalities exist in the measuring process for the various trophy categories. These are covered in the sections that follow. Certain general procedures and policies that apply to the Boone and Crockett system are covered in Chapters 17 and 18. These policies also apply to all entry categories and are presented in summary form for the interested trophy owner, sports person or measurer. ∎

MEASURING AND JUDGING
Bears and Cats

The Boone and Crockett Club recognizes four categories of bear—Alaska brown bear, black bear, grizzly bear, polar bear—and two categories of cats—cougar, jaguar—in its records. For some 25 years there was a moratorium on the acceptance of polar bear entries. In 1994, the Club renewed acceptance of polar bear entries. The Club is not currently accepting jaguar entries in the Awards Programs unless a CITES (Convention on International Trade of Endangered Species) permit is included with the entry materials, though the historic listings are maintained in the records books.

Measuring Skulls

Skulls of cats and bears require the simplest measurements of all trophies that are eligible for the records books. Only the length and width of the skull are recorded. However these measurements differ from all other trophy categories in that the measurements are taken to the nearest sixteenth of an inch (instead of to the nearest eighth of an inch).

All flesh, membrane, and cartilage must be removed from the skull before a measurement can be made. As with all trophies, a 60-day drying period must be observed before an official measurement for trophy entry can be performed. You should note that if the skull has been "boiled" to remove adherent flesh, the 60-day drying period starts with the boiling date. Similarly, if the skull has been frozen, or stored under any conditions other than normal atmospheric ones, an additional 60-day drying period,

FIGURE 4-A

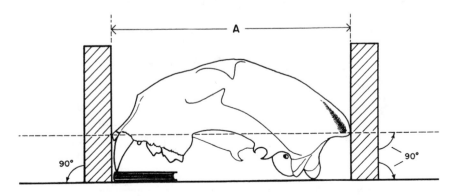

under normal atmospheric conditions, must be observed before measurements can be taken.

Skull measurements are made only with the lower jaw removed from the skull as the lower jaw is not part of the measured skull. Usually, the length measurement extends from the forward extension of the teeth to the rear of the skull. The width is taken across the zygomatic arches of the cheeks perpendicular to the length measurement. Skull measurements must always be taken at right angles to the skull axis. That is, the width must be taken at a right angle to the length, and the length must be taken at a right angle to the width.

The correct line of measurement for skull length is a straight line from the sagittal crest region at the rear of the skull to the frontal portion of the teeth. This line must be parallel to the surface on which the skull is resting. This means that the skull front may have to be elevated, as shown in **figure 4-A**, to achieve the proper measurement line.

If there are teeth protruding at a *noticeably* unusual angle (straight-out rather than generally down), or malformations of the skull that give a greater measurement than the skull deserves, adjust the measurement to credit only those normal features present. On bears, the point of contact is usually across the incisors; on cougar, the frontal point may be on the canines. If the teeth are missing, then the front starting point is to the front of the skull itself.

A large pair of calipers may be used to take skull measurements as demonstrated in **figure 4-B**. However, care must be exercised in closing them to exactly the right tension against the skull. If they are too "tight" against the surfaces, they will close slightly when removed, thus changing the measurement. Care must be taken when using calipers, especially

FIGURE 4-B

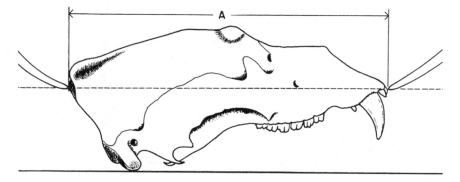

A BOONE AND CROCKETT CLUB FIELD GUIDE TO MEASURING AND JUDGING BIG GAME

on cougar, that the length is parallel to the longitudinal axis. If the frontal point of contact is a canine, then calipers cannot be used because a length measurement from the canine to the sagittal crest would be a diagonal to the axis of the skull rather than parallel. If this is the case, then another acceptable method for taking the length measurement must be used since the length measurement cannot be a diagonal to the skull's axis.

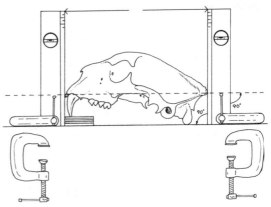

FIGURE 4-C

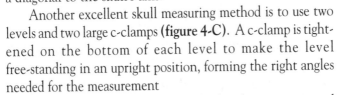

Another excellent skull measuring method is to use two levels and two large c-clamps **(figure 4-C)**. A c-clamp is tightened on the bottom of each level to make the level free-standing in an upright position, forming the right angles needed for the measurement

For the actual measurement, the levels are positioned snugly against the skull, and the bubbles are again checked. When both levels are perpendicular to the surface the skull is resting on (as shown by the bubbles), and are snugly against the skull, the measurement is then made between the two levels.

Another method used to obtain the length and width measurements accurately is to construct two large wooden blocks. These blocks are positioned at 90 degree angles on each side of the skull, at the proper location to reflect the greatest distance. Once the blocks have been snugly positioned so that no space can be discerned between block and skull, the skull width or length is then measured between the blocks. The best way to take this measurement is with a carpenter's folding rule. Obviously, this system demands *perfectly* square-cut, right-angle blocks and a perfectly flat surface for accuracy **(figure 4-A)**. Some measurers have used this concept to construct measuring boxes for skull measurement. Such boxes, when properly made, provide a convenient and easy-to-use tool.

Note that any loss of skull material cannot be compensated for in the measurement process. Often, bears and cats may be shot in the head, perhaps resulting in loss of mate-

FIGURE 4-D

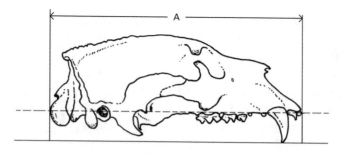

rial from a zygomatic arch (the cheek bone), thus potentially affecting the width measurement. Or, sometimes in freeing the skull from the backbone, careless use of an ax or saw may result in a portion of the rear of the skull being lost, obviously shortening the skull length measurement. No adjustment can be made for the lost material. *Only the intact, unrepaired skull can be measured.*

Related to this issue is the problem that may exist if the zygomatic arches are sprung. Often when cleaning a skull for display purposes, these arches slightly separate and spring outwards. Such separation might artificially inflate the width measurement. If so, the measurer should lightly press the arches back into their natural position before taking the width measurement.

On rare occasions, mostly with polar bears, the rear point of contact may be at the occipital condyles (the rounded edges of the spinal cord hole) rather than the sagittal crest (near the upper back of the skull). See **figure 4-D.** In such cases it is proper to record this measurement as the length measurement. Since the plane of measurement changes, you will have to rotate the skull either upward or downward to find out whether the rear contact is near the skull top or near the spinal opening. Remember to properly level the skull when taking this measurement. When the rear contact is across the occipital condyles, you cannot use a caliper to get the proper length (since the center, straight line passes through the spinal cord opening).

The measurements are recorded on the score chart, in sixteenths, and the final score is determined by adding the length and width measurements. There are no penalties in skull measurements since there are only the two measurements of length and width.

Field Judging Black Bears

Fuzzy teddy bear or ferocious menace? Man-eating or good eating? Endangered animal or common backyard pest? Big game trophy, bumbling clown, or wilderness icon? Rug or cure for arthritis? Big and bad or small and furtive? Which is it? The fact, is the black bear of North America have multiple personalities. They are the "Sybils" of the animal kingdom. Even calling a black bear "black" is a contradiction in terms; they can be black, blue, brown, red, cinnamon, blond, and even, in the case of the much-vaunted Kermode bear, white.

By Jim Shockey

Personality disorders aside, black bears are also the most widely distributed of all the huntable big game species in North America. They can be found coast to coast: rolling rocks for crabs on the shores of both the Pacific and Atlantic Oceans, slurping blueberries on the mid-Arctic tundra or gorging on high desert fruits south of Arizona.

Though some may disagree, black bears are one of the most sought after of all the big game species. Who hasn't desired a black bear rug? Next to whitetail deer, there is an argument to be made that black bears are the second most popular big game animal to hunt.

Popular to hunt they may be, but easy to field judge, they are not, and yet, in spite of the high degree of difficulty, everyone who hunts black bears wants a big one. A "meat bear" won't do. To whit, in all the many years I've outfitted for black bears, not one of my client-hunters has told me that his dream was to shoot a small bear for the freezer. It hasn't happened and it never will. The fascination we hunters have with big bears is ancient and primal; a combination of "fear" and "facing fear," another black bear dichotomy. It's akin to climbing up onto the roof of a building and looking over the edge, the higher the building (the bigger the bear), and the deeper the fascination.

Taking all this into consideration, why is it then that so many hunters have small or medium-sized black bear skin rugs on their wall? And more to the point of this article, why do they have small bear skulls in their dens? Why indeed. Ask them and virtually every one of them will say something to the effect of, "he (or she) looked huge to me." It is a standard and a fair evaluation of black bear hunting. Without doubt, the toughest part of taking a big black bear is knowing what "big" looks like. What follows in this article will hopefully help you correctly make what will be your toughest judging call of all.

First Things First

When my hunters ask me, and they all do, how to judge black bears, they invariably throw in what they know about judging black bears, the one or two tips they've read in some bear article, things like "look for small ears" and "big bears have small-looking heads." My pat response is that they are way ahead of themselves, looking at the size of a bear's ears or head isn't necessarily wrong, it just isn't the right thing to be doing first. The first thing they should be looking at when they see the bear they want to judge is the location of that bear.

Location

Big bears live, eat, and hang out in the best living, eating, and hanging out areas. Find the best looking bear habitat in whatever hunting area you are in and odds are, the bear you see there will be big, especially during prime evening hours. Small bears usually live in marginal habitat for their own safety, as well they should, since big black bears eat small bears. Often I hear hunters tell me that they spied an especially large bear right up near the edge of the timber, near the big trees. And they may well have, but odds are, the reason that bear is up there near all those good escape trees, is that the bear itself is small and the very tops of those nearby trees are the best insurance against ending up as a bear breakfast.

Of course, location is a relative thing. In my guiding area on Vancouver Island, a "good location" is a grassy meadow along a creek in the bottom country or a reclaimed road seeded to clover in the high country. In other areas, a good location may be a bait pile or oat field. Because of the huge diversity of black bear habitat across North America, good location is relative and impossible to qualify. Know your hunting area and you'll know what to look for, but remember, if there's a bear feeding on a prime spot at prime time, odds are it's a bear worth judging.

Attitude

Big bears are the toughest, meanest sons-of-a-guns in the valley and they act it. Watch a human bully walk down the street, he walks with a swagger and an attitude. A big bear walks the same way. He doesn't fit and start at every sound like a small bear will. A big bear doesn't have to; he believes he's got nothing to fear. Once you've spotted your bear on the prime feeding spot during prime time, it's time to get serious about how that bear is behaving.

It is important to note that long before you judge the size of the bear, you must judge the sex of that bear. A big, old sow will have all, or more correctly, almost all of the physical characteristics of a big, old boar. She'll have the nasty looking face that's seen one too many years in the ring, the potbelly and the sway back. The one thing (besides the obvious) that she won't have, except in exceptional cases, is the "I'm the biggest and baddest son of a gun in the valley" behavior that determines sex more effectively than if that bear was wearing a bikini.

Watch to see if the bear stands on his hind legs and rubs his back on a tree, that's a boar. If it walks along and straddles small trees, wiping its scent on that tree, it's a boar. If it stands up and breaks saplings over its shoulder, it's a boar. If it encounters another bear and gives chase, it's a boar and if it is following a smaller bear, it's a boar.

Believe it or not, if the bear has attitude, meaning if it displays any of the above behavior and is feeding on the best food source during the best part of the day, I will have already made up my mind for my client to take the bear. No looking at ears, head, belly or tail, if we're close enough, and the bear is about to disappear. I'll call the shot and live with the consequences. That's how important "location" and "attitude" are.

The simple fact of the matter is, no matter how much longer I look at that bear, I'm still not likely going to be any surer about the size of the bear's skull than I was when I first determined it was a boar! It isn't like judging any of the horned or antlered game—there's nothing to look at, and it's like judging the size of a whitetail buck's antlers when those antlers are inside a burlap sack. It can't be done, or at least not accurately.

Scale

There is one last general appearance tip to judging black bears that makes the top three in importance, and that is scale. A big bear looks big . . . but so does a closer, smaller bear. Here's a quantitative example of this. If the bear is 150 yards away but the hunter thinks the bear is 200 yards away, the hunter will overestimate the bear's relative size by somewhere near

25 percent. In other words, the hunter is in for a serious case of ground shrink when he walks up to his bear. Get as close to the bear as you can. The closer the bear, the less chance there is of misjudging the distance to the bear, and thereby misjudging the bear's relative size.

Specific Tips for Judging Black Bears

When I'm guiding, if the bear my client and I are judging fails any one of the above general conditions, then I will normally let the bear walk. It's tough and I've been wrong before, but at least there isn't a dead small bear lying on the ground. Call it a personal aversion to profuse apologies. If it does pass all the above criteria, and there is time to get fancy on the judging, I'll use every second I have to confirm what I already know. Normally I'll tell my hunter to be ready to shoot because at that particular instant I believe it's a big bear worth tagging, but the longer I can look at the bear the higher the odds that I'll be right.

1) **Body Shape:** Do you wear the same size pants as you did when you were in high school? Be honest, does your spouse poke you in the belly once in a while and tell you to cut back on the Twinkies? Bigger bears are older bears, and like most of us, they don't have the svelte bodies they once did. They tend to look "heavy" and out of shape. Remember, they monopolize the best feed and habitat, and therefore exert less energy to live.

2) **Head Shape:** A big bear (boar) will have a deeper, wider and longer snout than a smaller bear or a female. His ears will appear to be wide apart and small. If he is aware of you and looking your way, his ears won't stand up on top of his head like a dog's ears, they'll seem to be aimed out to the side of his head. A big bear will have well developed "bulging like Arnold," biting muscles on the top of his head.

3) **Legs:** A big bear will have massively developed front shoulders. His shoulders will look big and burly. A sow's wrist will pinch in directly above the foot. Not so with a boar. The lower forearm, wrist and the foot on a big boar are all the same width. A big bear often appears to have shorter legs because the body is so much thicker, but keep in mind that the best-scoring bears for the records book are often the lankier looking, longer-bodied bears.

PHOTO ANALYSIS OF BLACK BEAR
A Comparison in the Wild

- Wider snout on bigger bear
- Ears are wider apart and smaller as compared to the smaller bear in the inset photo
- Ears on big boars do not stand up like a dog's ears, rather point out to the side of his head

Let Boone and Crockett Sort Them Out

We've got a saying around my camp, "Let Boone and Crockett sort them out," and we live by it. There isn't a guide or hunter in the world who can accurately call the skull measurement of a black bear. It's impossible. There are simply too many variables that affect the final dried measurement. Sorry if it bursts any bubbles or offends other guides or hunters, but after outfitting for hundreds of black bears and seeing thousands upon thousands of them, I stand by what I said.

There are bears that have meatier heads; bears that look great and are great trophies, but that don't score well. There are others that have short skulls, block-headed beasts that look impressive, but that don't score well at all and there are lanky, skinny bears with donkey faces that score like the devil, but that a hunter seriously looking for a records book bear wouldn't walk across the street for. Black bear morphology is just too darn diversified to make a science out of judging. Trust me, I've been on both ends of the surprises when it comes to the actual score of the black bear I just told my hunter to take.

The best way to hunt for a records book boar is to simply shoot the bear that looks good to you and that hopefully you'll appreciate. If it's got a nice hide, be happy with your animal. If it has long claws and weighs a ton, good for you and congratulations. If it isn't as big as you'd like, don't fret, you're not alone and the rug on your wall will still look great. If it happens to be one of those rare few bears that has grown a skull that qualifies for the records book, thank your guide and your lucky stars and don't expect to repeat the feat in the near future. It won't be that bigger bears aren't around—they are—you just won't be able to tell them apart from the other bears in the area!

Field Judging Grizzly and Alaska Brown Bears

Field judgment of the size of the grizzly and Alaska brown bear (not polar) of the North American continent is really quite simple and well defined. The major points to consider are:

1) Legs—If a bear has what appear to be long, thin legs, it is a small bear. If it appears to have short, squatty legs, generally it is a big bear.

2) Walk—If a bear walks with an easy gait, without much movement of the rear end, it is a small bear. If a bear walks

PHOTO ANALYSIS OF GRIZZLY BEAR
A Comparison in the Wild

- Bigger bears have shorter, squatty legs compared to the smaller bear in the inset photo
- The ears on the bigger bear are barely discernible

with a duck waddle, with grossly exaggerated movement of the buttocks, it is usually a big bear

3) Ears—If a bear has prominent and relatively large and easily visible ears, it is a small bear. If the bear has apparently very small (or barely discernible) ears, it is usually a very large bear.

4) Relative size of the body—Obviously a very large-bodied bear will usually have a large head. However, you can be fooled with this observation. Occasionally you will find a large-bodied bear with a pinheaded skull, or you can have a relatively small (or average-bodied) bear with a jug-headed skull, which will score much higher than anticipated.

Of course, you have to take the time to scrutinize your bear to apply the above evaluation. Quite often when afield, there are only a few seconds to decide whether or not to shoot. You must therefore remember to apply your best evaluation character as soon as you spot your game. If you have enough time to apply all of them, you should know pretty well before you pull the trigger whether or not your bear has a chance of making the book. A readily visible difference in a big brown bear and a small one is that small bears don't appear to have a neck. A big brown bear will have a head-and-a-half between the hump and his ears. On a small bear you can barely see his head length between the hump and the ears.

On an old bear of any type, the head widens with age and tends to give the appearance that the ears come more and more out of the side of the head, rather than being on the top of the head as they are in a young bear.

Brown and grizzly bears can be especially tough to judge in the fall when they have put on a lot of weight in preparation for winter. If the bear is feeding right between his paws, he's probably a pretty short bear because he doesn't have much neck to reach down. A bigger bear will feed out in front of his feet by a couple of inches to as much as a foot.

Polar bears are evaluated differently because they're different shaped animals. The squared hide of the polar bear has more length than width, whereas the brown and grizzly bear have more width than length. Consequently, the big polar bears will develop a distinct rangy look. A big polar bear will have a long, lanky body, a long neck, and a very "snaky" appearance, overall.

Field Judging Cougars and Jaguar

Criteria for judging cougar and jaguar are quite similar to that for bear. The older specimens will almost always appear to have a large body for their skull, while the reverse is often true for young animals. As in bears, this is often due to the body of the older animals depositing fat. Invariably, when you see a large cat running, you are struck by the almost pendulous belly that swings from side to side as the cat runs. Younger animals are noticeably sleeker in appearance. Older cats appear short-legged for the body although the tracks will appear larger, with a very large track almost always indicating a very large cat.

In cougar hunting with dogs, there is usually ample time to view the animal after it is brought to bay. While the cougar is atop a rock or on a high tree limb, very accurate evaluation can be made by an experienced hunter. And, one is usually rather sure of the size of the cougar long before it is brought to bay from the size of the tracks and its general behavior The older cougar tend to give longer chases (unless full of meat from a recent kill), while younger cats will often bay quickly.

Jaguar furnish very different problems in evaluation afield. While they will be brought to bay by the dogs in most hunts, just as in cougar hunting, it will often be a confrontation on the ground which means the activities will generally proceed non-stop to the point of the shot. In fact, there may not really be a choice, the hunter may have to shoot in self-defense of himself and the dogs. Therefore, the evaluation must be on the tracks, deepness of the roar (if heard) and the behavior while being chased by the dogs. Generally, the hunter will have to rely strongly upon the expertise of his guide in jaguar hunting. ■

SCORECHART
Bear – all species

BOONE AND CROCKETT CLUB®

250 Station Drive
Missoula, MT 59801
(406) 542-1888

OFFICIAL SCORING SYSTEM FOR NORTH AMERICAN BIG GAME TROPHIES

BEAR

	MINIMUM SCORES		KIND OF BEAR (check one)
	AWARDS	ALL-TIME	
black bear	20	21	☐ black bear
grizzly bear	23	24	☐ grizzly
Alaska brown bear	26	28	☐ Alaska brown bear
polar bear	27	27	☐ polar

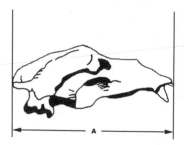

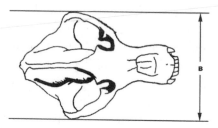

SEE OTHER SIDE FOR INSTRUCTIONS	MEASUREMENTS
A. Greatest Length Without Lower Jaw	
B. Greatest Width	
FINAL SCORE	

Exact Locality Where Killed:

Date Killed: Hunter:

Owner: Telephone #:

Owner's Address:

Guide's Name and Address:

Remarks: (Mention Any Abnormalities or Unique Qualities)

I, _____ , certify that I have measured this trophy on _____
    PRINT NAME   MM/DD/YYYYY

at _____
  STREET ADDRESS   CITY   STATE/PROVINCE

and that these measurements and data are, to the best of my knowledge and belief, made in accordance with the instructions given.

Witness:_____ Signature:_____ I.D. Number ☐☐☐☐
     B&C OFFICIAL MEASURER

INSTRUCTIONS FOR MEASURING BEAR

Measurements are taken with calipers or by using parallel perpendiculars, to the nearest **one-sixteenth** of an inch, without reduction of fractions. Official measurements cannot be taken until the skull has air dried for at least 60 days after the animal was killed. All adhering flesh, membrane and cartilage must be completely removed **before** official measurements are taken.

A. **Greatest Length** is measured between perpendiculars parallel to the long axis of the skull, without the lower jaw and excluding malformations.

B. **Greatest Width** is measured between perpendiculars at right angles to the long axis.

ENTRY AFFIDAVIT FOR ALL HUNTER-TAKEN TROPHIES

For the purpose of entry into the Boone and Crockett Club's® records, North American big game harvested by the use of the following methods or under the following conditions are ineligible:

I. Spotting or herding game from the air, followed by landing in its vicinity for the purpose of pursuit and shooting;
II. Herding or chasing with the aid of any motorized equipment;
III. Use of electronic communication devices, artificial lighting, or electronic light intensifying devices;
IV. Confined by artificial barriers, including escape-proof fenced enclosures;
V. Transplanted for the purpose of commercial shooting;
VI. By the use of traps or pharmaceuticals;
VII. While swimming, helpless in deep snow, or helpless in any other natural or artificial medium;
VIII. On another hunter's license;
IX. Not in full compliance with the game laws or regulations of the federal government or of any state, province, territory, or tribal council on reservations or tribal lands;

Please answer the following questions:

Were dogs used in conjunction with the pursuit and harvest of this animal?
☐ Yes   ☐ No

If the answer to the above question is yes, answer the following statements:

1. I was present on the hunt at the times the dogs were released to pursue this animal.
☐ True ☐ False

2. If electronic collars were attached to any of the dogs, receivers were not used to harvest this animal.
☐ True ☐ False

To the best of my knowledge the answers to the above statements are true. If the answer to either #1 or #2 above is false, please explain on a separate sheet.

I certify that the trophy scored on this chart was not taken in violation of the conditions listed above. In signing this statement, I understand that if the information provided on this entry is found to be misrepresented or fraudulent in any respect, it will not be accepted into the Awards Program and 1) all of my prior entries are subject to deletion from future editions of **Records of North American Big Game** 2) future entries may not be accepted.

FAIR CHASE, as defined by the Boone and Crockett Club®, is the ethical, sportsmanlike and lawful pursuit and taking of any free-ranging wild, native North American big game animal in a manner that does not give the hunter an improper advantage over such game animals.

The Boone and Crockett Club® may exclude the entry of any animal that it deems to have been taken in an unethical manner or under conditions deemed inappropriate by the Club.

Date:_____ Signature of Hunter:_____
(SIGNATURE MUST BE WITNESSED BY AN OFFICIAL MEASURER OR A NOTARY PUBLIC.)

Date:_____ Signature of Notary or Official Measurer:_____

SCORECHART
Cougar and Jaguar

BOONE AND CROCKETT CLUB®
OFFICIAL SCORING SYSTEM FOR NORTH AMERICAN BIG GAME TROPHIES

COUGAR AND JAGUAR

	MINIMUM SCORES	
	AWARDS	ALL-TIME
cougar	14 - 8/16	15
jaguar	14 - 8/16	14 - 8/16

KIND OF CAT (check one)
☐ cougar
☐ jaguar

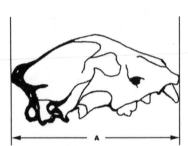

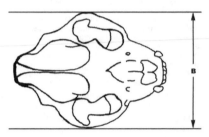

SEE OTHER SIDE FOR INSTRUCTIONS	MEASUREMENTS
A. Greatest Length Without Lower Jaw	
B. Greatest Width	
FINAL SCORE	

Exact Locality Where Killed:

Date Killed: _____ Hunter: _____

Owner: _____ Telephone #: _____

Owner's Address:

Guide's Name and Address:

Remarks: (Mention Any Abnormalities or Unique Qualities)

I, _____ , certify that I have measured this trophy on _____
  PRINT NAME   MM/DD/YYYYY

at _____
  STREET ADDRESS   CITY   STATE/PROVINCE

and that these measurements and data are, to the best of my knowledge and belief, made in accordance with the instructions given.

Witness: _____ Signature: _____ I.D. Number ☐ ☐ ☐ ☐
                                B&C OFFICIAL MEASURER

INSTRUCTIONS FOR MEASURING COUGAR AND JAGUAR

Measurements are taken with calipers or by using parallel perpendiculars, to the nearest **one-sixteenth** of an inch, without reduction of fractions. Official measurements cannot be taken until the skull has air dried for at least 60 days after the animal was killed. All adhering flesh, membrane and cartilage must be completely removed **before** official measurements are taken.

    A. **Greatest Length** is measured between perpendiculars parallel to the long axis of the skull, without the lower jaw and excluding malformations.

    B. **Greatest Width** is measured between perpendiculars at right angles to the long axis.

ENTRY AFFIDAVIT FOR ALL HUNTER-TAKEN TROPHIES

For the purpose of entry into the Boone and Crockett Club's® records, North American big game harvested by the use of the following methods or under the following conditions are ineligible:

    I.   Spotting or herding game from the air, followed by landing in its vicinity for the purpose of pursuit and shooting;

    II.   Herding or chasing with the aid of any motorized equipment;

    III.   Use of electronic communication devices, artificial lighting, or electronic light intensifying devices;

    IV.   Confined by artificial barriers, including escape-proof fenced enclosures;

    V.   Transplanted for the purpose of commercial shooting;

    VI.   By the use of traps or pharmaceuticals;

    VII.   While swimming, helpless in deep snow, or helpless in any other natural or artificial medium;

    VIII.   On another hunter's license;

    IX.   Not in full compliance with the game laws or regulations of the federal government or of any state, province, territory, or tribal council on reservations or tribal lands;

Please answer the following questions:

Were dogs used in conjunction with the pursuit and harvest of this animal?

    ☐ Yes   ☐ No

If the answer to the above question is yes, answer the following statements:

    1. I was present on the hunt at the times the dogs were released to pursue this animal.

        ☐ True ☐ False

    2. If electronic collars were attached to any of the dogs, receivers were not used to harvest this animal.

        ☐ True ☐ False

To the best of my knowledge the answers to the above statements are true. If the answer to either #1 or #2 above is false, please explain on a separate sheet.

I certify that the trophy scored on this chart was not taken in violation of the conditions listed above. In signing this statement, I understand that if the information provided on this entry is found to be misrepresented or fraudulent in any respect, it will not be accepted into the Awards Program and 1) all of my prior entries are subject to deletion from future editions of **Records of North American Big Game** 2) future entries may not be accepted.

FAIR CHASE, as defined by the Boone and Crockett Club®, is the ethical, sportsmanlike and lawful pursuit and taking of any free-ranging wild, native North American big game animal in a manner that does not give the hunter an improper advantage over such game animals.

The Boone and Crockett Club® may exclude the entry of any animal that it deems to have been taken in an unethical manner or under conditions deemed inappropriate by the Club.

Date:_____ Signature of Hunter:_____

                              (SIGNATURE MUST BE WITNESSED BY AN OFFICIAL MEASURER OR A NOTARY PUBLIC.)

Date:_____ Signature of Notary or Official Measurer:_____

MEASURING AND JUDGING
Whitetail and Coues' Deer

Coues' (pronounced "cows") deer and whitetails are subspecies of the same species, the familiar white-tailed deer. The Coues' deer is a smaller, desert-dwelling version of its larger cousin, the whitetail. Antler formation is similar, with mature Coues' deer racks being noticeably smaller and usually showing a limited degree of spread. Coues' deer are found in the deserts of southwestern New Mexico, Arizona, and northwestern Mexico. No part of their current range includes the larger whitetail. Thus, the geographic boundaries described in Chapter 2 provide adequate means of separating the two subspecies.

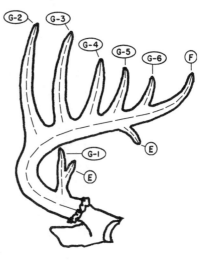

Whitetails can show an almost infinite variety in number and location of points. The non-typical category was established to properly recognize such trophies and there are typical and non-typical categories for both Coues' and whitetail trophies. If there are numerous abnormal points, the non-typical score chart should be used so that the additional points can add to the final score, rather than being subtracted from it. If the abnormal points are few in number and short in length(s), use the typical score chart that provides for a subtraction of the total of lengths of such points as a penalty for non-symmetry. If there is any doubt as to which score chart should be used, the trophy can be measured both ways. If the trophy qualifies for both the typical and non-typical categories, it **cannot** be listed in both. The final choice of the listing category in such instances rests with the trophy owner.

FIGURE 5-A

In the following material, the scoring procedure for whitetails will be described. Of course, the instructions apply equally well to Coues' deer, with the only difference being minimum entry scores. The typical pattern of mature whitetail antler development is an unbranched main beam that normally develops from three to seven (or more) unbranched points at spaced intervals **(figure 5-A)**. Usually, a brow tine develops in this pattern as the first point, G-1, and the second point, G-2, on each side

FIGURE 5-B
DETAIL OF A POINT
MEASUREMENT

is usually the longest of the sequence. As in other deer categories, the main beam tip is counted as a point but is not measured as a point. The length of main beam is a separate measurement, so the beam tip cannot also be measured as a point.

A point in whitetail and Coues' deer is any projection *at least one inch long and longer than wide at some location at least one inch from the tip of the projection.* (Each projection should be measured to ascertain whether it is or is not a point.) Once it is determined that a projection is a point then its entire point length is measured from its tip down to its base. As shown in **figure 5-B**, point base lines are established where the point joins either the main beam or another point. The base should reflect the normal antler configuration as if the point were not present.

The length of beam and antler point length measurement may be taken by the use of the flexible steel cable or a 1/4-inch wide steel clip-end tape. The use of a round, flexible steel cable (such as a bicycle brake cable) greatly speeds-up the measuring process while still yielding an accurate measurement. However, only the quarter inch steel tape can be used for circumference measurements. As with other categories for antlered species, the animal is not eligible for listing if the skull has been split.

For measurement of length, the cable is positioned along the outer curve of the beam or point. The end of the measurement is marked by attaching an alligator clip to the cable at the proper spot. The cable is then removed and held in a straight line against a clip-end tape or folding carpenter's rule to record the length measurement. The clip-end tape is often faster to use when antler points are generally straight as the clip-end can easily be hooked on the end of the antler point and the tape stretched across the point's base line. When using a 1/4-inch wide tape on a curved point or antler beam, the measurer will need to mark points of rotation along the line of measurement. The tape is then rotated at these marks. Be sure to align the tape at the appropriate length when the realignment is made.

The measurement for determining the length of an antler main beam is illustrated on the score chart, being generally a line from the antler burr, above the eye, to the beam tip, maintained along the outer side of the beam. It can be measured either from the tip to the burr or from the burr to the tip.

The measurement begins at the point where the center line along the outer side of the base intersects the burr. This point is above and slightly off center of the eye socket. To determine this starting point, view the antlers from the side lining up the far side with the near side. Find the middle of the burr as the antlers are viewed from this angle (i.e., the center of the burr on the outer side). It is neither at the lower front edge nor at the rear edge of the beam but rather at the outside center of the burr.

Once the starting location on the burr is noted, the length of the main beam measurement proceeds along the outer side of the beam towards the middle of the antler beam below the G-2 point as indicated on the diagram on the score chart (**figure 5-A**). From that location, it proceeds on out to the beam tip over the outer curve of the antler. In general, this line should stay near the middle of the beam on the outer side. It is sometimes helpful to first mark the base lines for the normal points as this may provide a visual reference for staying in the middle of the antler beam. The actual measurement is taken by the use of the flexible steel cable or steel clip-end tape. The use of a tape necessitates marking the antler with a soft lead pencil and swinging the tape at these marks as necessary as the antler curves. Either way should result in the same measurement if the correct line is chosen.

Prior to making the actual measurement by either method, it is often helpful to hold the rack in a normal, upright position at arm's length. This will show whether or not the chosen line properly follows the outer curve of the main beam.

If the antler beam roles inward, still stay near the middle of the beam even though the middle may now be on the top and not on the true outer side of the surface of the antler. If the beam hooks upward, still stay on the outer side of the antler near the middle (and not over the curve of the upper hook, which would place the measurement line along the bottom of the beam). If an abnormal point (or antler projection) is in the line of measurement, simply find the shortest path around the point either above or below the projection and continue the measurement.

In extreme cases where abnormalities occur such that the overall beam lengths and the subsequent overall score would be increased **unduly** as a result of the abnormalities, a caliper can be

FIGURE 5-C
ABNORMAL POINT
EXAMPLES
(SHADED)

5-C1

5-C2

5-C3

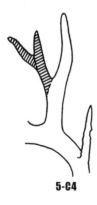

5-C4

used to determine the length of beam material under the abnormal projection(s). Measure the beam length to the abnormality. Then measure the length of beam under the abnormality with the caliper tips positioned on each side of it. Add this value to the first measurement and to the measurement of the remainder of the beam to obtain the overall beam length.

In the case of webbed antlers, special care must be taken when measuring beam lengths. You must first project the normal main beam as if there was no webbing. The length is then taken through the center of the projected main beam as usual. This measurement technique applies to any webbed antler, whether the webbing occurs on one or both antlers.

The next stage involves the measurement of point lengths. The designation of points as either normal or abnormal requires application of the following general rules:

1) Burr tines or "beauty points" (points arising from the antler burr) are always abnormal **(figure 5-C1)**.

2) Split or multiple brow tines mean that only one of these can be measured as the normal brow point. If one of these is a clear-cut branch of the other, the branch is designated as abnormal **(figure 5-C2)**. If both are separate points, without one being a branch of the other, choose as the normal G-1 point the one that best matches in shape and location usual G-1 points and the G-1 on the other antler. Generally this will be the longer point; the other(s) is then measured as abnormal.

3) Points arising from the side or bottom of the main beam are always abnormal **(figure 5-C3)**.

4) Point branches (those arising from points rather than from the main beam) are always abnormal **(figure 5-C4)**.

5) Extra points occurring below the brow tine are always abnormal points even though they may be paired.

6) If two points (other than brow points) have a common base origin on the top of the main beam, and one is not a branch of the other, and both "pair" with points on the opposite antler, both are considered normal (See earlier discussion of common base points).

7) Normal points arise from the top of the main beam at roughly spaced intervals and are usually paired with similar length points on the other antler in a more or less symmetrical pattern.

8) Paired points arising from the top of the beam are treated as normal points even though they may be shorter (or longer) than adjacent points and have slightly different spacing than other paired points. Thus, a pair of short points occurring between G-1 and the next set of taller points would be treated as G-2 points.

9) If a rack has two rows of side-by-side points on each antler, one row should be treated as abnormal points. Generally, the outer row points are measured as the normal points.

10) Extra, unpaired points at the end of the beam that project upward and generally in the usual spacing pattern are treated as normal points **(figure 5-D)**. Enter a dash or zero for the missing other side. Since these unmatched points at the end of the beam are "matched" against a zero value, their lengths will be subtracted in the difference column essentially negating their presence. The determination of these as normal points should be the same whether the trophy is entered in the typical or non-typical category.

11) If an "extra" point (unpaired, and **not** one of the normal pattern of points) arises from the top of the main beam and upsets the interval spacing/ pairing, it should be counted as abnormal (even though it is "normal" in origin) to avoid the artificial penalty for lack of symmetry between points that would occur if it were counted as a normal point. Such points are referred to as non-symmetry points and will be discussed in more detail in the material that follows.

12) There is no upper limit to how many normal points might occur on a whitetail trophy **(figure 5-E)**, but the usual pattern is seven or

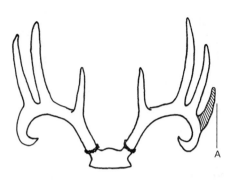

FIGURE 5-D

A IS AN UNPAIRED NORMAL POINT

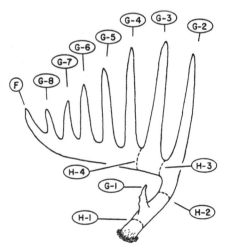

FIGURE 5-E

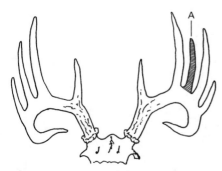

FIGURE 5-F
THE MOST
COMMON
UNMATCHED
POINT LOCATION

A IS AN
ABNORMAL POINT

fewer (plus beam tip) per antler, and the score chart reflects this pattern. In the extreme rarity that more than seven truly normal points occur, the measurements of the extra point(s) could be included as a separate additional line(s) and explained in the REMARKS section.

13) If a G-1 point (brow tine) is missing on one antler, it is proper to treat the existing brow tine on the opposite antler as a normal point, and match it against a blank or zero value for the missing G-1. Thus there are three, and only three occasions, when an unmatched point off the top of the beam is treated as a normal point—opposite a missing brow tine that never grew; opposite a broken normal point less than an inch long; and at the end of the main beam.

The lengths of the individual normal and abnormal points are recorded in the proper blanks on the score chart. If a normal point has been broken off to less than an inch long, record a zero or dash to indicate its condition and note the action in the REMARKS. Such action preserves the sequence and avoids any artificial penalty for non-symmetry.

Certain special cases—common base points, webbed points, burr points—that occur on all deer subspecies were covered in a previous chapter. Additional comments are in order for the treatment of non-symmetry points. The rule is simple—if an extra unmatched point, that is a normal point by definition, occurs at some position other than at the end of the beam, it is treated as an abnormal point. Such points are referred to as non-symmetry points. If this point were paired on the opposite beam, it would be treated as a normal point. Thus a rack must display more normal points on one side than the other to even be considered as one that has a non-symmetry point. While these unmatched points can occur at any location, they are most common between G-2 and G-3 as illustrated in **figure 5-F**. One specific situation that may give rise to this situation is the presence of a common base point with G-2 on one side and a forked G-2 on the other. In such a case it is likely the point sharing the common base with G-2 is extra as it may be "matched" against the fork, which is an abnormal point, on the other side.

The key determination is which point is unmatched. If the point is unmatched **at the end**, then it is **normal**. If it is unmatched **between normal points**, it is **abnormal**. The determination is the same whether or not the deer is being measured as a typical or non-typical entry. In many cases, the decision will result in an overall lower score for the buck, particularly if it is being entered in the typical category. Such a result should occur since the measuring system for typical entries is designed to reward highly symmetrical, balanced antlers. An extra point detracts from this symmetry. Again, this ruling does not apply to an unmatched G-1 point, nor an unmatched point at the beam's end. In cases where a point is ruled a non-symmetry point, please use the REMARKS to highlight this decision.

Points are measured either from the base lines established on the main beam to the tip of each point or from point tip to the base line, with both methods yielding the same result. Generally, points end in a sharp cone shape, with the measurement being to the tip of this cone. Should the point end in a noticeably blunted condition, somewhat like a human thumb, the measurement line can be continued to the midpoint of the rounding. If a point (or beam) is broken and not a round blunt end, use credit card or carpenter's square to "square off" the end in a fashion similar to the taking of the length of horn for sheep.

If a rack shows numerous points and/or many abnormal points, measurement of it can be aided by marking each point with bits of colored tape to designate normal points (perhaps green tape) and abnormal points (perhaps red tape). It is also very helpful to use a third color to indicate projections that do not qualify as points so that they are not inadvertently and incorrectly measured as points. As each point is measured to its proper base line, the tape is removed to show that the point has been measured. (Remember the beam tip is not measured as a point.)

Establishment of the base lines for individual point measurement is straightforward. The base line is established to identify that material properly called main beam from the material of the point (or separate a point branch from its "parent" point). Properly drawn, the base line should delineate the same amount of beam (or "parent") material below the point's center as can be ascertained on either side of the point being measured. A good method of marking base lines is to pull the steel measuring tape taut across the point base resting on top of the parent structure

FIGURE 5-G
DRAW A LINE
ACROSS THE
OUTSIDE CURVE
OF THE MAIN
BEAM (PERPEN-
DICULAR TO ITS
LENGTH) FROM
THE MIDPOINT OF
THE BASE OF THE
G-3 POINT. THEN
MEASURE THE
DISTANCE FROM
THE PERPENDICU-
LAR TO BEAM TIP.
THE LOCATION
FOR H-4 IS THEN
DETERMINED BY
DIVIDING THAT
DISTANCE BY 2.

antler material. Then the base line is marked with a lead pencil along the lower edge of the tape. Often a measuring cable makes it easier to establish the correct base line.

Antler points are then measured along the outside of their curve. In almost every case, the points G-2, 3, 4, and others in the sequence, curve inward and not outward. If a point should curve outward, it would be appropriate to measure it on the inside of the rack and thus reflect properly the outer curve of the point. In the case where it is not obvious which direction the point curves, measure both sides and record the longer measurement as the point length. It is never correct to measure along the sides of a point to determine its length. The same procedure of measuring points on the outside of their curve applies to abnormal points as well.

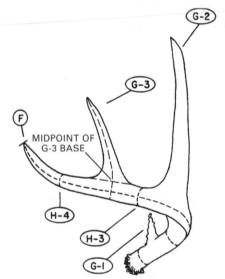

The brow tines, although usually straight, may be curved either backward or forward. If they are curved forward, they are measured on the backside in order to reflect the outer curve of the point. If they are curved backward, they are measured on the front side, again to reflect the outer curve. Note such actions in the REMARKS.

The four circumferences (H-1, 2, 3, and 4) are taken by use of the ring-end tape. The tape should be positioned in the general area of the indicated measurement by looping it around the main beam. Pull the tape together and gently move it along the beam until the smallest circumference measurement is obtained. If you use a clip-end tape to measure circumferences, overlap the tape at a full 10 inch increment to simplify the procedure. Be sure to subtract the amount of overlap before recording the measurement.

Almost without exception whitetail trophies large enough to reach the current all-time records book minimum entry score (170 for typical; 195 for non-typical) will have at least five normal points (including beam tip) on each antler. For such trophies the four circumferences will be taken between points as illustrated on the score chart. However, many Coues' deer will show only three measured points per antler, which will require that the H-4 circumference be taken halfway between

the G-3 point and the antler tip
(figure 5-G). To make this measurement properly, determine the
center of the base of G-3 where it
meets the main beam, then measure
from this center point to the beam

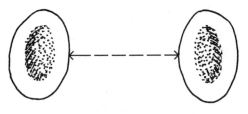

FIGURE 5-H

tip. The halfway point of this line is the correct location for
the H-4 circumference.

The inside spread should be taken with a folding
carpenter's rule, utilizing the extension to complete the measured line. Care must be exercised to properly position the
ruler for this measurement. The line of measurement should
be at a right angle to the long axis
of the skull. It must also be parallel to the skull cap. Thus, if one
beam should be positioned higher
than the other, it will be necessary
to utilize a straightedge against the
higher antler to properly locate the

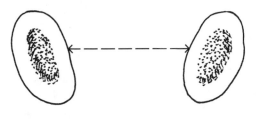

FIGURE 5-I

line. The actual measurement is taken to the center of the
main beams once it has been properly positioned.

The actual measurement is taken to the inside center of the
main beams once the antlers have been properly positioned. The
correct points of contact for taking
the inside spread measurement are
noted in **figure 5-H**, which represents
the cross sections of the main beams.
If the main beams roll inwards or tilt
outwards, the inside spread is taken
to the centers of the main beams as

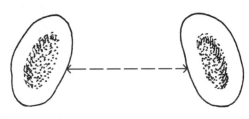

FIGURE 5-J

illustrated in **figure 5-I** and **figure 5-J**, respectively.

Note that spread credit (Column 1 of the score chart)
cannot exceed the length of the longer antler main beam. If
the spread measurement does exceed the longer main beam,
enter the longer main beam length (rather than the inside
spread measurement) in Column 1 of the score chart.

Rarely, one antler will curve inward in the normal fashion, while the other will flare outward. In such a case, the
point of measurement for inside spread should not be taken
on the flaring antler beyond where it begins to diverge from
the "normal" curvature as found on the other antler.

The supplementary data of tip to tip spread should also be

taken by use of the folding carpenter's rule or measuring tape. This measurement is simply from the center of the tip of one antler to the center of the tip of the other. Greatest spread is best taken by use of two perpendiculars, such as carpenter's levels held upright by large c-clamps or perfectly square-cut wooden blocks, that are positioned on each side of the rack. The measurement is then taken by a steel measuring tape or folding carpenter's rule between the perpendiculars.

Field Judging Whitetail Deer

By Jay Lesser

The Boone and Crockett Club recognizes two categories of whitetail deer. The larger and the more familiar to most of us is the common whitetail, which is found in Mexico, all but a handful of states in the United States, and in many parts of Canada. The other is the Coues' deer (correctly pronounced "cows"), a small-bodied whitetail with correspondingly smaller antlers that is found in the deserts and deciduous woodlands of southwestern New Mexico, Arizona, and northwestern Mexico. No part of the Coues' deer's current range is inhabited by the larger whitetail, thus separating the two subspecies.

The first thing you will notice about a large whitetail buck's rack is the overall height and width, followed by the number of points, and mass. When assessing a potential trophy's score, we need to look at the lengths of the main beams, lengths of the points, the inside spread of the main beams, and the mass or circumference of the main beams at four locations.

These things can be quickly evaluated in the field with a few simple calculations. To do this we need things of known sizes to visually compare the antlers to and in this case we will use the deer's ears, eyes, and nose. While this can be an inexact science considering the range of sizes from the diminutive Coues' deer to the bulky giants of Canada, we are going to throw out the biggest and the smallest and take an average of the most common whitetails found in the United States. The average buck, with his ears in an alert position, has an ear tip-to-tip spread of 16 inches. His ears will measures six inches from the base to the tip. The circumference of his eye is four inches, and from the center of the eye to the end of his nose should measure about eight inches. These will be our "rulers" for antler size estimation. If you are hunting in an area that traditionally produces huge-bodied deer,

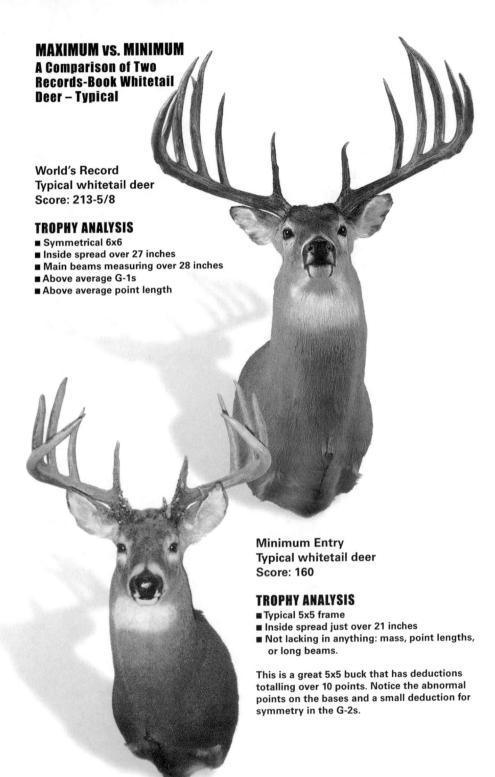

MAXIMUM vs. MINIMUM
A Comparison of Two Records-Book Whitetail Deer – Typical

World's Record
Typical whitetail deer
Score: 213-5/8

TROPHY ANALYSIS
- Symmetrical 6x6
- Inside spread over 27 inches
- Main beams measuring over 28 inches
- Above average G-1s
- Above average point length

Minimum Entry
Typical whitetail deer
Score: 160

TROPHY ANALYSIS
- Typical 5x5 frame
- Inside spread just over 21 inches
- Not lacking in anything: mass, point lengths, or long beams.

This is a great 5x5 buck that has deductions totalling over 10 points. Notice the abnormal points on the bases and a small deduction for symmetry in the G-2s.

or if you are hunting the little Coues' deer, you will need to adjust your "rulers" accordingly.

The Tally

Assuming you can get a frontal view, estimating a buck's inside spread should be easy. Is he outside of his ear tips? If so, by how much? For example, if his main beam appears to be half an ear or three inches outside the ear tip on each side, then by adding 6 to 16 we find that he has a 22-inch spread.

Judging the length of the main beams is next. A general rule of thumb is to look for a buck whose main beams appear to extend forward as far as the tip of his nose. However, by using this criterion alone, a long-beamed buck might be passed over if you only have a side view and the buck has a wide spread and/or its antlers turn sharply in so that the main beam tips nearly touch. Also, be aware of the buck whose beams tower above its head before sweeping forward as this adds valuable inches to an otherwise average looking main beam. The actual main beam length is estimated using our ear length and eye to nose "rulers."

Next, and to many, the most impressive features of a trophy whitetail are the number and lengths of the points on his rack. The Boone and Crockett Club defines a point on a whitetail or Coues' deer as "any projection at least one inch long and longer than it is wide at one inch or more of length." Since most whitetails are hunted in or near heavy cover where there may only be seconds to assess their antlers, we need a quick way to count points.

Points may be quickly counted by assuming that an overwhelming majority of mature whitetail bucks grow a brow tine on each antler and that the main beam tip usually lies almost horizontally. This allows us to count the standing normal points G-2, G-3, G-4, etc., and quickly add that to the number 2 (brow tine and beam tip). With this method you can quickly determine that a buck with two standing normal points per side is a 4x4 or 8-pointer, and with three standing points per side he is a 5x5 or 10-pointer, and so on, with the exception of Coues' whitetail. Nearly all the bucks that make the records book have at least five normal points per side. The length of the points can be estimated using the same "rulers" we used for the main beams.

The typical pattern of a mature whitetail's antler development is an unbranched main beam that normally develops

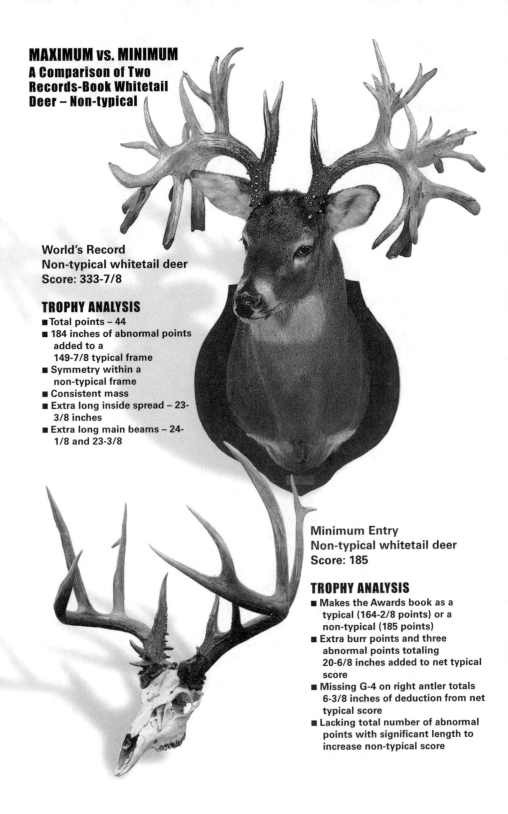

MAXIMUM vs. MINIMUM
A Comparison of Two Records-Book Whitetail Deer – Non-typical

World's Record
Non-typical whitetail deer
Score: 333-7/8

TROPHY ANALYSIS
- Total points – 44
- 184 inches of abnormal points added to a 149-7/8 typical frame
- Symmetry within a non-typical frame
- Consistent mass
- Extra long inside spread – 23-3/8 inches
- Extra long main beams – 24-1/8 and 23-3/8

Minimum Entry
Non-typical whitetail deer
Score: 185

TROPHY ANALYSIS
- Makes the Awards book as a typical (164-2/8 points) or a non-typical (185 points)
- Extra burr points and three abnormal points totaling 20-6/8 inches added to net typical score
- Missing G-4 on right antler totals 6-3/8 inches of deduction from net typical score
- Lacking total number of abnormal points with significant length to increase non-typical score

MAXIMUM vs. MINIMUM
A Comparison of Two Records-Book Coues' Whitetail Deer

World's Record
Typical Coues' whitetail deer
Score: 144-1/8

TROPHY ANALYSIS

- Mass, mass, and more mass
- 5x6 frame
- Extra long main beams – 20-2/8 and 20-5/8 inches
- Only 4-7/8 inches in symmetry deduction

Minimum Entry
Typical Coues' whitetail deer
Score: 104-1/8

TROPHY ANALYSIS

- 5x4 frame
- Only 2-6/8 inches in symmetry deduction
- Strong G-2s and G-3s – 9-6/8 and 9-2/8 inches, respectively
- Good main beams – 16 and 15 inches
- Lacks overall mass

from three to seven (sometimes more) unbranched points per antler at roughly spaced intervals. Any other points are considered "abnormal" and their lengths are deducted from the score if the buck is scored as a typical or added to the score if it is being scored as a non-typical.

Estimating the mass or circumference measurements of the antler is where we use our deer's four-inch eye circumference as the "ruler." Compare the antler at H-1, H-2, etc., to the eye. How much bigger is the antler? If it were half again bigger, the circumference measurement at that point would be about six inches.

Ideally, the rack should be viewed from the front and the side especially when judging the main beams. However, this isn't always possible and sometimes you will just have to go with your gut feeling. But beware of the rear view, as it can be deceiving. From this angle you get an exaggerated impression of the antler's height and spread.

The most practical way to practice your field-judging skills is to estimate the score of mounted heads. Use the buck's "rulers" to estimate the score, then check your calculations by actually measuring the rack. With a little practice, you will be surprised how close your estimates will become. One last word of advice, when the time comes to shoot, don't bother looking at the antlers one more time. It can cause your nervous system to do strange things.

Field Judging Coues' Whitetail

Coues' deer are miniature, desert-dwelling cousins of the familiar whitetail. Therefore, you are looking for the same features as in whitetails, only reduced in expression. Coues' deer antlers tend to form semi-circles, with the antler tips often pointing toward each other. Seldom will a Coues' deer show the "wide-open" look that is fairly common in whitetails. Often, there is very little distance between the antler tips, and some may nearly touch each other. A mature Coues' deer antler set may well look like a small whitetail set, although usually developed to a more "finished" look overall. Interestingly, the antler beams of Coues' deer may well be nearly as thick as those on a mature whitetail.

There will be at least three well-developed points (plus beam tip) on each antler for a near-book typical Coues' deer trophy, and the inside spread will need to be near 15 inches. The general look of the rack will be mature, with the second point on each antler being usually the longest of the side and the antler tips pointing toward each other.

A large non-typical Coues' deer will show these qualities plus several noticeable abnormal points. Roughly, the abnormal points will need to total about 10 inches (current typical all-time records book minimum entry score is 110 and that for non-typical is 120), which means generally about three or four abnormal points on the rack. ■

SCORECHART
Whitetail – Typical

BOONE AND CROCKETT CLUB®
OFFICIAL SCORING SYSTEM FOR NORTH AMERICAN BIG GAME TROPHIES

TYPICAL WHITETAIL AND COUES' DEER

MINIMUM SCORES		
	AWARDS	ALL-TIME
whitetail	160	170
Coues'	100	110

KIND OF DEER (check one)
- ☐ whitetail
- ☐ Coues'

Detail of Point Measurement

Abnormal Points	
Right Antler	Left Antler
SUBTOTALS	
TOTAL TO E	

SEE OTHER SIDE FOR INSTRUCTIONS

				COLUMN 1	COLUMN 2	COLUMN 3	COLUMN 4
A. No. Points on Right Antler		No. Points on Left Antler		Spread Credit	Right Antler	Left Antler	Difference
B. Tip to Tip Spread		C. Greatest Spread					
D. Inside Spread of Main Beams		SPREAD CREDIT MAY EQUAL BUT NOT EXCEED LONGER MAIN BEAM					
E. Total of Lengths of Abnormal Points							
F. Length of Main Beam							
G-1. Length of First Point							
G-2. Length of Second Point							
G-3. Length of Third Point							
G-4. Length of Fourth Point, If Present							
G-5. Length of Fifth Point, If Present							
G-6. Length of Sixth Point, If Present							
G-7. Length of Seventh Point, If Present							
H-1. Circumference at Smallest Place Between Burr and First Point							
H-2. Circumference at Smallest Place Between First and Second Points							
H-3. Circumference at Smallest Place Between Second and Third Points							
H-4. Circumference at Smallest Place Between Third and Fourth Points							
			TOTALS				

ADD	Column 1		Exact Locality Where Killed:
	Column 2		Date Killed: Hunter:
	Column 3		Owner: Telephone #:
	Subtotal		Owner's Address:
SUBTRACT Column 4			Guide's Name and Address:
FINAL SCORE			Remarks: (Mention Any Abnormalities or Unique Qualities)

I, _____ , certify that I have measured this trophy on _____
PRINT NAME   MM/DD/YYYYY

at _____
STREET ADDRESS   CITY   STATE/PROVINCE
and that these measurements and data are, to the best of my knowledge and belief, made in accordance with the instructions given.

Witness: _____ Signature: _____ I.D. Number [ ][ ][ ][ ]
B&C OFFICIAL MEASURER

INSTRUCTIONS FOR MEASURING TYPICAL WHITETAIL AND COUES' DEER

All measurements must be made with a 1/4-inch wide flexible steel tape to the nearest one-eighth of an inch. (Note: A flexible steel cable can be used to measure points and main beams only.) Enter fractional figures in eighths, without reduction. Official measurements cannot be taken until the antlers have air dried for at least 60 days after the animal was killed.

    A. Number of Points on Each Antler: To be counted a point, the projection must be at least one inch long, with the length exceeding width at one inch or more of length. All points are measured from tip of point to nearest edge of beam as illustrated. Beam tip is counted as a point but not measured as a point.

    B. Tip to Tip Spread is measured between tips of main beams.

    C. Greatest Spread is measured between perpendiculars at a right angle to the center line of the skull at widest part, whether across main beams or points.

    D. Inside Spread of Main Beams is measured at a right angle to the center line of the skull at widest point between main beams. Enter this measurement again as the Spread Credit if it is less than or equal to the length of the longer main beam; if greater, enter longer main beam length for Spread Credit.

    E. Total of Lengths of all Abnormal Points: Abnormal Points are those non-typical in location (such as points originating from a point or from bottom or sides of main beam) or extra points beyond the normal pattern of points. Measure in usual manner and enter in appropriate blanks.

    F. Length of Main Beam is measured from the center of the lowest outside edge of burr over the outer side to the most distant point of the main beam. The point of beginning is that point on the burr where the center line along the outer side of the beam intersects the burr, then following generally the line of the illustration.

    G-1-2-3-4-5-6-7. Length of Normal Points: Normal points project from the top of the main beam. They are measured from nearest edge of main beam over outer curve to tip. Lay the tape along the outer curve of the beam so that the top edge of the tape coincides with the top edge of the beam on both sides of the point to determine the baseline for point measurements. Record point lengths in appropriate blanks.

    H-1-2-3-4. Circumferences are taken as detailed in illustration for each measurement. If brow point is missing, take H-1 and H-2 at smallest place between burr and G-2. If G-4 is missing, take H-4 halfway between G-3 and tip of main beam.

ENTRY AFFIDAVIT FOR ALL HUNTER-TAKEN TROPHIES

For the purpose of entry into the Boone and Crockett Club's® records, North American big game harvested by the use of the following methods or under the following conditions are ineligible:

    I.   Spotting or herding game from the air, followed by landing in its vicinity for the purpose of pursuit and shooting;

    II. Herding or chasing with the aid of any motorized equipment;

    III. Use of electronic communication devices, artificial lighting, or electronic light intensifying devices;

    IV. Confined by artificial barriers, including escape-proof fenced enclosures;

    V. Transplanted for the purpose of commercial shooting;

    VI. By the use of traps or pharmaceuticals;

    VII. While swimming, helpless in deep snow, or helpless in any other natural or artificial medium;

    VIII. On another hunter's license;

    IX. Not in full compliance with the game laws or regulations of the federal government or of any state, province, territory, or tribal council on reservations or tribal lands;

I certify that the trophy scored on this chart was not taken in violation of the conditions listed above. In signing this statement, I understand that if the information provided on this entry is found to be misrepresented or fraudulent in any respect, it will not be accepted into the Awards Program and 1) all of my prior entries are subject to deletion from future editions of **Records of North American Big Game** 2) future entries may not be accepted.

FAIR CHASE, as defined by the Boone and Crockett Club®, is the ethical, sportsmanlike and lawful pursuit and taking of any free-ranging wild, native North American big game animal in a manner that does not give the hunter an improper advantage over such game animals.

The Boone and Crockett Club® may exclude the entry of any animal that it deems to have been taken in an unethical manner or under conditions deemed inappropriate by the Club.

Date: _____ Signature of Hunter: _____
(SIGNATURE MUST BE WITNESSED BY AN OFFICIAL MEASURER OR A NOTARY PUBLIC.)

Date: _____ Signature of Notary or Official Measurer: _____

SCORECHART
Whitetail – Non-Typical

250 Station Drive
Missoula, MT 59801
(406) 542-1888

BOONE AND CROCKETT CLUB®
OFFICIAL SCORING SYSTEM FOR NORTH AMERICAN BIG GAME TROPHIES

NON-TYPICAL
WHITETAIL AND COUES' DEER

MINIMUM SCORES		
	AWARDS	ALL-TIME
whitetail	185	195
Coues'	105	120

KIND OF DEER (check one)
☐ whitetail
☐ Coues'

Abnormal Points	
Right Antler	Left Antler

Detail of Point Measurement

SUBTOTALS	
E. TOTAL	

SEE OTHER SIDE FOR INSTRUCTIONS			COLUMN 1	COLUMN 2	COLUMN 3	COLUMN 4
A. No. Points on Right Antler		No. Points on Left Antler	Spread Credit	Right Antler	Left Antler	Difference
B. Tip to Tip Spread		C. Greatest Spread				
D. Inside Spread of Main Beams		SPREAD CREDIT MAY EQUAL BUT NOT EXCEED LONGER MAIN BEAM				
F. Length of Main Beam						
G-1. Length of First Point						
G-2. Length of Second Point						
G-3. Length of Third Point						
G-4. Length of Fourth Point, If Present						
G-5. Length of Fifth Point, If Present						
G-6. Length of Sixth Point, If Present						
G-7. Length of Seventh Point, If Present						
H-1. Circumference at Smallest Place Between Burr and First Point						
H-2. Circumference at Smallest Place Between First and Second Points						
H-3. Circumference at Smallest Place Between Second and Third Points						
H-4. Circumference at Smallest Place Between Third and Fourth Points						
		TOTALS				

	Column 1		Exact Locality Where Killed:
ADD	Column 2		Date Killed: Hunter:
	Column 3		Owner: Telephone #:
	Subtotal		Owner's Address:
SUBTRACT Column 4			Guide's Name and Address:
	Subtotal		Remarks: (Mention Any Abnormalities or Unique Qualities)
	ADD Line E Total		
	FINAL SCORE		

I, _____, certify that I have measured this trophy on _____
 PRINT NAME   MM/DD/YYYYY

at _____
 STREET ADDRESS   CITY   STATE/PROVINCE

and that these measurements and data are, to the best of my knowledge and belief, made in accordance with the instructions given.

Witness: _____ Signature: _____ I.D. Number ☐☐☐
                                                           B&C OFFICIAL MEASURER

INSTRUCTIONS FOR MEASURING NON-TYPICAL WHITETAIL AND COUES' DEER

All measurements must be made with a 1/4-inch wide flexible steel tape to the nearest one-eighth of an inch. (Note: A flexible steel cable can be used to measure points and main beams only.) Enter fractional figures in eighths, without reduction. Official measurements cannot be taken until the antlers have air dried for at least 60 days after the animal was killed.

A. Number of Points on Each Antler: To be counted a point, the projection must be at least one inch long, with the length exceeding width at one inch or more of length. All points are measured from tip of point to nearest edge of beam as illustrated. Beam tip is counted as a point but not measured as a point.

B. Tip to Tip Spread is measured between tips of main beams.

C. Greatest Spread is measured between perpendiculars at a right angle to the center line of the skull at widest part, whether across main beams or points.

D. Inside Spread of Main Beams is measured at a right angle to the center line of the skull at widest point between main beams. Enter this measurement again as the Spread Credit I f it is less than or equal to the length of the longer main beam; if greater, enter longer main beam length for Spread Credit.

E. Total of Lengths of all Abnormal Points: Abnormal Points are those non-typical in location (such as points originating from a point or from bottom or sides of main beam) or extra points beyond the normal pattern of points. Measure in usual manner and enter in appropriate blanks.

F. Length of Main Beam is measured from the center of the lowest outside edge of burr over the outer side to the most distant point of the main beam. The point of beginning is that point on the burr where the center line along the outer side of the beam intersects the burr, then following generally the line of the illustration.

G-1-2-3-4-5-6-7. Length of Normal Points: Normal points project from the top of the main beam. They are measured from nearest edge of main beam over outer curve to tip. Lay the tape along the outer curve of the beam so that the top edge of the tape coincides with the top edge of the beam on both sides of the point to determine the baseline for point measurement. Record point lengths in appropriate blanks.

H-1-2-3-4. Circumferences are taken as detailed in illustration for each measurement. If brow point is missing, take H-1 and H-2 at smallest place between burr and G-2. If G-4 is missing, take H-4 halfway between G-3 and tip of main beam.

ENTRY AFFIDAVIT FOR ALL HUNTER-TAKEN TROPHIES

For the purpose of entry into the Boone and Crockett Club's® records, North American big game harvested by the use of the following methods or under the following conditions are ineligible:

I. Spotting or herding game from the air, followed by landing in its vicinity for the purpose of pursuit and shooting;
II. Herding or chasing with the aid of any motorized equipment;
III. Use of electronic communication devices, artificial lighting, or electronic light intensifying devices;
IV. Confined by artificial barriers, including escape-proof fenced enclosures;
V. Transplanted for the purpose of commercial shooting;
VI. By the use of traps or pharmaceuticals;
VII. While swimming, helpless in deep snow, or helpless in any other natural or artificial medium;
VIII. On another hunter's license;
IX. Not in full compliance with the game laws or regulations of the federal government or of any state, province, territory, or tribal council on reservations or tribal lands;

I certify that the trophy scored on this chart was not taken in violation of the conditions listed above. In signing this statement, I understand that if the information provided on this entry is found to be misrepresented or fraudulent in any respect, it will not be accepted into the Awards Program and 1) all of my prior entries are subject to deletion from future editions of **Records of North American Big Game** 2) future entries may not be accepted.

FAIR CHASE, as defined by the Boone and Crockett Club®, is the ethical, sportsmanlike and lawful pursuit and taking of any free-ranging wild, native North American big game animal in a manner that does not give the hunter an improper advantage over such game animals.

The Boone and Crockett Club® may exclude the entry of any animal that it deems to have been taken in an unethical manner or under conditions deemed inappropriate by the Club.

Date: _____ Signature of Hunter: _____
                                              (SIGNATURE MUST BE WITNESSED BY AN OFFICIAL MEASURER OR A NOTARY PUBLIC.)

Date: _____ Signature of Notary or Official Measurer: _____

MEASURING AND JUDGING
Mule and Blacktail Deer

Columbia and Sitka blacktail deer and mule deer are sub-species of the same species. They are separated by geographically defined boundary lines for records keeping purposes. Antler formation is similar, with mature Sitka blacktail racks being noticeably smaller than those of Columbia blacktail, which in turn are much smaller than mature mule deer. In the text that follows all references to mule deer will apply as well to Sitka and Columbia blacktail deer.

From a structural standpoint typical mule deer are actually the easiest of all the deer to measure as there can be no more than five normal points per antler, including the brow point (G-1) and the main beam tip (figure 6-A). All other measurable points must be considered abnormal and so entered on the score chart. A measurable point is any projection *at least one inch long and longer than wide at some location at least one inch from the tip of the projection.* (Each projection should be measured to ascertain whether it is or is not a point.) Once it is determined that a projection is a point the entire point length is measured from its tip down to its base. As shown in figure 6-B, point base lines are established where the point joins either the main beam or another point. The base should reflect the normal antler configuration as if the point were not present.

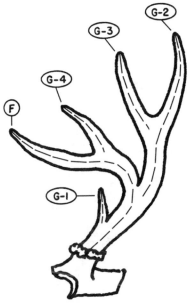

FIGURE 6-A

If an antler lacks the brow point or G-1 point, as sometimes happens, there can be only four normal points, including the main beam tip. Sitka blacktail sometimes fail to develop G-3 points, and thus resemble the usual whitetail pattern of points from a single, unbranched main beam.

Once the five normal points (if the brow and G-3 points are present) have been identified on each antler, the remaining points should be assessed to determine if a typical or non-typical score chart should be used. If there are numer-

FIGURE 6-B
DETAIL OF A POINT
MEASUREMENT

ous abnormal points, the non-typical score chart should be used so that the abnormal point lengths can be added to the final score, rather than being subtracted from it. If the abnormal points are few in number and short in length, use the typical score chart that provides for a subtraction of the total of lengths of such points as a penalty for non-symmetry. If there is any doubt as to which score chart should be used, the trophy can be measured both ways, choosing the scoring that gives better recognition for the trophy. If the trophy qualifies for both the typical and non-typical categories, it cannot be listed in both. The final choice of the listing category in such instances rests with the trophy owner.

The length of beam and antler point length measurements may be taken by the use of the flexible steel cable or a 1/4 inch wide steel clip-end tape. The use of a round, flexible steel cable (such as a bicycle brake cable) greatly speeds-up the measuring process while still yielding an accurate measurement. However, only the steel tape can be used for circumference measurements. As with other categories for antlered species, the animal is not eligible for listing if the skull has been split.

For measurement of length, the cable is positioned along the outer curve of the beam or point. The end of the measurement is marked by attaching an alligator clip to the cable at the proper spot. The cable is then removed and held in a straight line against a clip-end tape or folding carpenter's rule to record the length measurement. The clip-end tape is often faster to use when antler points are generally straight as the clip-end can easily be hooked on the end of the antler point and the tape stretched across the point's base line. When using a 1/4 inch wide tape on a curved point or antler beam, the measurer will need to mark locations of rotation along the line of measurement. The tape is then rotated at these marks. Be sure to align the tape at the appropriate length when the realignment is made.

The length of antler main beam measurement is illustrated on the score chart, being generally a line from the antler burr to the beam tip. The measurement begins at the point where the center line along the outer side of the base intersects the burr. This point is above and slightly off center of the eye socket. To determine this starting point, view the antlers from the side, lining up the far side with the near side. Find the

middle of the burr as the antlers are viewed from this angle
(i.e., the center of the burr on
the outer side). It is neither at
the lower front edge nor at the
rear edge of the beam but rather
at the outside center of the burr.
Once the starting location on
the burr is noted, the length of
the main beam measurement

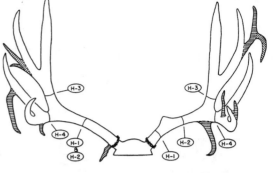

proceeds along the outer side of the beam toward the middle of
the antler beam below the G-2 point as indicated on the diagram on the score chart (figure 6-A).

From that location, it proceeds on out to the beam tip
over the outer curve of the antler. In general, this line should
stay near the middle of the beam on the outer side. The line
can be measured from either the burr to the tip or the tip to
the burr. If the antler beam rolls inward, still stay near the
middle of the beam even though the middle may not be on
the true outer side surface of the antler. If the beam hooks
upward, still stay on the outer side of the antler near the
middle (and not over the curve of the upper hook which
would place the measurement line along the bottom of the
beam). If an abnormal point (or antler projection) is in the
line of measurement, simply find the shortest path around
the point either above or below the projection and continue
the measurement.

After the main beam lengths are recorded, the lengths of
G-1, G-2, and G-4 are measured from their base lines on the
main beam. The base line for the G-3 point is along the edge of
the G-2 point from which it arises. Since a point is measured
over its outer curve, the base line can be on either the inside or
the outside of the rack depending on the curvature of the point.
If normal points are missing on one or both antlers (e.g. G-1,
G-3 or G-4), enter a zero or dash on the score chart to indicate
their absence. This is necessary to properly maintain the rest of
the point sequence.

The designation of points as either normal or abnormal
requires some judgment, especially if there are numerous
paired points. **Figure 6-C** demonstrates some abnormal configurations. Keep in mind the following general rules for mule
and blacktail deer points:

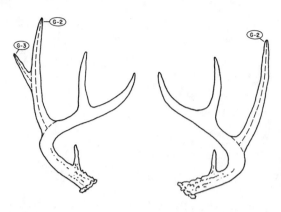

FIGURE 6-D

1) Burr tines or "beauty points" (points arising from or near the antler burr) are always abnormal.

2) Split or multiple brow tines mean that only one of these can be measured as the normal brow point. If one of these is a clear-cut branch of the other, the branch is designated as abnormal. If both are separate points, without one being a branch of the other, choose as the normal G-1 point the one that best matches in shape and location usual G-1 points and the G-1 point on the other antler. Generally this will be the longer point; the other(s) is then measured as abnormal.

3) Often a cluster of projections and points will be present, especially on G-1. In order for more than one projection to be treated as a point, each projection *separately* must meet the definition of a point (longer than wide at one inch or more of length). In such cases, the base of secondary projections may be back to the main beam *only* if they share a common base, or back to the parent point if they do not.

4) Except for the G-3 point, point branches (those arising from points rather than the main beam) are always abnormal.

5) Points arising from the side or bottom of the main beam are always abnormal.

6) Normal points occur in the "Y" branching pattern, with two such forks (G-2 and G-3 plus G-4 and beam tip) comprising the normal condition.

The lengths of the individual normal points, and also any abnormal points present, are recorded in the proper blanks on the score chart, with zero or a dash being recorded for the obvious absence of a point in the normal sequence. Points are measured either from the base lines established on the main beam to the tip of each point or from the point tip to the base line. Either method should yield the same result. Generally, points end in a sharp cone shape, with the measurement being to the tip of this cone. Should the point end in a noticeably blunted condition, somewhat like a human thumb, the measurement line can be continued to the midpoint of the rounding. In measuring points, the measurement line should be along the outer curve of the point to properly record its greatest length. Abnormal points are measured in exactly the same manner as normal points.

If the trophy has numerous extra points, it may be difficult to remember which are normal and which are abnormal as the measurement of individual points is begun. Marking the points with bits of colored tape can be a distinct help. Use one color (perhaps green) for the normal points and another (perhaps red) for the abnormal ones. Also be sure to designate projections that do not qualify as points with some form of tape or mark so they are not inadvertently recorded as points. Once all points have been so tagged, the individual point measurement is begun. As each point is measured, the tape is removed to show measurement of that point has been completed. When all tape bits have been removed, the measurement of individual points is complete (again, a main beam tip is not measured as an individual point because its length is recorded as length of main beam.)

When measuring nontypical entries, it is very helpful to record the abnormal points in a systematic fashion. Start near the base and measure each point up the main beam to G-2; then measure all abnormal points off G-2 (and G-3). Continue along the main beam and G-4 until you have recorded all abnormal points on that side of the antler. If you inadvertently fail to measure one point, it will be far easier to determine which point is missing if you have proceeded in this manner.

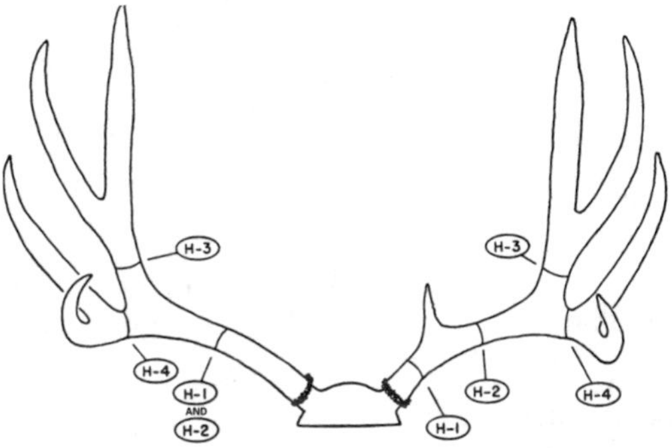

FIGURE 6-E
THE FOUR CIRCUMFERENCE MEASUREMENTS.

Some Columbia blacktail, Sitka blacktail and an occasional mule deer will be missing a G-3 point on one antler and will display an apparent reversal of the usual pattern of the G-2 and G-3 points on the other. Normally, the third point (G-3) projects forward and to the outside from G-2. In some cases, the shorter branch point will project backwards as **figure 6-D** displays. In such a case, if the rear-most point is designated as G-2 (as is normally done), the resulting pairing with the other antler will match this short point with the longer G-2 of the other side. Except for this reversal, the rack may be very symmetrical and matching the long G-2 with the short, "reversed" point would produce a large deduction. In such cases (one where the G-3 point is missing on one side and where the rear point on the other is a shorter branch), it is permissible to label the rear pointing projection as G-3, which will better pair the two longer points that come off the main beam. It is important to note this ruling applies *only when a G-3 point is missing from only one of the antlers.* If the deer has G-2 and G-3 points present on both antlers, then the rear, inner points are *always* G-2 and the forward projecting, outer points are *always* G-3 regardless of their configuration.

Four circumferences are always taken regardless of the number of normal points. The four circumference locations (H-1, 2, 3, and 4) shown in **figure 6-E** are taken by use of the ring-end tape. The tape should be positioned in the general area of the indicated measurement by looping it around the main beam. Then pull the tape together and gently move it along the beam until the smallest circumference measurement is obtained. If you use a clip-end tape to measure circumferences, overlap the tape at a full 10 inch increment to simplify the procedure. Be sure to subtract the amount of overlap before recording the measurement.

If the G-1 point is completely missing **(figure 6-E)** then H-1 and H-2 are taken at the same location, the smallest circumference between the G-2 point and the burr. However, if there is an indication of the presence of the G-1 point even though the projection (or broken point) does not qualify as G-1 then it is proper to take the H-1 and H-2 measurements on either side of the projection, as would normally be done. Some mule deer fail to develop the third point (G-3) branching from G-2, thus lack the usual point of location for the third circumference (H-3). In such a case, measure the G-2 point length and then mark its midpoint as the proper location to take the third circumference **(figure 6-F)**. Likewise if G-4 is totally missing, the H-4 measurement is taken halfway from the center of the base of the G-2 point on the main beam to the beam tip **(figure 6-G)**.

FIGURE 6-F
DIVIDE AB BY TWO
AND MARK C.
TAKE H-3 AT C.

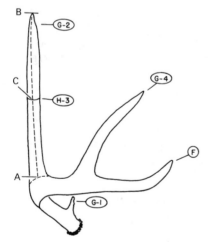

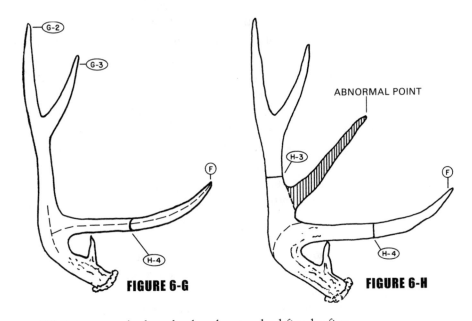

FIGURE 6-G

FIGURE 6-H

While most mule deer display the standard five by five antler configuration, some added problems may arise. Sometimes a projection that appears at first glance to be the G-4 point may actually project from the G-2 point **(figure 6-H)** instead of the main beam, as it should. When this antler configuration occurs, there is no G-4 point and the point off G-2 is treated as abnormal. This ruling will also affect the location of the H-4 measurement. Some mule deer, may have common base G-2 and G-4 points. If this occurs only on one side of the rack, there is no problem and the points (G-2 and G-4) are measured to the beam **(figure 6-I)**. If the G-2 and G-4 points on *both* antlers are common base, their lengths (on both sides) are taken as illustrated in **figure 6-J**. This procedure is the same as the method for common base points described earlier in the manual.

The inside spread (D) should be taken with a folding carpenter's rule, utilizing the extension to complete the measurement **(figure 6-K)**. Care must be exercised to properly position the ruler for this measurement. The line of measurement should be at a right angle to the long axis of the skull. It must also be parallel to the skull cap. Thus, if one beam should be positioned appreciably higher than the other, it will be necessary to utilize a straightedge against the higher antler to properly locate the line. The actual measurement will reflect the greatest distance between the inside edges of the two main beams, making sure to keep the line oriented as noted above. Since the beams may roll inward or outward this measurement is taken from near the center of one beam to near the center of the other at the widest location.

On rare occasions, one antler will curve inward in the normal fashion, while the other will **excessively** flare outward. In such a case, the inside spread measurement cannot include spread caused by the excessive flaring of the antler beam. The measurement is then taken at the greatest inside spread from the location where the antler begins to diverge from the "normal" curvature back to the burr.

Note that spread credit (Column 1 of the score chart) **cannot** exceed the length of the longer antler main beam. If the inside spread measurement does exceed the longer main beam, enter the longer main beam length (rather than the inside spread measurement) in Column 1 of the score chart. Although the inside spread on a whitetail rarely, if ever, is greater than the length of the longer antler, this situation is fairly common in mule deer. Many non-typical mule deer display exceptionally wide spreads; thus, the measurer must watch for this situation to occur.

The supplementary data of tip to tip spread **(figure 6-K)** should also be taken with a folding carpenter's rule or

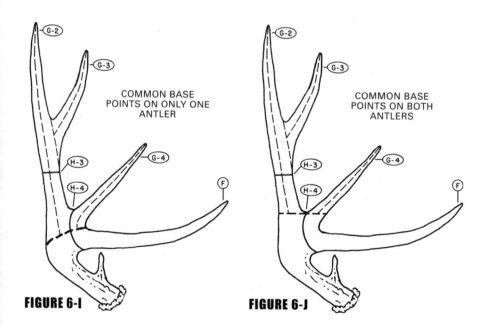

COMMON BASE
POINTS ON ONLY ONE
ANTLER

COMMON BASE
POINTS ON BOTH
ANTLERS

FIGURE 6-I

FIGURE 6-J

steel tape. This measurement (B) is simply from the center of the tip of one antler to the center of the tip of the other. On mule deer that flare out in a general fashion (not excessively divergent), the inside spread may occur near the beam tips and be nearly the same as the tip to tip measurement.

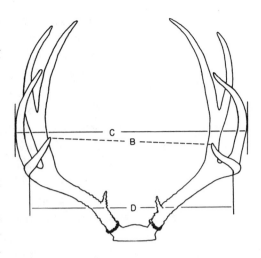

FIGURE 6-K
SPREAD
MEASUREMENTS

Greatest spread (C) is best taken by use of two perpendiculars **(figure 6-K)**, such as carpenter's levels held upright by large c-clamps or perfectly square-cut wooden blocks. The measurement is then taken by yardstick or folding carpenter's rule between the perpendiculars, after they are positioned snugly against the rack. If perpendiculars are not available, a floor and wall can be used for one perpendicular, with the second being improvised from a carpenter's level or a straight, square-cut board. In no case should the human eye be relied upon for establishment of the second perpendicular line.

Field Judging Mule Deer

By Jay Lesser

Mule deer may not have as much going on above their heads as other members of the deer family, like elk and moose, but judging them in the field can be just as tricky. Accurately field judging a mule deer buck's trophy status starts with knowing the basics of scoring a mule deer. Under the Boone and Crockett Club's scoring system, the gross score for a typical mule deer is the sum total of measurements of his inside spread, length of his main beams, length of points, and eight mass or circumference measurements. By definition, a typical mule deer will have four points per side, plus eye guards. Under field conditions we don't always have the time to pull out a calculator, however, there are a few things we can quickly look for to determine whether a buck would be a record book qualifier.

Once you've located your buck the first thing to check is his overall frame. This is the part where, "If he looks big, he is big" can come into play. A buck's frame takes into account all factors used in scoring — the inside spread, length of points, length of the main beams, and mass. If you're looking at a high racked buck with long points and a spread past his ears, you just might be looking at a buck that warrants a full evaluation. As a rule, high, wide, and heavy is what to look for, especially if you're beyond trophy and thinking record book.

After frame, try and get a clean look at the number of points, fork depth, and symmetry. Any additional or "abnormal" points are subtracted from the typical score. However, if there are enough abnormal points, a buck may be scored as a non-typical and the length of the abnormal points are added to the score. The overwhelming majority of bucks that make the book are five-point bucks (western count — four points per side, plus the eye guards). A buck with good eye guards (3+ inches) is a bonus. If he is at least a 5x5, including the brow tines, move on to fork depth. Deep forks translate into long tines and high scores. The deeper his forks, front and back, the longer his tines will be.

While sizing up his forks, pay attention to fork symmetry. Do the back forks and front forks match their counterparts on the opposite antler in depth and tine length? In scoring, symmetry is a factor. It is common to see bucks with strong back forks but weak fronts (crab claws) and vise-versa.

Next, check for mass. The mass or circumference of the main beam is also a consideration in scoring, but it can be tough to judge in the field. Mass can be estimated by comparing the circumference of the antler to the buck's eye. A mule deer's eye will measure about four inches in circumference. By using his eye as a gauge you can visualize whether his bases and main beams are at least 4-inches or larger. Heavy bases (6+ inches) with this kind of mass carried out through his main beams (5 to 4 inches), means a buck will receive high marks in the circumference category.

Your last check is spread. By now you've already accessed his spread when checking his frame, but it will help to pin down a spread measurement before you tally everything. To accurately judge antler spread, we can use a buck's ear width as a gauge. On the average mature mule deer buck, with its ears in an alert position, he will have an ear span of 20 to 22 inches tip-to-tip. But I have measured large specimens with ear tip to tip spans up to 26 inches. However, if you always use the 20 to 22 inch estimate your buck is less likely to suffer "ground shrinkage." So with this estimate a buck's rack past his ears by two inches means an inside spread in the neighborhood of 24 inches — more than enough to put him in the book if the rest adds up.

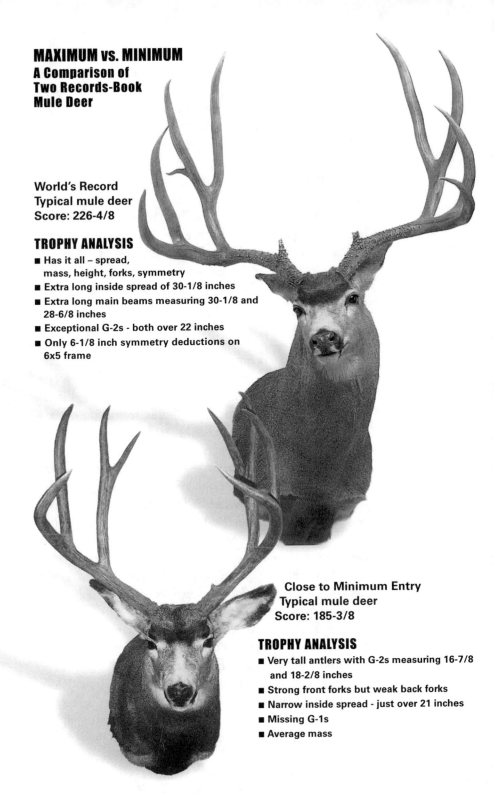

MAXIMUM vs. MINIMUM
A Comparison of Two Records-Book Mule Deer

World's Record
Typical mule deer
Score: 226-4/8

TROPHY ANALYSIS

- Has it all – spread, mass, height, forks, symmetry
- Extra long inside spread of 30-1/8 inches
- Extra long main beams measuring 30-1/8 and 28-6/8 inches
- Exceptional G-2s - both over 22 inches
- Only 6-1/8 inch symmetry deductions on 6x5 frame

Close to Minimum Entry
Typical mule deer
Score: 185-3/8

TROPHY ANALYSIS

- Very tall antlers with G-2s measuring 16-7/8 and 18-2/8 inches
- Strong front forks but weak back forks
- Narrow inside spread - just over 21 inches
- Missing G-1s
- Average mass

The Tally

After judging all these antler features you should be able to put your buck into one of three categories; obviously a shooter and book contender, a buck on the bubble that may require actually adding up the numbers to see if he will make 180 (B&C typical minimum), or just one heck of a nice buck. If he's on the edge, you might have to put a number on each feature that counts in final scoring and mentally add them up for a rough score to make your decision. Here, you can use his ears again to estimate each number. On most mature bucks it is approximately eight inches from the white spot at the base of the ear to the ear tip. If you visually superimpose this feature to the antler, you can accurately estimate things like length of main beam, height of the rack and length of the points.

The Traps

There can be a lot of hurdles to overcome in accurate field judging. Getting enough time to look your buck over closely is one. Seeing all the angles so you can count points and access fork depth is another. There are also a few "X" factors that can throw you a curve, like antler coloration and background. Bucks sporting darker horns can appear to have more mass than a tape can give them credit for. Conversely, lighter colored antlers can appear to be thinner than they really are. Background can also trick you. If your buck is standing with snow as a backdrop, antler mass can appear greater. If he is standing in the shadows or in low light, his antlers can also appear to be thinner. Another common illusion in all field judging is the power of your optics. If you are viewing, at fairly close range, with your spotting scope on 60x, even an average 5x5 can look like a monster. Back off your power to a reasonable setting so you can compare him to his body features.

Bucks on the move leave little time for a really good look. You may not be able to get past frame and mass before you have to make a decision. Bucks traveling away from you always appear bigger than they are, and watch for other bucks. Having other bucks in view to compare with can be helpful. They can also trick you if you don't pay close attention to how big they really are compared to the best buck in the bunch.

Also, if it's been a while since you've seen a quality buck, either from season to season, or if you have gone a few days on the same hunt without seeing one, the first buck you see may

MAXIMUM vs. MINIMUM
A Comparison of Two Records-Book Non-typical Mule Deer

World's Record
Non-typical
mule deer
Score: 355-2/8

TROPHY ANALYSIS
- 43 scoreable points
- 147-7/8 inches of abnormal points on a 207-3/8 typical frame
- Excellent mass, height, and width

Close to Minimum Entry
Non-typical mule deer
Score: 227-5/8

TROPHY ANALYSIS
- 19 scoreable points
- Exceptional mass
- 50-6/8 inches of abnormal points on a 176-7/8 typical frame

MAXIMUM vs. MINIMUM
A Comparison of Two Records-Book Columbia Blacktail Deer

World's Record
Typical Columbia blacktail deer
Score: 182-2/8

TROPHY ANALYSIS
- The only blacktail that surpasses the typical mule deer minimum score
- Mule deer-like 5x5 frame – G-1s are not always present in blacktail
- Extra long main beams – both over 24 inches

Close to Minimum Entry
Typical Columbia Blacktail Deer
Score: 129-7/8

TROPHY ANALYSIS
- Lacking G-3s, but brow tines make it a 4x4
- Strong G-2s measuring 12-4/8 and 11-6/8 inches.
- Average mass
- Symmetrical – only 4-3/8 inches in deductions

seem bigger than he really is. If you have the time, settle down and run your mental checklist.

Lastly, a 30-inch spread is the ideological benchmark most mule deer enthusiasts look for in a trophy. Often times outside spread is all that gets noticed, as illustrated by my new-found hunting buddy mentioned earlier. Keep in mind, spread looks good on the wall, but in scoring, inside spread between the main beams is all that counts and it's only one measurement. There are plenty of bucks in the record book with 25-inch inside spreads.

As with all acquired skills, accurate field judging comes with practice. The more bucks you have a chance to put a mental tape on the better you will become at judging them before deciding to tag 'em or pass 'em. Nothing beats sizing up live game under field conditions when the pressure is on. This builds confidence and speed in your assessment. But, if you are

MAXIMUM vs. MINIMUM
A Comparison of Two Records-Book Sitka Blacktail Deer

World's Record
Typical Sitka blacktail deer
Score: 133

TROPHY ANALYSIS

- Both height and width exceptional for a Sitka blacktail
- Outstanding inside spread of 19-6/8 inches – 5 inches more than the top 25 average.
- Strong main beams averaging 20 inches
- Average mass – all measuring over 3 inches

Close to Minimum Entry
Typical Sitka blacktail deer
Score: 108-4/8

TROPHY ANALYSIS

- Above average inside spread of 16-4/8 inches
- Extremely symmetrical frame – 1-2/8 inch in deductions
- Small overall frame offset by the above features
- Short G-2s – Both 6-6/8 inches

like most of us, time in the field seeing trophy-class bucks can be hard to come by. The next best thing is to estimate the score of mounted heads, then put a tape on them. You'll be surprised how close you can come with a little practice. ∎

SCORECHART
Mule Deer and Blacktail – Typical

Records of
North American
Big Game

250 Station Drive
Missoula, MT 59801
(406) 542-1888

BOONE AND CROCKETT CLUB®
OFFICIAL SCORING SYSTEM FOR NORTH AMERICAN BIG GAME TROPHIES

TYPICAL
MULE DEER AND BLACKTAIL DEER

MINIMUM SCORES	AWARDS	ALL-TIME
mule deer	180	190
Columbia blacktail	125	135
Sitka blacktail	100	108

KIND OF DEER (check one)
☐ mule deer
☐ Columbia blacktail
☐ Sitka blacktail

Detail of Point
Measurement

Abnormal Points	
Right Antler	Left Antler

SUBTOTALS		
TOTAL TO E		

SEE OTHER SIDE FOR INSTRUCTIONS			COLUMN 1	COLUMN 2	COLUMN 3	COLUMN 4
			Spread Credit	Right Antler	Left Antler	Difference
A. No. Points on Right Antler		No. Points on Left Antler				
B. Tip to Tip Spread		C. Greatest Spread				
D. Inside Spread of Main Beams		SPREAD CREDIT MAY EQUAL BUT NOT EXCEED LONGER MAIN BEAM				
E. Total of Lengths of Abnormal Points						
F. Length of Main Beam						
G-1. Length of First Point, If Present						
G-2. Length of Second Point						
G-3. Length of Third Point, If Present						
G-4. Length of Fourth Point, If Present						
H-1. Circumference at Smallest Place Between Burr and First Point						
H-2. Circumference at Smallest Place Between First and Second Points						
H-3. Circumference at Smallest Place Between Main Beam and Third Point						
H-4. Circumference at Smallest Place Between Second and Fourth Points						
		TOTALS				

ADD	Column 1		Exact Locality Where Killed:
	Column 2		Date Killed: Hunter:
	Column 3		Owner: Telephone #:
	Subtotal		Owner's Address:
SUBTRACT Column 4		Guide's Name and Address:
FINAL SCORE		Remarks: (Mention Any Abnormalities or Unique Qualities)

COPYRIGHT © 2000 BY BOONE AND CROCKETT CLUB®

I, _____, certify that I have measured this trophy on _____
        PRINT NAME   MM/DD/YYYYY

at _____
    STREET ADDRESS   CITY   STATE/PROVINCE

and that these measurements and data are, to the best of my knowledge and belief, made in accordance with the instructions given.

Witness: _____ Signature: _____ I.D. Number [ ][ ][ ][ ]
                                                      B&C OFFICIAL MEASURER

INSTRUCTIONS FOR MEASURING TYPICAL MULE AND BLACKTAIL DEER

All measurements must be made with a 1/4-inch wide flexible steel tape to the nearest one-eighth of an inch. (Note: A flexible steel cable can be used to measure points and main beams only.) Enter fractional figures in eighths, without reduction. Official measurements cannot be taken until the antlers have air dried for at least 60 days after the animal was killed.

    A. Number of Points on Each Antler: To be counted a point, the projection must be at least one inch long, with length exceeding width at one inch or more of length. All points are measured from tip of point to nearest edge of beam. Beam tip is counted as a point but not measured as a point.

    B. Tip to Tip Spread is measured between tips of main beams.

    C. Greatest Spread is measured between perpendiculars at a right angle to the center line of the skull at widest part, whether across main beams or points.

    D. Inside Spread of Main Beams is measured at a right angle to the center line of the skull at widest point between main beams. Enter this measurement again as the Spread Credit if it is less than or equal to the length of the longer main beam; if greater, enter longer main beam length for Spread Credit.

    E. Total of Lengths of all Abnormal Points: Abnormal Points are those non-typical in location such as points originating from a point (exception: G-3 originates from G-2 in perfectly normal fashion) or from bottom or sides of main beam, or any points beyond the normal pattern of five (including beam tip) per antler. Measure each abnormal point in usual manner and enter in appropriate blanks.

    F. Length of Main Beam is measured from the center of the lowest outside edge of burr over the outer side to the most distant point of the Main Beam. The point of beginning is that point on the burr where the center line along the outer side of the beam intersects the burr, then following generally the line of the illustration.

    G-1-2-3-4. Length of Normal Points: Normal points are the brow tines and the upper and lower forks as shown in the illustration. They are measured from nearest edge of main beam over outer curve to tip. Lay the tape along the outer curve of the beam so that the top edge of the tape coincides with the top edge of the beam on both sides of point to determine the baseline for point measurement. Record point lengths in appropriate blanks.

    H-1-2-3-4. Circumferences are taken as detailed in illustration for each measurement. If brow point is missing, take H-1 and H-2 at smallest place between burr and G-2. If G-3 is missing, take H-3 halfway between the base and tip of G-2. If G-4 is missing, take H-4 halfway between G-2 and tip of main beam.

ENTRY AFFIDAVIT FOR ALL HUNTER-TAKEN TROPHIES

For the purpose of entry into the Boone and Crockett Club's® records, North American big game harvested by the use of the following methods or under the following conditions are ineligible:

    I.   Spotting or herding game from the air, followed by landing in its vicinity for the purpose of pursuit and shooting;
    II. Herding or chasing with the aid of any motorized equipment;
    III. Use of electronic communication devices, artificial lighting, or electronic light intensifying devices;
    IV. Confined by artificial barriers, including escape-proof fenced enclosures;
    V.   Transplanted for the purpose of commercial shooting;
    VI. By the use of traps or pharmaceuticals;
    VII. While swimming, helpless in deep snow, or helpless in any other natural or artificial medium;
    VIII. On another hunter's license;
    IX. Not in full compliance with the game laws or regulations of the federal government or of any state, province, territory, or tribal council on reservations or tribal lands;

I certify that the trophy scored on this chart was not taken in violation of the conditions listed above. In signing this statement, I understand that if the information provided on this entry is found to be misrepresented or fraudulent in any respect, it will not be accepted into the Awards Program and 1) all of my prior entries are subject to deletion from future editions of **Records of North American Big Game** 2) future entries may not be accepted.

FAIR CHASE, as defined by the Boone and Crockett Club®, is the ethical, sportsmanlike and lawful pursuit and taking of any free-ranging wild, native North American big game animal in a manner that does not give the hunter an improper advantage over such game animals.

The Boone and Crockett Club® may exclude the entry of any animal that it deems to have been taken in an unethical manner or under conditions deemed inappropriate by the Club.

Date: _____ Signature of Hunter: _____
                                            (SIGNATURE MUST BE WITNESSED BY AN OFFICIAL MEASURER OR A NOTARY PUBLIC.)

Date: _____ Signature of Notary or Official Measurer: _____

SCORECHART
Mule Deer and Blacktail – Non-Typical

Records of
North American
Big Game

BOONE AND CROCKETT CLUB®
OFFICIAL SCORING SYSTEM FOR NORTH AMERICAN BIG GAME TROPHIES

250 Station Drive
Missoula, MT 59801
(406) 542-1888

NON-TYPICAL
MULE DEER AND BLACKTAIL DEER

	MINIMUM SCORES	
	AWARDS	ALL-TIME
mule deer	215	230
Columbia blacktail	155	155
Sitka blacktail	118	118

KIND OF DEER (check one)
☐ mule deer
☐ Columbia blacktail
☐ Sitka blacktail

Detail of Point
Measurement

Abnormal Points	
Right Antler	Left Antler
SUBTOTALS	
E. TOTAL	

SEE OTHER SIDE FOR INSTRUCTIONS			COLUMN 1	COLUMN 2	COLUMN 3	COLUMN 4
A. No. Points on Right Antler		No. Points on Left Antler	Spread Credit	Right Antler	Left Antler	Difference
B. Tip to Tip Spread		C. Greatest Spread				
D. Inside Spread of Main Beams		SPREAD CREDIT MAY EQUAL BUT NOT EXCEED LONGER MAIN BEAM				
F. Length of Main Beam						
G-1. Length of First Point, If Present						
G-2. Length of Second Point						
G-3. Length of Third Point, If Present						
G-4. Length of Fourth Point, If Present						
H-1. Circumference at Smallest Place Between Burr and First Point						
H-2. Circumference at Smallest Place Between First and Second Points						
H-3. Circumference at Smallest Place Between Main Beam and Third Point						
H-4. Circumference at Smallest Place Between Second and Fourth Points						
		TOTALS				

ADD	Column 1		Exact Locality Where Killed:
	Column 2		Date Killed: Hunter:
	Column 3		Owner: Telephone #:
	Subtotal		Owner's Address:
SUBTRACT Column 4			Guide's Name and Address:
	Subtotal		Remarks: (Mention Any Abnormalities or Unique Qualities)
	ADD Line E Total		
	FINAL SCORE		

COPYRIGHT © 2000 BY BOONE AND CROCKETT CLUB®

I, _____ , certify that I have measured this trophy on _____
PRINT NAME   MM/DD/YYYYY

at _____
STREET ADDRESS   CITY   STATE/PROVINCE

and that these measurements and data are, to the best of my knowledge and belief, made in accordance with the instructions given.

Witness: _____ Signature: _____ I.D. Number ☐☐☐☐
                                               B&C OFFICIAL MEASURER

INSTRUCTIONS FOR MEASURING NON-TYPICAL MULE DEER

All measurements must be made with a 1/4-inch wide flexible steel tape to the nearest one-eighth of an inch. (Note: A flexible steel cable can be used to measure points and main beams only.) Enter fractional figures in eighths, without reduction. Official measurements cannot be taken until the antlers have air dried for at least 60 days after the animal was killed.

A. Number of Points on Each Antler: To be counted a point, the projection must be at least one inch long, with length exceeding width at one inch or more of length. All points are measured from tip of point to nearest edge of beam as illustrated. Beam tip is counted as a point but not measured as a point.

B. Tip to Tip Spread is measured between tips of main beams.

C. Greatest Spread is measured between perpendiculars at a right angle to the center line of the skull at widest part, whether across main beams or points.

D. Inside Spread of Main Beams is measured at a right angle to the center line of the skull at widest point between main beams. Enter this measurement again as the Spread Credit If it is less than or equal to the length of the longer main beam; if greater, enter longer main beam length for Spread Credit.

E. Total of Lengths of all Abnormal Points: Abnormal Points are those non-typical in location such as points originating from a point (exception: G-3 originates from G-2 in perfectly normal fashion) or from bottom or sides of main beam, or any points beyond the normal pattern of five (including beam tip) per antler. Measure each abnormal point in usual manner and enter in appropriate blanks.

F. Length of Main Beam is measured from the center of the lowest outside edge of burr over the outer side to the most distant point of the main beam. The point of beginning is that point on the burr where the center line along the outer side of the beam intersects the burr, then following generally the line of the illustration.

G-1-2-3-4. Length of Normal Points: Normal points are the brow tines and the upper and lower forks as shown in the illustration. They are measured from nearest edge of main beam over outer curve to tip. Lay the tape along the outer curve of the beam so that the top edge of the tape coincides with the top edge of the beam on both sides of point to determine the baseline for point measurement. Record point lengths in appropriate blanks.

H-1-2-3-4. Circumferences are taken as detailed in illustration for each measurement. If brow point is missing, take H-1 and H-2 at smallest place between burr and G-2. If G-3 is missing, take H-3 halfway between the base and tip of G-2. If G-4 is missing, take H-4 halfway between G-2 and tip of main beam.

ENTRY AFFIDAVIT FOR ALL HUNTER-TAKEN TROPHIES

For the purpose of entry into the Boone and Crockett Club's® records, North American big game harvested by the use of the following methods or under the following conditions are ineligible:

   I.   Spotting or herding game from the air, followed by landing in its vicinity for the purpose of pursuit and shooting;
   II. Herding or chasing with the aid of any motorized equipment;
   III. Use of electronic communication devices, artificial lighting, or electronic light intensifying devices;
   IV. Confined by artificial barriers, including escape-proof fenced enclosures;
   V.   Transplanted for the purpose of commercial shooting;
   VI. By the use of traps or pharmaceuticals;
   VII. While swimming, helpless in deep snow, or helpless in any other natural or artificial medium;
   VIII. On another hunter's license;
   IX. Not in full compliance with the game laws or regulations of the federal government or of any state, province, territory, or tribal council on reservations or tribal lands;

I certify that the trophy scored on this chart was not taken in violation of the conditions listed above. In signing this statement, I understand that if the information provided on this entry is found to be misrepresented or fraudulent in any respect, it will not be accepted into the Awards Program and 1) all of my prior entries are subject to deletion from future editions of **Records of North American Big Game** 2) future entries may not be accepted.

FAIR CHASE, as defined by the Boone and Crockett Club®, is the ethical, sportsmanlike and lawful pursuit and taking of any free-ranging wild, native North American big game animal in a manner that does not give the hunter an improper advantage over such game animals.

The Boone and Crockett Club® may exclude the entry of any animal that it deems to have been taken in an unethical manner or under conditions deemed inappropriate by the Club.

Date: _____ Signature of Hunter: _____
                                               (SIGNATURE MUST BE WITNESSED BY AN OFFICIAL MEASURER OR A NOTARY PUBLIC.)

Date: _____ Signature of Notary or Official Measurer: _____

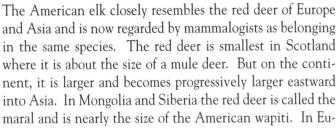

MEASURING AND JUDGING
American, Roosevelt's, and Tule Elk

The American elk closely resembles the red deer of Europe and Asia and is now regarded by mammalogists as belonging in the same species. The red deer is smallest in Scotland where it is about the size of a mule deer. But on the continent, it is larger and becomes progressively larger eastward into Asia. In Mongolia and Siberia the red deer is called the maral and is nearly the size of the American wapiti. In Europe, Scandinavia and eastward, the animal we call the moose is referred to as elk. This can cause some confusion when American sportsmen are discussing trophy hunting with their European counterparts.

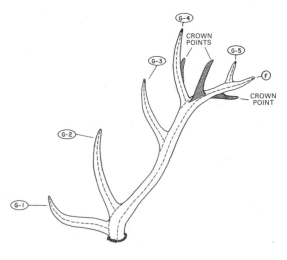

In North America there are three primary subspecies of elk: the American elk of the Rocky Mountains, which grow the largest antlers; the Roosevelt's elk of the coastal areas of the northwest, which are the largest bodied elk; and the smaller tule elk of the valleys of central California. American elk, Roosevelt's elk and tule elk are separated by the boundary lines described in Chapter 2.

The measurement of American elk differs from Roosevelt's and tule elk. Racks of mature American elk bulls normally show six points on each side (including main beam tip as a counted, but not individually measured, point). Trophies with seven, eight, or even more normal points are occasionally found. American elk racks are often very symmetrical.

FIGURE 7-A

Roosevelt's and tule elk are more inclined to form several extra points adjacent to and above the major G-4 point as shown in **figure 7-A**. These extra points are called "crown points" (the presence of several often produces a cup-shaped "crown," thus the name), just as they are in red deer. These

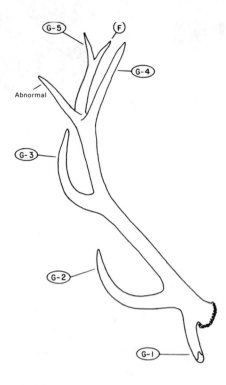

FIGURE 7-B

crown points often develop in a very non-symmetric pattern especially on very large, mature bulls and are a highly desirable characteristic of these elk. For this reason, these extra points on or above G-4 are rewarded in the measuring system by adding their lengths into the total score without a deduction for lack of symmetry.

American elk also display some tendency to develop crown points but to a lesser extent. Often a mature American elk may have points immediately above G-4 that protrude more from the side of the beam than from the top **(figure 7-B)**. These points do not follow the usual highly structured pattern of American elk and are treated as abnormal points. Other abnormal points may be present on mature bulls. Since the occurrence of bulls with abnormal points is common, a separate non-typical American elk category exists. As Roosevelt's and tule elk are measured in a different fashion, there is no need for non-typical categories for these subspecies of elk.

As indicated in Chapter 4, a measurable point is any projection *at least one inch long and longer than wide at some location at least one inch from the tip of the projection.* (Each projection should be measured to ascertain whether it is or is not a point.) Once it is determined that a projection is a point then the entire point length is measured from its tip down to its base. Point base lines are established where the point joins either the main beam or another point. The base should reflect the normal antler configuration as if the point was not present.

When one is measuring an American elk, once the normal points have been identified on each antler, the remaining points should be assessed to determine if a typical or non-typical score chart should be used. If there are numerous abnormal points, or only one or two that are long, the non-typical score chart should be used so that the abnormal point lengths can be added to the final score, rather than being subtracted from it. If the abnormal points are few in number and short in length, use the typical score chart that provides for a subtraction of the total of lengths of such points as a penalty for lack of symmetry. If there is any doubt as to which score chart should be used, the trophy can be measured both ways. If the trophy qualifies for both the typical and non-typical categories, it **cannot** be listed in both. The final choice of the listing category in such instances rests with the trophy owner.

The length of beam and antler point length measurement may be taken by the use of the flexible steel cable or a 1/4-inch wide steel clip-end tape. The use of a round, flexible steel cable (such as a bicycle brake cable) greatly speeds-up the measuring process while still yielding an accurate measurement. However, only the steel tape can be used for circumference measurements. As with other categories for antlered species, the animal is not eligible for listing if the skull has been split.

For measurement of length, the cable is positioned along the outer curve of the beam or point. The end of the measurement is marked by attaching an alligator clip to the cable at the proper spot. The cable is then removed and held in a straight line against a clip-end tape or folding carpenter's rule to record the length measurement. The clip-end tape is often faster to use when antler points are generally straight as the clip-end can easily be hooked on the end of the antler point and the tape stretched across the point's base line. When using a 1/4-inch wide tape on a curved point or antler beam, the measurer will need to mark points of rotation along the line of measurement. The tape is then rotated at these marks. Be sure to align the tape at the appropriate length when the realignment is made.

The length of antler beam measurement is illustrated on the score chart, being generally a line from the antler burr to the beam tip. The measurement begins at the point where the center line of the antler along the outer side intersects the burr. To determine the starting point, find the middle of the burr as the antlers are viewed from the side. It is neither at the lower front edge, nor at the rear edge of the beam, but rather at the outside center of the burr.

The measurement proceeds on the outer side the beam on out to the beam tip. In general, this line should stay near the

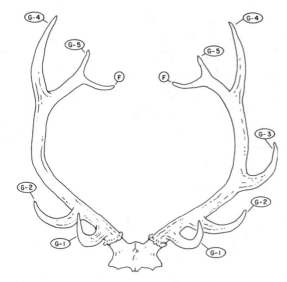

FIGURE 7-C
UNMATCHED G-3 POINT

middle of the beam on the outer side. Since the antler beams on most mature elk tend to roll, it is very helpful to first mark the point bases for the normal points. These base lines will provide reference points that help the measurer stay near the middle of the beam. The line can be measured from either the burr to the tip or from the tip to the burr. If an abnormal point (or antler projection) is in the line of measurement, simply find the shortest path around the point and continue the measurement.

After the measurement of the beam lengths, the lengths of the normal points are recorded. Keep in mind the following general rules for elk points:

1) Normal points arise from the top of the main beam (or the front and outer side for the case of G-1, G-2 and G-3 points) at roughly spaced intervals and are usually paired with similar points on the other antler in a symmetrical pattern.

2) Points arising from the side or bottom of the main beam are always abnormal or crown points (see the discussion that follows for clarification of crown points).

3) If an extra pair of points occurs, one on each antler, below the large *dagger* point, which is usually G-4, then it is proper to record this extra pair of points as normal points.

4) If an elk has an unmatched G-1, G-2, or G-3 point **(figure 7-C)**, this point should be treated as a normal point. It should be entered on the score chart as a normal point and (like G-1 on mule deer) a zero or dash entered on the opposite side for the missing point. Above G-4, one cannot have an unmatched normal point on American elk unless the point is matched against one that is completely broken off or unless the unmatched point is at the end of the beam. For American elk, if an unmatched point occurs between two normal points above G-4, it is treated as an abnormal (non-symmetry) point. On Roosevelt's and tule elk, it would be measured as a normal point. Below G-4 an unmatched point that is not a G-1, G-2, or G-3 point is an abnormal (non-symmetry) point for all three species of elk.

5) While the score chart shows space for recording only seven such points, there is no upper limit to how many normal points can occur on an elk antler. In the extreme rarity that more than seven normal points (not including the beam tip) occur, the measurements of the extra point(s) may be included as a separate, additional line or as a separate attachment. Be sure to explain this action in the REMARKS section.

The scoring of Roosevelt's and tule elk differs from American elk in regards to the treatment of "crown" points. Roosevelt's and tule elk may have one to several extra points on or above the G-4 dagger point. These "crown points" may display a wide variety of configurations and may not match from side to side on the antlers. On Roosevelt's and tule elk, the measurer must still identify normal points past G-4 if they exist. Normal points past G-4 project upward from the top of the beam. Often the G-5 point may be sepa-

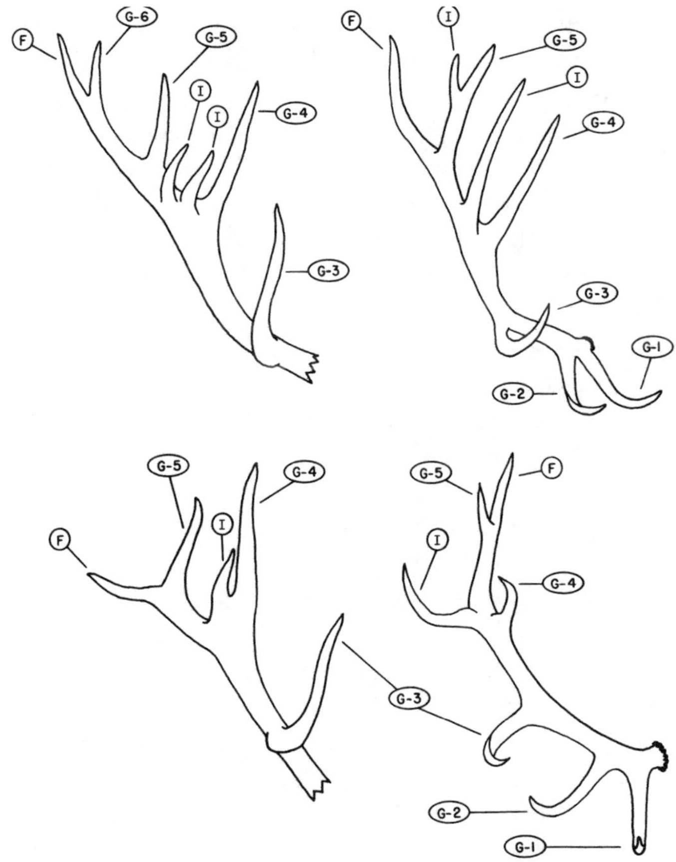

FIGURE 7-D
VARIOUS ILLUSTRATIONS OF CROWN POINTS

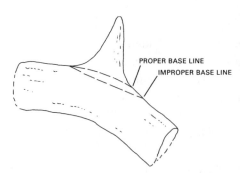

PROPER BASE LINE
IMPROPER BASE LINE

FIGURE 7-E

rated from the G-4 point by several other points that project from the side of the beam. **Figure 7-D** presents various illustrations of crown points. The normal points are recorded in their proper blanks on the score chart. All other points on or in the vicinity of G-4, or above G-4, on Roosevelt's and tule elk are measured as **crown points** and entered separately in appropriate blanks on the upper right of the score chart.

The total of the lengths of the crown points is added in as a step in obtaining the final score. Roosevelt's and tule elk may have abnormal points as well as crown points. The total of the lengths of the abnormal points for both Roosevelt's and tule elk (like typical American elk) is deducted from the score total.

Another difference occurs in the treatment of point length differences. Since the pattern of points above G-4 on Roosevelt's and tule elk may be highly influenced by crown points, no point length deductions are taken for normal points beyond G-4.

To summarize, differences in the treatment of points on American elk and both Roosevelt's and tule elk are:

1) Abnormal points on Roosevelt's and tule elk (points off other points, points from underside of beam, extra unpaired points not G-1, G-2, or G-3) occur only below G-4.

2) Roosevelt's and tule elk crown points would be considered abnormal points on American elk. One common occurrence of this on American elk is the presence of a pair (one on each antler) of large points immediately past G-4 that project more from the side (tilt out) than from the top. As previously noted, these are abnormal points on American elk.

3) On Roosevelt's and tule elk abnormal, non-symmetry points can only occur below G-4; on American elk they can be either above or below G-4.

4) Point branches are abnormal points. On Roosevelt's and tule elk such branches on or above G-4 are treated as crown points.

The lengths of the individual points are recorded in the proper blanks on the score chart. Points are measured either from the base lines established on the main beam to the tip of each point or from point tip to the base line. Either method should yield the same result. Generally, points end in a sharp cone shape, with the measurement being to the tip of this cone. Should the point end in a noticeably blunted condition, somewhat like a human thumb, the measurement line can be continued to the midpoint of the rounding.

Establishment of the base lines for individual point measurement is straightforward. The base line is established to separate that material properly called main beam from the material of the point (or to separate an abnormal point from its "parent" point). Properly drawn, the base line should delineate the same amount of beam (or "parent" point) material below it as can be ascertained on either side of the point. This is especially critical in elk as the beam often twists and decreases in diameter at some point locations. One should remain parallel with the contour of the lower edge of the beam when establishing a base line to ensure that the point base line has not cut too deeply into the main beam **(figure 7-E)**.

Antler points are measured along the outer side of their curve. In most cases the normal points curve inward and are simply measured on the outside of the rack. But, should a point curve outward (often G-6 points will), it would be appropriate to measure it on the inside of the rack and thus reflect properly the outer curve of the point.

One item to note is the taking of the length of the G-1 point. The base line for G-1 is drawn from the top of the beam just next to the burr to the top of the beam between G-1 and G-2 on the *outer side* of the beam. The length of G-1 is then measured from the tip, over the curve, to the center of this point on the outer side. It is **not** taken over **FIGURE 7-F**

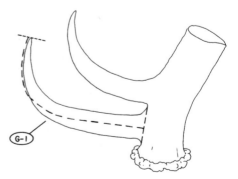

the curve to the burr! The proper line of measurement begins at the tip and proceeds over the curve of G-1 and then angles across the point to the center mark that is on the outer side as shown in **figure 7-F**. If the G-1 point is "bent" downward rather than in the usual upward fashion, the measurement of its length is taken in same way except now the line is coming up from the tip of the point. The same procedure of following the outer curve applies to abnormal points as well.

The four circumferences (H-1, 2, 3, and 4) are taken by the use of a ring-end tape by looping the tape around the beam, with the zero mark up. Pull the tape together and gently move it along the beam until the smallest circumference measurement is obtained. This value is then recorded as the circumference for that location. If you use a clip-end tape to measure circumferences, overlap the tape a full 10 inch increment to simplify the procedure. Be sure to subtract the amount of overlap before recording the measurement.

Undoubtedly, elk trophies large enough to reach the current all-time records book minimums will have at least five normal points (not including the beam tip) on each antler. For such trophies the four circumferences will be taken between points in the usual manner described on the score chart. However, should there be only four normal points (not including the beam tip) on the antler, the H-4 circumference should be taken halfway between the G-4 point and the antler tip. To take this measurement properly, determine the center of the base of G-4 where it meets the main beam measurement line, then measure from this point to the beam tip. The halfway point of this line is the correct location for the H-4 circumference.

If a point is broken completely off, take the measurement in the usual locations. If a G-2 point is completely missing on one antler, then take H-1 and H-2 at the same location, the smallest place between G-1 and G-3.

The presence of crown points can make the taking of H-4 tricky. As **figure 7-G** displays, the measurer must take the circumference at the smallest location between the normal G-4 point and the *normal* G-5 point. Several crown points may interrupt the spacing and necessitate the trial measurement of several locations in order to find the smallest.

The inside spread should be taken with a folding carpenter's rule, utilizing the extension to complete the measured line. Care must be exercised to properly position the ruler for this measurement. The line of measurement should be at a right angle to the long axis of the skull. It must also be parallel to the skull cap. Thus, if one beam should be positioned higher than the other, it will be necessary to utilize a straightedge against the higher antler to properly locate the line. The actual measurement will reflect the greatest distance between the inside edges of the two main beams at their center, making sure to keep the measurement oriented as noted above.

Rarely, one or both antlers will curve outward *excessively* near their tips. In such rare cases credit should not be given the elk for such abnormal spread. Thus, the inside spread measurement must be taken where the "flaring" antler(s) begins to diverge from the normal curvature or at a location below the point of divergence, whichever is greater.

Note that spread credit (Column 1 of the score chart) **cannot** exceed the length of the longer main beam. If the spread measurement does exceed the longer main beam, enter the longer main beam length (rather than the inside spread measurement) in Column 1 of the score chart for the spread credit.

The tip to tip spread and greatest spread are supplementary measurements and are not figured into the final score. They are recorded on the score chart as they do indicate the general conformation of the rack, and with the other measurements give a rather complete picture of antler formation for the trophy.

The supplementary data of tip to tip spread should also be taken by use of the folding carpenter's rule or steel tape. This measurement is simply from the center of the tip of one antler to the center of the tip of the other. If the main beams are essentially the same length as one another, the inside spread measurement could be nearly the same length as the tip to tip if the bull's antlers gradually (not excessively) widen. Such situations occur on Roosevelt's elk, less frequently on American elk.

Greatest spread is best taken by use of two perpendiculars, such as carpenter's levels held upright by large c-clamps or perfectly square-cut wooden blocks. The measurement is then taken by using a steel tape or folding carpenter's rule between the perpendiculars. If perpendiculars are not available, a floor and wall can be used for one perpendicular with the second being improvised from a

FIGURE 7-G
PROPER LOCATION OF H-4 WITH THE PRESENCE OF CROWN POINTS

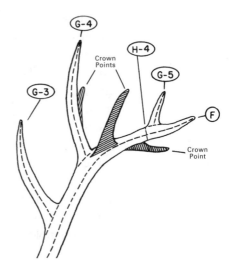

carpenter's level or a straight, square-cut board. In no case should the human eye be relied upon for establishment of the second perpendicular line.

By
Craig Boddington

Field Judging American Elk

A bull elk is one of North America's most majestic creatures, and a really big bull elk is the best of the best, one of the most regal, most dramatic, and most impressive creatures in the entire world. There is a big difference between a nice, normal, respectable, good bull and a monster that will make the records book. It isn't hard to tell the difference, but the first decision you need to make is whether or not you care.

Although it's possible for a huge bull to turn up almost anywhere these big deer are found, there aren't large numbers of really big bulls anywhere. In a lot of elk country any bull at all is truly a fine trophy, and any six-point bull is a great trophy. As with all trophy hunting, you can't shoot a big one unless you're willing to turn down lesser animals. This may not be the best course of action for all elk hunters in all areas, especially not for those who like to eat elk meat. Let's start with the clear understanding that there aren't enough big bulls to go around, and it isn't always sensible to spend a lot of time counting antler points, let alone computing Boone and Crockett scores. However, sometimes there is time, and in some times and places there are lots of elk, enough that you really can size them up and try to find the bull of a lifetime. Will you know him if you see him?

Counting Points

Relatively few elk hunters go afield with a certain records book score in mind, but lots of elk hunters go in search of a "six-point bull." This isn't a bad plan, provided you understand that a six-point bull isn't necessarily a monster, nor even fully mature, and that there are huge 5x5s wandering around that dwarf many 6x6s. That said, six points per side (including the main beam tip) is the normal configuration for most American elk. Some bulls never grow the sixth point, and some grow a seventh and (rarely) even more, but most mature bull elk are 6x6s. It is normal for an elk's first antlers to be spikes. It is just as normal for a spike to go straight to a 5-point rack as a 2-1/2-year-old, and then to a small six-point rack as a 3-1/2-year-old.

MAXIMUM vs. MINIMUM
A Comparison of Two Records-Book Typical American Elk

**World's Record
Typical American elk
Score: 442-5/8**

TROPHY ANALYSIS

- 8x7 typical frame
- Exceptional G-1s and G-2s – between 22 and 29 inches
- Exceptional mass – H-1s both over 10 inches
- Above average spread credit of 47-4/8 inches
- Strong G-3s – both over 22 inches If a bull has a weakness it is usually found here.
- Good symmetry

**Close to Minimum Entry
Typical American elk
Score: 362-3/8**

TROPHY ANALYSIS

- 6x6 typical frame
- Strong main beams – both near 50 inches
- Average G-1s and G-2s – between 16 and 18 inches
- Average mass – H-1s just over 8 inches
- Exceptional symmetry – only 6-5/8 deductions
- Weak G-3s – just over 20 inches combined
- Lack of overall tine length kept this bull out of the All-time book

Often the process is slower and, rarely, it can be faster. But a 3-1/2, 4-1/2, or even 5-1/2-year-old bull is a long way from full maturity, regardless of how many points he is carrying. It depends on the country, but a bull elk's best set of antlers will probably come in his 10th, 11th, or even 12th year. There's a lot of growing to do between his first six-point rack and his best rack, so there are six-pointers and then there are six-pointers.

However, simply identifying, in an instant, a six-point bull is not difficult. Elk antlers grow with a main beam that goes up and slightly back, usually curving rearward toward the tip of the main beam. Points tend to grow forward and slightly outward from the main beam. In the normal configuration there are two brow tines that project forward, a third point that projects from the side of the antler, and fourth and subsequent points that grow from the top of the main beam. The fourth point is normally the longest and most dominant point. Sometimes called the dagger point or the sword point, this is usually the single most distinctive feature of an elk rack, and you'll pick it up in an almost instantaneous glance.

If the main beam tip goes straight back from the dagger point you're almost certainly looking at a five-point antler. If there's another point rising upward behind this prominent dagger point, perhaps making a horizontal "Y," then you're looking at a six-point antler. Again, the dagger point is almost always the longest and thickest point, and unless something is missing (broken off or not grown), it will be the fourth point. Points behind the dagger point are generally shorter. So, not counting the main beam tip, one point behind the dagger means a six-pointer. Two points behind the dagger means the rare seven-pointer, with the sixth tine usually considerably shorter than the fifth tine.

Going by the Book

If a "six-point bull" is what you have in mind, this is all you need to know, but don't take it too literally because I've seen hunters pass huge five-pointers in favor of much smaller six-pointers! Now, let's progress to records book score. Elk are measured by a combination of beam lengths, point lengths, circumferences at four different places on the main beam, and inside spread. The minimum is lower for Roosevelt's elk than for American elk, also known as Rocky Mountain elk, and lower still for tule elk, but in all cases the minimum is very, very high, and it takes a real whopper to make the grade in any category. Although the basic criteria of beams, points, circumferences, and inside spread are the same, Roosevelt's and tule elk are measured differently because they often grow additional points near the dagger point, forming a cluster or "crown" of points like a European red deer. American elk, which rarely crown, are divided into typical and non-typical categories. We will focus initially on the most plentiful and widespread American elk, with notes on Roosevelt's and tule elk at the conclusion.

For American elk it requires a minimum of 375 points for entry into the All-time records book as a typical bull and 360 points to enter in the Awards book. The non-typical minimum is 385 points for both the Awards and All-time records books. As an indicator of how large such a bull really is, most nice, representative, good 6x6 elk will measure somewhere between 260 and 290 Boone and Crockett points. Relatively few people will ever see a true record-class bull, but the yardstick by which you would know them are the same for lesser bulls.

A Combination of Factors

With any antlered game it's important to understand that all the criteria are important. No rack is perfect, not even a World's Record. Since there are more points than anything else, point length is very important, but what you really want is a combination of long points, long beams, good mass, and a wide spread. Since no wapiti has all of this in equal proportion, you have to look at the overall rack, longer points make up for short beams, extreme mass makes up for a narrower spread, and so forth. It's important to look at the entire rack and not become fixated on one feature, whether outstanding or weak. That said, some criteria are more important than others. We'll look at each.

Beam Length

Long beams are not sufficient to put an elk in the records book. You need all the rest, but most great elk have long main beams. In the all-time records book, main beams of American elk range from a very few heads with a beam length in the mid-40s, all the way to beams well over 60 inches in length. The average beam length of the top 10 typical heads is over 58 inches.

Interestingly, however, the average beam length of the bottom ten typical heads is 55-4/8 inches, not much difference. Note that the top 10 typical American elk average 426 points; the bottom 10 average just over 375 points. That's a 50-inch difference, but the difference in beam length averages just 2-4/8 inches.

What this should tell you is that most great elk have very long beams. There are exceptions, and they must have the rest as well, but long beams matter. It's very difficult to quantify beam length when you're looking at an elk through binoculars, but it isn't difficult to see that a bull has exceptionally long beams. With the head carried normally, antlers erect, look for antlers that are significantly taller than the elk's shoulder height. With the head thrown back, perhaps to bugle, look for main beams that appear to reach as far back as the haunches. It is difficult to precisely estimate beam length against body size, but this business about "being able to scratch his rear end with his antlers" is valid. An elk with really long beams can almost do this. Another good visual clue on a six-pointer is extreme length behind the last point, and, on any elk, the apparent length behind the dagger point, preferably at least 20 inches.

Inside Spread

This is a measurement that many hunters don't like. It's a measurement of air, not antler. Looking at typical American elk (the category with by far the most entries) the range is quite considerable. The narrowest head in the book has an inside spread of just 32-2/8 inches, exceptionally narrow for a mature bull. At a total of 384-1/8 B&C points, this bull actually outscores the widest bull, 55-6/8 inches (total score 380-2/8). This suggests that spread isn't everything! Indeed it isn't, and this is borne out by the averages of the top 10 and bottom 10 entries. The top 10 typical American elk range from 38-2/8 inches inside spread to 53 inches, with an average of 46-2/8 inches. The bottom 10 range from 38 inches to 49-4/8 inches, with an average of 42-4/8 inches. Again, this is not significant against the 50-inch difference that separates these elk in Boone and Crockett's scoring system.

In the field, this is not a criteria I would worry about too much, except in the relatively rare case where you're looking at a very narrow, straight-up-and-down rack. Most "big" elk

MAXIMUM vs. MINIMUM
A Comparison of Two Records-Book Non-typical American Elk

World's Record Non-Typical American elk Score: 465-5/8

TROPHY ANALYSIS
- Strongest overall feature – a 410-2/8 typical frame with 55 inches of abnormal points
- 9x11 Frame
- Exception G-1s and G-2s – between 23 and 26 inches
- Strong G-3s – both over 22 inches
- Above average main beams measuring 49-2/8 and 46-3/8 inches
- Average mass with H-1s almost 9 inches

Close to Minimum Entry Non-Typical American elk Score: 390-2/8

TROPHY ANALYSIS
- Similar amount of abnormal points to the World's Record, but on a 335-2/8 typical frame
- 10x11 frame
- Narrow spread credit of 38-2/8 inches
- Above average main beams both measuring over 46 inches
- Weak G-1s and G-3s, but average G-2s

will come well outside the ears or, from the rear, will have antlers that extend well outside the body profile. This will put you somewhere in the low to mid-40s, and that's all you need be concerned about. A really wide bull gives you a bonus, and that's good. A really narrow bull may be a problem, but not if the beams and points are spectacular. Note that the fourth typical American elk in the all-time records book has an inside spread of just 39 inches, and the ninth head in the same listing has an inside spread of just 38-2/8 inches.

Mass

As a bull reaches full maturity, he may or may not grow additional points, and he may or may not add significant length to his rack, but his antlers will become more massive. Most really good elk have heavy antlers and carry the mass the length of the main beam. An individual circumference measurement is not a large number, but there are four circumference measurements on each side, so they add up. "H-1" is taken at the smallest place between the first (brow) tine (G-1) and the second tine (G-2). H-2 is taken between the second and third (G-3) tines, H-3 between the third and fourth (G-4, normally the dagger) tines, and H-4 is taken between the dagger point and next point (G-5) or, if a G-5 is lacking (a five-point rack), then the measurement is taken halfway between the G-4 and the end of the main beam.

Mass is very hard to judge, and isn't something worth spending a lot of time on. Few elk that are "big" in the more visible characteristics have thin antlers. The average H-1 (between first and second point) on the top 10 typical American elk is 10-4/8 inches, which is very massive. The average H-1 of the bottom 10 is 8-6/8 inches. That is a fairly significant difference, especially if you figure this average difference of 1-4/8 inches is carried through all 8 circumference measurements. However, the next-to-last head in the all-time book has an unusually small H-1 of 6-7/8. This is the very rare "big bull" that is not at least reasonably heavy. Throw that one out and the average goes up to nine inches.

You want to look for antlers that are visibly as large or larger in circumference than the ear bases, and, more importantly, maintain the appearance of thickness at least to the fifth point. It's unusual to have a lot of time to look at a big bull, and mass is not where you should spend most of it.

Tines Count

On even the most massive-beamed bull elk the total circumference measurements will not approach 20% of the total points. Spread is worth perhaps as little as 10%, but never much more than 15%. Beam length matters, a lot. The total of both the beam lengths can easily exceed 100 points, and on a "record-class" bull, will surely exceed 90 points, so it is worth close to 25% of the total score on a big bull. Do the math. That means tine length accounts for at least 40% of the total, sometimes more, but rarely less.

If you have time to really study a bull, look at the main beams and really look at the tines. Obviously you want to count points. Because there are additional points to measure, 7x7s score well and the rare bulls with additional typical points score even better, provided they match. Tines that are not matched on the other antler are deducted, unless they're non-typical points and the animal is measured as a non-typical. So a big 6x6 will out score an equally big 7x6 every time. Broken points also count against you, so you do want to look for symmetry, but don't get carried away looking for a 7x7. Elk with more than six points dominate the first page of the records book listings, but after that the most common configuration among record-class elk is the same as the most common configuration among mature bulls: 6x6.

This being the case, it should be obvious that point length is the single most important criteria, regardless of how many points the bull has. There are many 7x7s that won't make the magical minimum, while a lot of 6x6s have. It is even possible for a bull to "make it" without the sixth point. There are currently no 5x5 bulls in the all-time records book, but there is one 6x5, scoring 378-6/8 points. Remembering that differences in symmetry are deducted, thus the length of the sixth point on the one side was subtracted. This was one big elk.

The good news is that point length is one of the easiest things to judge because there is a yardstick. On a big American elk the distance from the eye to the tip of the nose is about 12-4/8 to 13 inches. Perhaps better, the distance from the base of the burr to the tip of the nose is about 15-4/8 inches. There are variances, but they're slight, and this is not an exact science, nor will you normally have time to make it so. The most important thing on a big elk is long points, as many and as long as possible.

Start at the bottom and work up. The brow tines are usually strong. You want them to extend at least to the end of the nose, preferably longer and with some curve, which greatly adds to the length. A curved brow that appears to reach the end of the nose should be about 18-inches long. The G-2s and G-3s are often a bit weaker, but they can't be too weak. They, too, need to approach the distance from burr to tip of nose. Now comes the truth-teller, the dagger point. The dagger point is usually the longest point, and there are a lot of potential inches there. You want it to be considerably longer than the burr-to-nose distance, approaching double the eye-to-nose yardstick. If it's a clean 6x6, the G-5 point matters a lot. It has to be strong, at least 8 or 10 inches. This is less important if the bull is a 7x7, but you still need some inches in the top of the rack.

The Perfect Elk

The best people in the world at judging elk are the veteran guides at the White Mountain Apache Reservation, because they have seen more big elk taken than anyone else in the world. Typically, they take an average for mass based on "feel," and they take an average for inside spread based on a "narrow, wide, or normal" judgment. Where they spend the time is working out the beam lengths and the point lengths because that's where it's at.

So let's look through the spotting scope at a really good 6x6. Get your notebook out. He seems to have really long beams, almost scratching his rump. We'll give him 55 inches on each beam. Spread is fairly wide, not noticeably splayed out, but wide. We'll give him 45 inches of inside spread. Mass isn't huge, but is pretty good. We'll figure he starts at a normally heavy 9 inches and keeps it pretty well, maybe 30 inches of circumference on each antler, 60 total.

Now we're going to work out the points. The brow tines curve nicely and seem to pass the tip of the nose. Let's give them 18 inches. The G-2s and G-3s are also good, but not quite so long, and they seem about equal. Let's give them 16 inches each. The G-4s are quite good, about half again the burr-to-nose distance. Let's give them 22 inches. The back fork is also pretty good. We'll call the G-5s at least eight inches each.

Now let's look again for visible differences from one side to another. No, no points are missing, and while there will cer-

MAXIMUM vs. MINIMUM
A Comparison of Two Records-Book Roosevelt's Elk

**World's Record
Roosevelt's Elk
Score: 404-6/8**

TROPHY ANALYSIS
- 9x8 Frame
- 11-5/8 inches of crown points
- Truly exceptional main beams – both measuring over 54 inches
- Above average spread credit – over 40 inches
- Strong G-1s and G-2s measuring between 15 and 20 inches
- Above average G-3s – averaging 17 inches
- Exceptional G-4s – both over 22 inches
- Average H-1s – 8-2/8 and 9-4/8 inches
- Over 12 inches of symmetry deductions

**Close to Minimum Entry
Roosevelt's Elk
Score: 290-1/8**

TROPHY ANALYSIS
- 7x7 Frame
- 7-3/8 inches of crown points
- Average G-1s and G-2s – between 12-4/8 and 14-2/8 inches
- Weak G-3s measuring 9 and 9-6/8 inches
- Narrow spread credit – 37-6/8 inches
- Score held up with only 3-5/8 inches in symmetry deductions

tainly be subtle differences, none are obvious. Okay, do the math. We've got 110 inches on the beams, 60 inches in circumference, and 45 inches of inside spread. The point length is 80 inches per side, total of 160. If you're right, you're looking at a bull that will score 375 points. Hopefully you've been conservative rather than generous in your estimation, and hopefully you haven't missed any significant deductions. If these two things are true, you're looking at a Boone and Crockett typical bull.

Non-Typicals

The only non-typical elk category is for the American elk. A non-typical point is not a mismatched point from one side to the other, but a point that grows somewhere other than in the typical pattern, perhaps a drop point or a horizontal point coming off the main beam. As is the case with deer, the possibilities are almost endless, but, if anything, non-typical elk are less common than non-typical deer, and it's rare to see more than a handful of true non-typical points. Reflecting this, the non-typical minimum is 385 points. This means that only 10 inches of true non-typical points are required above a typical measurement of 375. In theory, a couple of non-typical "kickers" of five or six inches would take the "perfect bull" we described above out of the typical and into the non-typical category. Non-typical bulls are extremely hard to judge, but you can measure the points by the same criteria. The trick is to make sure you're looking at non-typical points and not deductions.

Notes on Roosevelt's and Tule Elk

Roosevelt's elk and tule elk are generally measured in the same way with one major exception. Both subspecies often grow irregular "crown" points near or above the G-4 or dagger point. These points are measured separately and added into the total score. Abnormal points below the G-4 are deducted, and there is no category for non-typical Roosevelt's or tule elk.

The other major difference is the racks are more compact. Roosevelt's elk are giants in the body, with the eye-to-nose and burr-to-nose distances maybe 1/2 inch longer than with American elk. The racks on the best bulls tend to be just as heavy, but main beams are considerably shorter. Beam lengths above 50 inches are rare, with most of the best Roosevelt's elk having beams in the mid-40s. Reflecting this, the minimum score for Roosevelt's elk is 290 points.

MAXIMUM vs. MINIMUM
A Comparison of Two Records-Book Tule Elk

World's Record Tule Elk
Score: 351

TROPHY ANALYSIS

- 21-7/8 inches of crown points added to a 339-7/8 inch frame
- Exceptional spread credit – 48-6/8 inches
- Above average G-1s and G-2s measuring between 12-5/8 and 16-4/8 inches
- Respectable G-3s averaging 10 inches
- Above average mass with H-3s over 6 inches

All-time Minimum Tule Elk
Score: 284-6/8

TROPHY ANALYSIS

- 8-6/8 inches of crown points added to a 283-1/8 inch frame
- Average spread credit just over 40 inches
- Average G-1s and G-2s measuring between 10-1/8 and 12-2/8 inches
- Weak G-3s just over 7 inches

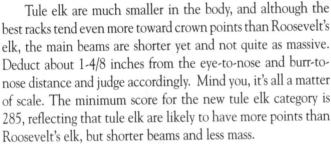

Tule elk are much smaller in the body, and although the best racks tend even more toward crown points than Roosevelt's elk, the main beams are shorter yet and not quite as massive. Deduct about 1-4/8 inches from the eye-to-nose and burr-to-nose distance and judge accordingly. Mind you, it's all a matter of scale. The minimum score for the new tule elk category is 285, reflecting that tule elk are likely to have more points than Roosevelt's elk, but shorter beams and less mass.

During hunting season there won't be many occasions when you have the time to get out your notebook and try to figure all this out. Nor should you. Sometimes, when elk are feeding on a distant hillside, you can sit down and work it out. But "the big ones look big," and if he looks that big, your time may be better spent making a stalk. On the other hand, the more time you spend really judging elk the better (and faster) you will be at it. This is a great exercise for off-season scouting, or while game viewing in a park. It takes practice and no one will reach perfection. The more time you spend looking and judging elk, the better prepared you will be when you see a big bull in the field. As with all antlered game, the secret is to look at the whole rack, not just one feature, and to know what you're looking at.

SCORECHART
American Elk – Typical

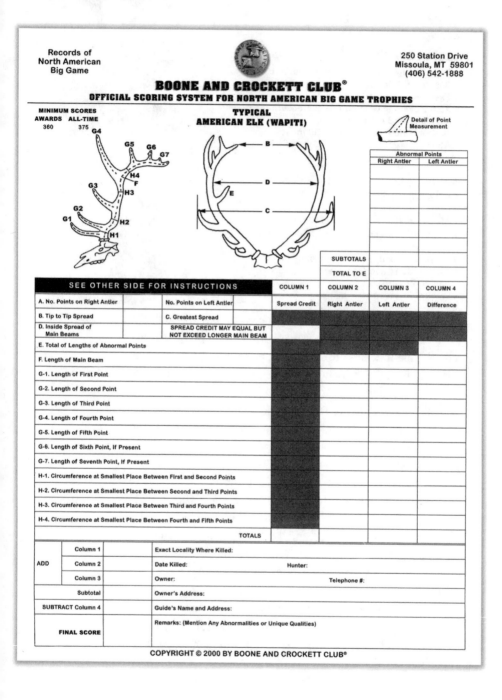

Records of
North American
Big Game

250 Station Drive
Missoula, MT 59801
(406) 542-1888

BOONE AND CROCKETT CLUB®
OFFICIAL SCORING SYSTEM FOR NORTH AMERICAN BIG GAME TROPHIES

MINIMUM SCORES

AWARDS	ALL-TIME
360	375

TYPICAL AMERICAN ELK (WAPITI)

Detail of Point Measurement

Abnormal Points	
Right Antler	Left Antler
SUBTOTALS	
TOTAL TO E	

SEE OTHER SIDE FOR INSTRUCTIONS

				COLUMN 1	COLUMN 2	COLUMN 3	COLUMN 4
A. No. Points on Right Antler		No. Points on Left Antler		Spread Credit	Right Antler	Left Antler	Difference
B. Tip to Tip Spread		C. Greatest Spread					
D. Inside Spread of Main Beams		SPREAD CREDIT MAY EQUAL BUT NOT EXCEED LONGER MAIN BEAM					
E. Total of Lengths of Abnormal Points							
F. Length of Main Beam							
G-1. Length of First Point							
G-2. Length of Second Point							
G-3. Length of Third Point							
G-4. Length of Fourth Point							
G-5. Length of Fifth Point							
G-6. Length of Sixth Point, If Present							
G-7. Length of Seventh Point, If Present							
H-1. Circumference at Smallest Place Between First and Second Points							
H-2. Circumference at Smallest Place Between Second and Third Points							
H-3. Circumference at Smallest Place Between Third and Fourth Points							
H-4. Circumference at Smallest Place Between Fourth and Fifth Points							
			TOTALS				

ADD	Column 1		Exact Locality Where Killed:	
	Column 2		Date Killed:	Hunter:
	Column 3		Owner:	Telephone #:
	Subtotal		Owner's Address:	
SUBTRACT Column 4			Guide's Name and Address:	
FINAL SCORE			Remarks: (Mention Any Abnormalities or Unique Qualities)	

COPYRIGHT © 2000 BY BOONE AND CROCKETT CLUB®

I, _____ , certify that I have measured this trophy on _____
　　　　PRINT NAME　　　　　　　　　　　　　　　　　　　　　　　　　　　　　　　　MM/DD/YYYY

at _____
　　STREET ADDRESS　　　　　　　　　　　　　　　　　　　　　CITY　　　　　　　　　STATE/PROVINCE

and that these measurements and data are, to the best of my knowledge and belief, made in accordance with the instructions given.

Witness: _____ Signature: _____ I.D. Number [ ][ ][ ][ ]
　　　　　　　　　　　　　　　　　　　　　　　B&C OFFICIAL MEASURER

INSTRUCTIONS FOR MEASURING TYPICAL AMERICAN ELK (WAPITI)

All measurements must be made with a 1/4-inch wide flexible steel tape to the nearest one-eighth of an inch. (Note: A flexible steel cable can be used to measure points and main beams only.) Enter fractional figures in eighths, without reduction. Official measurements cannot be taken until the antlers have air dried for at least 60 days after the animal was killed.

- **A. Number of Points on Each Antler:** To be counted a point, the projection must be at least one inch long, with length exceeding width at one inch or more of length. All points are measured from tip of point to nearest edge of beam as illustrated. Beam tip is counted as a point but not measured as a point.
- **B. Tip to Tip Spread** is measured between tips of main beams.
- **C. Greatest Spread** is measured between perpendiculars at a right angle to the center line of the skull at widest part, whether across main beams or points.
- **D. Inside Spread of Main Beams** is measured at a right angle to the center line of the skull at widest point between main beams. Enter this measurement again as the Spread Credit if it is less than or equal to the length of the longer main beam; if greater, enter longer main beam length for Spread Credit.
- **E. Total of Lengths of all Abnormal Points:** Abnormal Points are those non-typical in location (such as points originating from a point or from bottom or sides of main beam) or pattern (extra points, not generally paired). Measure in usual manner and record in appropriate blanks.
- **F. Length of Main Beam** is measured from the center of the lowest outside edge of burr over the outer side to the most distant point of the main beam. The point of beginning is that point on the burr where the center line along the outer side of the beam intersects the burr, then following generally the line of the illustration.
- **G-1-2-3-4-5-6-7. Length of Normal Points:** Normal points project from the top or front of the main beam in the general pattern illustrated. They are measured from nearest edge of main beam over outer curve to tip. Lay the tape along the outer curve of the beam so that the top edge of the tape coincides with the top edge of the beam on both sides of point to determine the baseline for point measurement. Record point length in appropriate blanks.
- **H-1-2-3-4. Circumferences** are taken as detailed in illustration for each measurement.

ENTRY AFFIDAVIT FOR ALL HUNTER-TAKEN TROPHIES

For the purpose of entry into the Boone and Crockett Club's® records, North American big game harvested by the use of the following methods or under the following conditions are ineligible:

- I.　Spotting or herding game from the air, followed by landing in its vicinity for the purpose of pursuit and shooting;
- II.　Herding or chasing with the aid of any motorized equipment;
- III.　Use of electronic communication devices, artificial lighting, or electronic light intensifying devices;
- IV.　Confined by artificial barriers, including escape-proof fenced enclosures;
- V.　Transplanted for the purpose of commercial shooting;
- VI.　By the use of traps or pharmaceuticals;
- VII.　While swimming, helpless in deep snow, or helpless in any other natural or artificial medium;
- VIII.　On another hunter's license;
- IX.　Not in full compliance with the game laws or regulations of the federal government or of any state, province, territory, or tribal council on reservations or tribal lands;

I certify that the trophy scored on this chart was not taken in violation of the conditions listed above. In signing this statement, I understand that if the information provided on this entry is found to be misrepresented or fraudulent in any respect, it will not be accepted into the Awards Program and 1) all of my prior entries are subject to deletion from future editions of **Records of North American Big Game** 2) future entries may not be accepted.

FAIR CHASE, as defined by the Boone and Crockett Club®, is the ethical, sportsmanlike and lawful pursuit and taking of any free-ranging wild, native North American big game animal in a manner that does not give the hunter an improper advantage over such game animals.

The Boone and Crockett Club® may exclude the entry of any animal that it deems to have been taken in an unethical manner or under conditions deemed inappropriate by the Club.

Date: _____ Signature of Hunter: _____
　　　　　　　　　　　　　　　　　　　　　(SIGNATURE MUST BE WITNESSED BY AN OFFICIAL MEASURER OR A NOTARY PUBLIC.)

Date: _____ Signature of Notary or Official Measurer: _____

SCORECHART
American Elk – Non-Typical

Records of
North American
Big Game

250 Station Drive
Missoula, MT 59801
(406) 542-1888

BOONE AND CROCKETT CLUB®
OFFICIAL SCORING SYSTEM FOR NORTH AMERICAN BIG GAME TROPHIES

NON-TYPICAL AMERICAN ELK (WAPITI)

MINIMUM SCORES
AWARDS	ALL-TIME
385	385

Detail of Point Measurement

Abnormal Points	
Right Antler	Left Antler
SUBTOTALS	
E. TOTAL	

SEE OTHER SIDE FOR INSTRUCTIONS				COLUMN 1	COLUMN 2	COLUMN 3	COLUMN 4
				Spread Credit	Right Antler	Left Antler	Difference
A. No. Points on Right Antler		No. Points on Left Antler					
B. Tip to Tip Spread		C. Greatest Spread					
D. Inside Spread of Main Beams		SPREAD CREDIT MAY EQUAL BUT NOT EXCEED LONGER MAIN BEAM					
F. Length of Main Beam							
G-1. Length of First Point							
G-2. Length of Second Point							
G-3. Length of Third Point							
G-4. Length of Fourth Point							
G-5. Length of Fifth Point							
G-6. Length of Sixth Point, If Present							
G-7. Length of Seventh Point, If Present							
H-1. Circumference at Smallest Place Between First and Second Points							
H-2. Circumference at Smallest Place Between Second and Third Points							
H-3. Circumference at Smallest Place Between Third and Fourth Points							
H-4. Circumference at Smallest Place Between Fourth and Fifth Points							
		TOTALS					

ADD	Column 1		Exact Locality Where Killed:
	Column 2		Date Killed: Hunter:
	Column 3		Owner: Telephone #:
	Subtotal		Owner's Address:
SUBTRACT Column 4			Guide's Name and Address:
	Subtotal		Remarks: (Mention Any Abnormalities or Unique Qualities)
	Add Line E Total		
	FINAL SCORE		

I, _____ , certify that I have measured this trophy on _____
    PRINT NAME   MM/DD/YYYYY

at _____
    STREET ADDRESS   CITY   STATE/PROVINCE

and that these measurements and data are, to the best of my knowledge and belief, made in accordance with the instructions given.

Witness: _____ Signature: _____ I.D. Number [ ][ ][ ][ ]
                                               B&C OFFICIAL MEASURER

INSTRUCTIONS FOR MEASURING NON-TYPICAL AMERICAN ELK (WAPITI)

All measurements must be made with a 1/4-inch wide flexible steel tape to the nearest one-eighth of an inch. (Note: A flexible steel cable can be used to measure points and main beams only.) Enter fractional figures in eighths, without reduction. Official measurements cannot be taken until the antlers have air dried for at least 60 days after the animal was killed.

    A. Number of Points on Each Antler: To be counted a point, the projection must be at least one inch long, with length exceeding width at one inch or more of length. All points are measured from tip of point to nearest edge of beam as illustrated. Beam tip is counted as a point but not measured as a point.

    B. Tip to Tip Spread is measured between tips of main beams.

    C. Greatest Spread is measured between perpendiculars at a right angle to the center line of the skull at widest part, whether across main beams or points.

    D. Inside Spread of Main Beams is measured at a right angle to the center line of the skull at widest point between main beams. Enter this measurement again as the Spread Credit if it is less than or equal to the length of the longer main beam; if greater, enter longer main beam length for Spread Credit.

    E. Total of Lengths of all Abnormal Points: Abnormal Points are those non-typical in location (such as points originating from a point or from bottom or sides of main beam) or pattern (extra points, not generally paired). Measure in usual manner and record in appropriate blanks.

    F. Length of Main Beam is measured from the center of the lowest outside edge of burr over the outer side to the most distant point of the main beam. The point of beginning is that point on the burr where the center line along the outer side of the beam intersects the burr, then following generally the line of the illustration.

    G-1-2-3-4-5-6-7. Length of Normal Points: Normal points project from the top or front of the main beam in the general pattern illustrated. They are measured from nearest edge of main beam over outer curve to tip. Lay the tape along the outer curve of the beam so that the top edge of the tape coincides with the top edge of the beam on both sides of point to determine the baseline for point measurement. Record point length in appropriate blanks.

    H-1-2-3-4. Circumferences are taken as detailed in illustration for each measurement.

ENTRY AFFIDAVIT FOR ALL HUNTER-TAKEN TROPHIES

For the purpose of entry into the Boone and Crockett Club's® records, North American big game harvested by the use of the following methods or under the following conditions are ineligible:

    I. Spotting or herding game from the air, followed by landing in its vicinity for the purpose of pursuit and shooting;

    II. Herding or chasing with the aid of any motorized equipment;

    III. Use of electronic communication devices, artificial lighting, or electronic light intensifying devices;

    IV. Confined by artificial barriers, including escape-proof fenced enclosures;

    V. Transplanted for the purpose of commercial shooting;

    VI. By the use of traps or pharmaceuticals;

    VII. While swimming, helpless in deep snow, or helpless in any other natural or artificial medium;

    VIII. On another hunter's license;

    IX. Not in full compliance with the game laws or regulations of the federal government or of any state, province, territory, or tribal council on reservations or tribal lands;

I certify that the trophy scored on this chart was not taken in violation of the conditions listed above. In signing this statement, I understand that if the information provided on this entry is found to be misrepresented or fraudulent in any respect, it will not be accepted into the Awards Program and 1) all of my prior entries are subject to deletion from future editions of **Records of North American Big Game** 2) future entries may not be accepted.

FAIR CHASE, as defined by the Boone and Crockett Club®, is the ethical, sportsmanlike and lawful pursuit and taking of any free-ranging wild, native North American big game animal in a manner that does not give the hunter an improper advantage over such game animals.

The Boone and Crockett Club® may exclude the entry of any animal that it deems to have been taken in an unethical manner or under conditions deemed inappropriate by the Club.

Date: _____ Signature of Hunter: _____
                                              (SIGNATURE MUST BE WITNESSED BY AN OFFICIAL MEASURER OR A NOTARY PUBLIC.)

Date: _____ Signature of Notary or Official Measurer: _____

SCORECHART
Roosevelt's and Tule Elk

Records of
North American
Big Game

250 Station Drive
Missoula, MT 59801
(406) 542-1888

BOONE AND CROCKETT CLUB®
OFFICIAL SCORING SYSTEM FOR NORTH AMERICAN BIG GAME TROPHIES

ROOSEVELT'S AND TULE ELK

MINIMUM SCORES		
	AWARDS	ALL-TIME
Roosevelt's	275	290
Tule	270	285

KIND OF ELK (check one)
☐ Roosevelt's
☐ Tule

Crown Points	
Right Antler	Left Antler

I. Crown Points Total

Abnormal Points	
Right Antler	Left Antler

Detail of Point Measurement

TOTAL TO E

SEE OTHER SIDE FOR INSTRUCTIONS		COLUMN 1	COLUMN 2	COLUMN 3	COLUMN 4
A. No. Points on Right Antler	No. Points on Left Antler	Spread Credit	Right Antler	Left Antler	Difference
B. Tip to Tip Spread	C. Greatest Spread				
D. Inside Spread of Main Beams	SPREAD CREDIT MAY EQUAL BUT NOT EXCEED LONGER MAIN BEAM				
E. Total of Lengths of Abnormal Points					
F. Length of Main Beam					
G-1. Length of First Point					
G-2. Length of Second Point					
G-3. Length of Third Point					
G-4. Length of Fourth Point					
G-5. Length of Fifth Point					
G-6. Length of Sixth Point, If Present					
G-7. Length of Seventh Point, If Present					
H-1. Circumference at Smallest Place Between First and Second Points					
H-2. Circumference at Smallest Place Between Second and Third Points					
H-3. Circumference at Smallest Place Between Third and Fourth Points					
H-4. Circumference at Smallest Place Between Fourth and Fifth Points					
TOTALS					

ADD	Column 1		Exact Locality Where Killed:
	Column 2		Date Killed: Hunter:
	Column 3		Owner: Telephone #:
	Total of I		Owner's Address:
	Subtotal		Guide's Name and Address:
SUBTRACT Column 4			Remarks: (Mention Any Abnormalities or Unique Qualities)
FINAL SCORE			

COPYRIGHT © 2000 BY BOONE AND CROCKETT CLUB®

I, _____, certify that I have measured this trophy on _____

PRINT NAME   MM/DD/YYYYY

at _____

STREET ADDRESS   CITY   STATE/PROVINCE

and that these measurements and data are, to the best of my knowledge and belief, made in accordance with the instructions given.

Witness: _____ Signature: _____ I.D. Number ☐☐☐☐

B&C OFFICIAL MEASURER

INSTRUCTIONS FOR MEASURING ROOSEVELT'S AND TULE ELK

All measurements must be made with a 1/4-inch wide flexible steel tape to the nearest one-eighth of an inch. (Note: A flexible steel cable can be used to measure points and main beams only.) Enter fractional figures in eighths, without reduction. Official measurements cannot be taken until the antlers have air dried for at least 60 days after the animal was killed.

A. **Number of Points on Each Antler:** to be counted a point, the projection must be at least one inch long, with length exceeding width at one inch or more of length. All points are measured from tip of point to nearest edge of beam as illustrated. Beam tip is counted as a point but not measured as a point.

B. **Tip to Tip Spread** is measured between tips of main beams.

C. **Greatest Spread** is measured between perpendiculars at a right angle to the center line of the skull at widest part, whether across main beams or points.

D. **Inside Spread of Main Beams** is measured at a right angle to the center line of the skull at widest point between main beams. Enter this measurement again as the Spread Credit if it is less than or equal to the length of the longer main beam; if greater, enter longer main beam length for Spread Credit.

E. **Total of Lengths of all Abnormal Points:** Abnormal Points are those non-typical in location or pattern occurring below G-4. Measure in usual manner and record in appropriate blanks. **Note: do not confuse with Crown Points that may occur in the vicinity of G-4, G-5, G-6, etc.**

F. **Length of Main Beam** is measured from the center of the lowest outside edge of burr over the outer side to the most distant point of the main beam. The point of beginning is that point on the burr where the center line along the outer side of the beam intersects the burr, then following generally the line of the illustration.

G-1-2-3-4-5-6-7. **Length of Normal Points:** Normal points project from the top or front of the main beam in the general pattern illustrated. They are measured from nearest edge of main beam over outer curve to tip. Lay the tape along the outer curve of the beam so that the top edge of the tape coincides with the top edge of the beam on both sides of point to determine the baseline for point measurement. Record point length in appropriate blanks.

H-1-2-3-4. **Circumferences** are taken as detailed in illustration for each measurement.

I. **Crown Points:** From the well-defined Royal on out to end of beam, all points other than the normal points in their typical locations are Crown Points. This includes points occurring on the Royal, on other normal points, on Crown Points, and on the bottom and sides of main beam after the Royal. Measure and record in appropriate blanks provided and add to score below.

ENTRY AFFIDAVIT FOR ALL HUNTER-TAKEN TROPHIES

For the purpose of entry into the Boone and Crockett Club's® records, North American big game harvested by the use of the following methods or under the following conditions are ineligible:

    I. Spotting or herding game from the air, followed by landing in its vicinity for the purpose of pursuit and shooting;

    II. Herding or chasing with the aid of any motorized equipment;

    III. Use of electronic communication devices, artificial lighting, or electronic light intensifying devices;

    IV. Confined by artificial barriers, including escape-proof fenced enclosures;

    V. Transplanted for the purpose of commercial shooting;

    VI. By the use of traps or pharmaceuticals;

    VII. While swimming, helpless in deep snow, or helpless in any other natural or artificial medium;

    VIII. On another hunter's license;

    IX. Not in full compliance with the game laws or regulations of the federal government or of any state, province, territory, or tribal council on reservations or tribal lands;

I certify that the trophy scored on this chart was not taken in violation of the conditions listed above. In signing this statement, I understand that if the information provided on this entry is found to be misrepresented or fraudulent in any respect, it will not be accepted into the Awards Program and 1) all of my prior entries are subject to deletion from future editions of **Records of North American Big Game** 2) future entries may not be accepted.

FAIR CHASE, as defined by the Boone and Crockett Club®, is the ethical, sportsmanlike and lawful pursuit and taking of any free-ranging wild, native North American big game animal in a manner that does not give the hunter an improper advantage over such game animals.

The Boone and Crockett Club® may exclude the entry of any animal that it deems to have been taken in an unethical manner or under conditions deemed inappropriate by the Club.

Date: _____ Signature of Hunter: _____

(SIGNATURE MUST BE WITNESSED BY AN OFFICIAL MEASURER OR A NOTARY PUBLIC.)

Date: _____ Signature of Notary or Official Measurer: _____

MEASURING AND JUDGING
Moose

As detailed in the section on geographic boundaries, there are three categories of North American moose recognized for entry in the Boone and Crockett Club's Awards Programs. Alaska-Yukon moose are the largest bodied and heaviest antlered; Wyoming (Shiras') moose are the lightest; Canada moose are intermediate in both respects. Fewer measurements are taken for moose than for the other antlered categories. Despite this, moose can be one of the most complex trophies to measure. If the skull on a moose rack is split, the moose cannot be entered into the records.

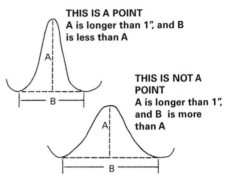

THIS IS A POINT
A is longer than 1", and B is less than A

THIS IS NOT A POINT
A is longer than 1", and B is more than A

FIGURE 8-A

Rather than having their length measured, points on moose antlers are simply counted. The reason point lengths are not recorded is that moose with well-developed palms with short points are considered more desirable trophies. Long points develop as a result of the lack of palm material. Including point length measurements would thus discriminate against the more desirable character of well-developed palms.

In moose, a point is any projection at least one inch long and with a width, at the point of measurement at one inch or more from the tip, less than the length **(figure 8-A)**. Point width is taken perpendicular to the axis of the point as **figure 8-B** shows.

Normal points arise *only* from the outer edge of a palm. Abnormal points are not common on moose racks. Any point that grows from the palm face on the front or back surface, or on the inside edge of the palm, or on any other unusual location is regarded as abnormal. Sometimes moose will have double palmation on one or both sides. Any points projecting from the secondary, abnormal palm must be treated as abnormal points as well. Show the count of such points in the box on the upper right side of the score chart and enter the total count into the abnormal point total on the score chart line B where it will be a deduction from the score. There is no requirement that antler points must be matched with

FIGURE 8-B
DETAIL OF A POINT
MEASUREMENT

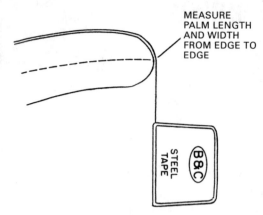

MEASURE
PALM LENGTH
AND WIDTH
FROM EDGE TO
EDGE

STEEL TAPE
B&C

FIGURE 8-C
**MEASURE PALM
LENGTH AND
WIDTH FROM
EDGE TO EDGE**

corresponding points on the opposite antler to be regarded as normal. But, points on moose antlers are best rewarded if there are an equal number of normal points on each side. Record the appropriate point count for each antler on line C of the score chart.

There is a tendency for measurers to count every major projection on a moose antler as a point. When moose antlers are remeasured at panel judging sessions, the biggest discrepancy in scores arises from incorrect, initial point counts. Many projections on moose antlers appear to be points when in fact they are not as the width of the point remains greater than the length at all points of measurement. Such projections do not meet the definition of a point and, thus, are not to be included in the point count. Often, the only way to tell if an individual projection qualifies as a point or not is to measure each one.

After determination of and recording of the number of points present, the length of palm measurements are taken. In taking both length and width of palm measurements, the start and finish of the measurement lines should be the midpoints of the edge of the palm. This approach recognizes the thickness of the palm material, a desirable characteristic, as part of the measurements. **Figure 8-C** illustrates this approach.

FIGURE 8-D

INCORRECT

CORRECT E
MEASUREMENT

To begin the length of palm measurement, turn the rack upside down and lay out a strip of masking tape *parallel* to the inside edge of the palm. Then consider alternative ways the length of palm could be measured so that the measuring tape will remain parallel to the inner edge line established by the masking tape. In moose with well developed lower palms and top structure, there may be several possible measurement lines. It is helpful to lay out possible lines with masking tape (even if there is only one possibility). These alternate masking tape lines provide visual reference for the comparison of possibilities. See **figure 8-D** for an illustration.

The correct length of palm measurement is the longest line that can be measured in contact with the antler surface that is also the most parallel to the inside edge of the palm. Typically this line will extend from the bottom of a dip on the palm top to the bottom of the valley between points on the brow. Since many large moose racks do not have any countable points on the palm top, the line can be started from any dip (notch) or indentation along the top edge. This line can never be taken from the tip of a point.

Often the length line crosses an open bay on the outer edge of the palm. This is acceptable as long as the line is the longest, most parallel line **(figure 8-E)**. However, the line can never pass over open space on the inner edge of the palm as **figure 8-F** shows.

If the brow is palmated with several points, the line extends from the top of the upper palm to the bottom edge between points. If the brow is forked and without other points, the line should extend to the bottom of the fork. Unlike the beginning of the length measurement on the top of the palm, the end of the measurement on the lower edge must *always* be between points (if present), not simply to dips or indentations along the lower, brow palm.

If the brow is unforked, and is really only a spike extending forward, the edge of the main palm then becomes the termination of the palm length measurement line. **Figure 8-G** shows this situation. The proper length line on moose with a spike as the brow palm is the longest parallel line to the inner edge *that does not cross an open bay* on the outer palm edge.

Once the palm length has been properly established, the palm width can be taken. Palm width is taken at a right angle to the inner edge of the palm. Use the masking tape line that was initially established as the line parallel to the inner edge of the palm as the reference line

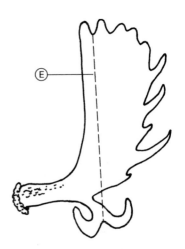

FIGURE 8-E
LENGTH OF PALM
MEASUREMENT
CROSSING
OPEN BAY

FIGURE 8-F
A-B IMPROPER
LENGTH
OF PALM
MEASUREMENT

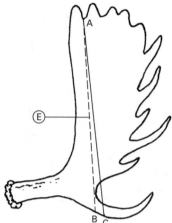

FIGURE 8-G

**A-B PROPER
MEASUREMENT**

**A-C IMPROPER
MEASUREMENT**

for this measurement. Just as in palm length, the measurement line is begun at a spot between point dips and continued *in contact* with the palm's under (back) surface (this will be the "upper" surface if antlers are turned upside-down as previously suggested). The measurement extends from the palm edge across the back of the palm to the center of the palm's inner edge. The proper width is the greatest width of the possible widths that originate at the bottom of the dip between points to the middle of the palm edge of the *upper* palm.

There may be some question as to how far down the top palm this measurement may be taken. The width may be recorded as far down the top palm as the upper edge of the horizontal plane of the main beam. Palm width cannot be taken on brow palm.

A single circumference of each main beam is measured by looping a ring-end tape around the beam, with the zero mark up. Pull the tape together and gently move it along the beam until the smallest circumference measurement is obtained. If you use a clip-end tape to measure circumferences, overlap the tape at a full 10-inch increment to simplify the procedure. Be sure to subtract the amount of overlap before recording the measurement.

The greatest spread is best determined by use of two perpendiculars (such as carpenter's levels supported upright by large c-clamps), or by use of a floor and wall (providing it is a true 90 degree angle) for one perpendicular and a carpenter's level held upright by a large c-clamp, or a carpenter's square for the other. When the perpendiculars have been properly established against the rack, the greatest spread is measured between them in a straight line, at a right angle to the skull center line, by using the folding carpenter's rule. Usually, the antlers and attached skull are turned upside-down, resting on a level floor, for this measurement. Obviously, care must be taken that the line of measurement is at a right angle to the center line of the skull to ensure the measurement is not improperly at a diagonal. Unlike other antlered species, the greatest spread for a moose is directly part of the final score.

The greatest spread *cannot* include any portion of an abnormal point. If an abnormal point impacts the greatest spread measurement, find the greatest spread that does not include the abnormality. Note this action in the REMARKS section of the score chart. The greatest spread can occur across the brow palms as well as across the top palm. In fact, the point of contact on one side for greatest spread may be at the tip of a point along the outer edge of the top palm and on the edge of the brow palm on the other as long the measurement line remains square to the center line of the skull.

Rarely, a moose palm will show ridges and valleys or even a highly corrugated, folded surface of palm. In such a case, it would not be fair to simply measure the length and width of palm in the usual fashion. If the ridges and/or corrugations were "ironed-out," the palm would be either longer or wider, or both. The solution for this condition is establishment of the usual lines of measurement but with the actual measurement taken by following the edge of heavy, craft-like paper, cut perfectly straight, that is laid across the ridges and into the valleys. The paper is forced into the valleys to properly contact surface material of the palm along the entire line of measurement. The number and location of the corrugations or valleys can obviously alter the placement of the measurement lines. Trial-and-error measurements must be used in such cases, keeping in mind the correct location of length and width measurement lines in relation to the inner edge of the palm.

The total mass of antler material of a large Alaska-Yukon moose is greater than that of any other living member of the deer family. Alaska-Yukon moose racks may exceed 60 pounds when fully dried. Large Canada moose racks may weigh in excess of 50 pounds and Shiras' moose antlers may weigh more than 30 pounds. Information on rack weight is requested as supplemental information on the back of the hunter, guide and hunt information form.

Field Judging Moose

Of all the living members of the deer family, moose have the greatest amount of antler material. They also show great variation in size, with the smallest racks coming from Idaho, Montana, Utah and Wyoming, and the largest from Alaska, Yukon, and the Northwest Territories. A records book sized Wyoming (Shiras) moose would not be even a desirable trophy in Alaska.

Although the widest spread antlers are sought in all cat-

MAXIMUM vs. MINIMUM
A Comparison of Two
Records-Book Wyoming Moose

World's Record Wyoming moose
Score: 205-4/8

TROPHY ANALYSIS

- 15 points per antler
- No distinguishable weaknesses
- Exceptional width of palm averaging 16 inches
- Above average spread of 53 inches and length of palm 38" plus
- Average mass close to 7 inches

Close to minimum Wyoming moose
Score: 140-2/8

TROPHY ANALYSIS

- 9x10 point frame
- Average spread of 41-6/8 inches
- Average length of palm – both over 24 inches
- Average mass – both over 6 inches
- Narrow width of palm – averaging 10 inches

egories for the records, strong development of antler palmation in both length and width is even more desirable. Many Shiras moose show only a single spike brow point on each antler, rather than a well-developed brow palm. This is undesirable since the length-of-palm is measured to a notch between brow points. The single spike brow dictates that the length of palm measurement must be ended at the edge of the main palm, obviously losing some potential that would have been fulfilled if the brow were palmate or even forked. High-scoring Canada or Alaska-Yukon moose have three or more brow points, on broad, well-developed brow palms that increase the length-of-palm measurement. This feature, along with broad main palms, markedly improves the score potential.

Although an Alaska-Yukon moose may have 15 or more points on each antler, not all projections count as points, especially if they are blunt in shape. One cannot accurately count the antler points on most trophy moose when the animal is in

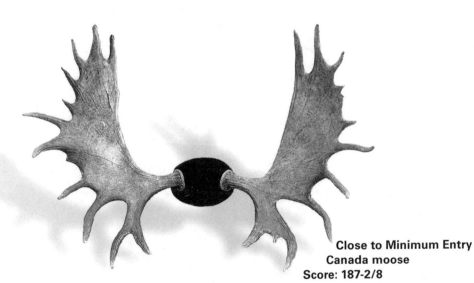

**World's Record
Canada moose
Score: 242**

TROPHY ANALYSIS
- 15x16 point frame
- All areas exceptional
- Spread over 63 inches
- Width of palm averaging 22 inches
- Length of palm – 44-5/8 and 45 inches

**Close to Minimum Entry
Canada moose
Score: 187-2/8**

TROPHY ANALYSIS
- 11x11 point frame
- Above average spread over 54 inches
- Above average mass measuring 7-7/8 and 7-6/8 inches
- Average width of palm averaging 12 inches
- Average length of palm – both over 36 inches

MAXIMUM vs. MINIMUM
A Comparison of Two Records-Book Alaska-Yukon Moose

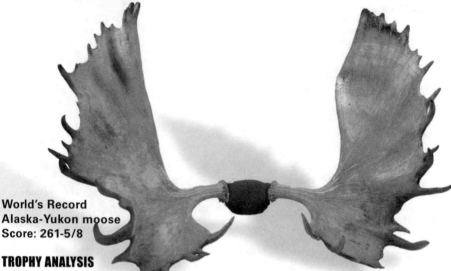

World's Record
Alaska-Yukon moose
Score: 261-5/8

TROPHY ANALYSIS

- 19x15 point frame
- Exceptional palms – width averaging 22 inches and length averaging 54 inches
- Exceptional mass – both circumferences over 8 inches
- Above average spread measuring over 65 inches
- Only bull in the book over 260 points

Minimum Entry
Alaska-Yukon moose
Score: 210

TROPHY ANALYSIS

- 12x14 point frame
- Above average spread over 66 inches
- Above average mass – both circumferences measuring 7-5/8 inches
- Average palms – both measure 14-1/8 inches wide and length averages just under 39 inches

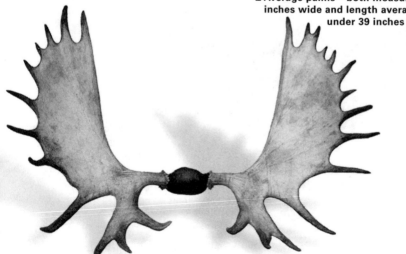

the field, so evaluation must generally be made on the basis of the amount of palm material present and the greatest spread.

Big trophy moose of all three classes tend to have the main palms lying flat to produce a wide spread, whereas smaller antlers are more apt to show cup-shaped palms and a narrow spread. Even though moose can often be studied carefully in the field, and an experienced guide may make reasonable estimate of the greatest spread, it is very difficult to estimate the scores accurately at a distance. This is because the length, width, and symmetry of the palms are all hard to judge when seen from the side. A frontal view, with the animal's head down and antlers nearly vertical, gives a much better chance for accurate evaluation, but may not be available under field conditions. ■

SCORECHART
Moose

Records of
North American
Big Game

250 Station Drive
Missoula, MT 59801
(406) 542-1888

BOONE AND CROCKETT CLUB®
OFFICIAL SCORING SYSTEM FOR NORTH AMERICAN BIG GAME TROPHIES

MOOSE

MINIMUM SCORES	AWARDS	ALL-TIME
Canada	185	195
Alaska-Yukon	210	224
Wyoming	140	155

KIND OF MOOSE (check one)
- ☐ Canada
- ☐ Alaska-Yukon
- ☐ Wyoming

Detail of Point
Measurement

	Abnormal Points	
	Right Antler	Left Antler
NUMBER OF POINTS		
TOTAL TO B.		

SEE OTHER SIDE FOR INSTRUCTIONS	COLUMN 1	COLUMN 2	COLUMN 3	COLUMN 4
		Right Antler	Left Antler	Difference
A. Greatest Spread				
B. Number of Abnormal Points on Both Antlers				
C. Number of Normal Points				
D. Width of Palm				
E. Length of Palm Including Brow Palm				
F. Circumference of Beam at Smallest Place				
TOTALS				

ADD			Exact Locality Where Killed:
	Column 1		
	Column 2		Date Killed: Hunter:
	Column 3		Owner: Telephone #:
	Subtotal		Owner's Address:
SUBTRACT Column 4			Guide's Name and Address:
FINAL SCORE			Remarks: (Mention Any Abnormalities or Unique Qualities)

I, _____ , certify that I have measured this trophy on _____

PRINT NAME   MM/DD/YYYYY

at _____

STREET ADDRESS   CITY   STATE/PROVINCE

and that these measurements and data are, to the best of my knowledge and belief, made in accordance with the instructions given.

Witness: _____ Signature: _____ I.D. Number ☐☐☐☐

B&C OFFICIAL MEASURER

INSTRUCTIONS FOR MEASURING MOOSE

Measurements must be made with a 1/4-inch wide flexible steel tape to the nearest one-eighth of an inch. Enter fractional figures in eighths, without reduction. Official measurements cannot be taken until antlers have air dried for at least 60 days after animal was killed.

A. **Greatest Spread** is measured between perpendiculars in a straight line at a right angle to the center line of the skull.

B. **Number of Abnormal Points on Both Antlers:** Abnormal points are those projections originating from normal points or from the upper or lower palm surface, or from the inner edge of palm (see illustration). Abnormal points must be at least one inch long, with length exceeding width at one inch or more of length.

C. **Number of Normal Points:** Normal points originate from the outer edge of palm. To be counted a point, a projection must be at least one inch long, with the length exceeding width at one inch or more of length. Be sure to verify whether or not each projection qualifies as a point.

D. **Width of Palm** is taken in contact with the under surface of palm, at a right angle to the inner edge of palm. The line of measurement should begin and end at the midpoint of the palm edge, which gives credit for the desirable character of palm thickness.

E. **Length of Palm** including Brow Palm is taken in contact with the surface along the underside of the palm, **parallel** to the inner edge, from dips between points at the top to dips between points (if present) at the bottom. If a bay is present, measure across the open bay if the proper line of measurement, parallel to **inner edge**, follows this path. The line of measurement should begin and end at the midpoint of the palm edge, which gives credit for the desirable character of palm thickness.

F. **Circumference** of Beam at Smallest Place is taken as illustrated.

ENTRY AFFIDAVIT FOR ALL HUNTER-TAKEN TROPHIES

For the purpose of entry into the Boone and Crockett Club's® records, North American big game harvested by the use of the following methods or under the following conditions are ineligible:

I. Spotting or herding game from the air, followed by landing in its vicinity for the purpose of pursuit and shooting;

II. Herding or chasing with the aid of any motorized equipment;

III. Use of electronic communication devices, artificial lighting, or electronic light intensifying devices;

IV. Confined by artificial barriers, including escape-proof fenced enclosures;

V. Transplanted for the purpose of commercial shooting;

VI. By the use of traps or pharmaceuticals;

VII. While swimming, helpless in deep snow, or helpless in any other natural or artificial medium;

VIII. On another hunter's license;

IX. Not in full compliance with the game laws or regulations of the federal government or of any state, province, territory, or tribal council on reservations or tribal lands;

I certify that the trophy scored on this chart was not taken in violation of the conditions listed above. In signing this statement, I understand that if the information provided on this entry is found to be misrepresented or fraudulent in any respect, it will not be accepted into the Awards Program and 1) all of my prior entries are subject to deletion from future editions of **Records of North American Big Game** 2) future entries may not be accepted.

FAIR CHASE, as defined by the Boone and Crockett Club®, is the ethical, sportsmanlike and lawful pursuit and taking of any free-ranging wild, native North American big game animal in a manner that does not give the hunter an improper advantage over such game animals.

The Boone and Crockett Club® may exclude the entry of any animal that it deems to have been taken in an unethical manner or under conditions deemed inappropriate by the Club.

Date:_____ Signature of Hunter:_____
(SIGNATURE MUST BE WITNESSED BY AN OFFICIAL MEASURER OR A NOTARY PUBLIC.)

Date:_____ Signature of Notary or Official Measurer:_____

A BOONE AND CROCKETT CLUB FIELD GUIDE TO MEASURING AND JUDGING BIG GAME

MEASURING AND JUDGING
Caribou

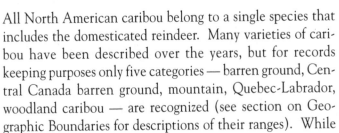

All North American caribou belong to a single species that includes the domesticated reindeer. Many varieties of caribou have been described over the years, but for records keeping purposes only five categories — barren ground, Central Canada barren ground, mountain, Quebec-Labrador, woodland caribou — are recognized (see section on Geographic Boundaries for descriptions of their ranges). While certain categories display more pronounced features than others, and individual caribou racks vary widely in conformation, all caribou have the same basic antler structure. Thus the scoring system is the same for all five categories.

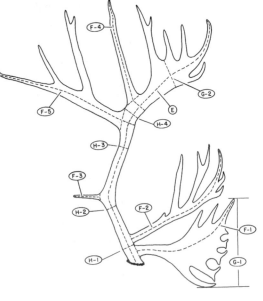

As displayed in **figure 9-A**, mature caribou racks show a usual pattern of five main features:

1) a main beam, E, that arises from the skull and grows outward and backward and then usually forward to a tip, much like a gigantic whitetail

2) a brow palm, F-1, sometimes called a "shovel" and often found on only one antler, that projects in a perpendicular fashion forward over the face and that may show any stage of development from a single spike to a many-pointed, broad palm

3) a bez point (pronounced "bay"), F-2, growing forward from the main beam just above the brow palm, usually with two or more branches and often showing some palmation

4) a rear point, F-3, that usually develops as an unbranched spike projecting backward from about the middle of the main beam

5) a series of distinct, separate points that develop at the top of the antler main beam, with the beam often showing distinct palmation at this location

FIGURE 9-A
THIS IS A POINT
A is longer than 1″, and B is less than A

THIS IS NOT A POINT
A is longer than 1″, and B is more than A

FIGURE 9-B
DETAIL OF A POINT
MEASUREMENT

While caribou generally display these five features, no other antlered species shows greater variety in the development of antler points. For this reason, there is no such thing as an abnormal point in caribou. The point definition in caribou differs from the general definition used for all other antlered game. For purposes of determining points in caribou, a point is any projection at least **one-half** inch long, and longer than wide at any length of one half-inch or more, measuring from the tip. Any projection meeting this definition is considered a point **(figure 9-B)**. The determination of points on a caribou can be a detailed process as some bulls may have in excess of 50 points. Many of the points, especially on the brow palm and bez may be quite short and curved requiring careful examination by the measurer. A projection is measured over its outer curve when determining its length and its width is taken perpendicular to the center line of the length measurement.

The first step in caribou scoring is determination of all points on both antlers, keeping in mind the above definition of a point. The total number of points including the beam tip but **excluding** any points on the brow palm is first counted. Next, the points on each brow palm (when the brow palm is present) are determined *separately* from the points for the rest of the antler and entered on the appropriate line on the score chart. *Be careful not to count the brow palm points twice* (once as brow palm points and again as points on each antler); this is a common measuring error.

Figure 9-C illustrates the proper point count for three situations dealing with brow palm configurations. On the left diagram, there is only one point on the brow palm; for the middle sketch, two points would be recorded; the right sketch displays three separate points. One reason for this is that the brow palm length for the brow palm on the left would be recorded to the upper tip of the palm. Thus that tip is then the brow palm and not a separate point off the rest of that palm. In the other two diagrams one (center sketch) and then two (right sketch) other points occur as once again the top tip counts as one and the lower structure counts as either a second, or second and third points.

If the brow palm, bez, rear or top points are missing on one or both antlers, record them as zero(s) or dashes (-) on the score chart to properly identify the point sequence. Since many caribou may have only a single brow palm or a brow palm and a spike, there is no difference penalty for lack of symmetry on all brow palm measurements.

The length of beam and antler point length measurements may be taken by the use of the flexible steel cable or a 1/4 inch wide steel clip-end tape. The use of a round, flexible steel cable (such as a bicycle brake cable) greatly speeds-up the measuring process while still yielding an accurate measurement. However, only the steel tape can be used for circumference measurements. As with other categories for antlered species where inside spread is an integral part of the final score, the animal is not eligible for listing if the skull has been split.

For measurement of length, the cable is positioned along the outer curve of the beam or point. The end of the measurement is marked by attaching an alligator clip to the cable at the proper spot. The cable is then removed and held in a straight line against a clip-end tape or folding carpenter's rule to record the length measurement. The clip-end tape is often faster to use when antler points are generally straight as the clip-end can easily be hooked on the end of the antler point and the tape stretched to the point's base line. When using a 1/4 inch wide tape on a curved point or antler beam, the measurer will need to mark points of rotation along the line of measurement. The tape is then rotated at these marks. Be sure to align the tape at the appropriate length when the re-alignment is made.

The next step is to measure the main beam lengths. The score chart indicates the end of the beam length measurement is the most distant point of the main beam. In determining which points of the antler tops are to be regarded as the main beam tips, both antlers should be studied. Generally, symmetrical and matching location points are selected as the tips of the measurable beams. These points should be the **FIGURE 9-C**

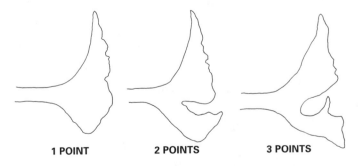

| 1 POINT | 2 POINTS | 3 POINTS |

FIGURE 9-D
TYPICAL BEZES

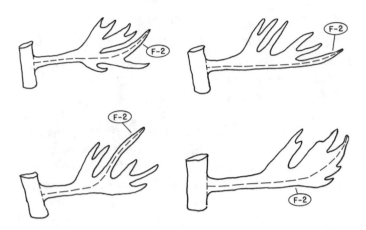

longest forward projecting points. Almost all caribou show the main beams growing forward with the tips over the top of the skull. On many caribou racks, the main beam tip is the lowest point on the forward directed main beam. Very *rarely* the main beam grows backward, reminiscent of a wapiti antler, so that the top points are reversed in their position as they come off the main beam.

The measurement for determining the length of antler main beam is illustrated on the score chart and on **figure 9-A**, being generally a line from the antler burr, above the eye, to the beam tip, maintained along the outer side of the beam. It can be measured either from the tip to the burr or from the burr to the tip. Either way should result in the same measurement if the correct line is chosen.

The correct line begins at that location where the center line of the beam intersects the burr. It is neither at the lower front edge nor at the rear edge of the beam but rather at the outside center of the burr.

The measurement generally follows the center of the outside of the main beam. The area of most difficulty often is across the top palm of the antler. The line of measurement follows the most massive structure to the beam tip. Essentially the measurer is following the center of the antler beam on out to the tip.

Measurement of the length of brow palm (F-1) and bez (F-2) is similar to point measurement in deer and elk. Point base lines are established for these points where they join main beam material. The edge of the beam, and, hence, the starting location for the base line for the brow palm, may be quite forward and somewhat under the brow palm itself, so care needs to be taken when marking the brow palm's base. The length is then taken from the center of the brow's base over the outer curve to the tip. This measurement may be taken either on the outside or on the inside of the brow palm, depending on the curvature of the brow. The lengths of the brow palms and bez points are recorded in the proper blanks on the score chart, with zero being recorded for the obvious absence of a point in the normal sequence.

FIGURE 9-E
NO BROW PALM

Since the brow palm and bez may possess multiple branches, there may be several choices for placement of the measurement line. The correct choice is that line extending into the most distant projection of the point. **Figure 9-D** illustrates some possible F-2 length measurements. Particularly on the bez, the greatest length may be up one of the points that branches from the bez prior to its tip. It is also important to note that both the brow palm and the bez **must** project from the main beam itself. On occasion, a brow palm-like structure comes not off the beam but off the bez as shown in **figure 9-E**. In such a case, that structure cannot be treated as a brow palm but rather as points on the bez. The brow palm is missing and the condition noted in the REMARKS section.

FIGURE 9-F
REAR POINT VARIATIONS
AD IS 1/2 INCH OR LONGER AND LONGER THAN THE WIDTH BC. MEASURE LENGTH AE

Rear points (F-3) are often missing on caribou. If the rear point qualifies as a point in terms of being longer than wide at some point one-half inch or more from the point tip, its length is measured

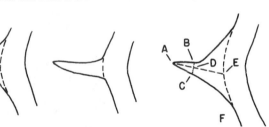

from its tip to its base line on the main beam. Often, the rear point may be quite blunt and triangular in shape. **Figure 9-F** illustrates these cases. If a projection doesn't qualify as a point, it is obviously not counted nor measured as a point. However, if any sign of a rear point development is present, it is used to properly locate the second and third circumferences of main beam (H-2 and H-3).

Credit can be given for only a single rear point (if present) on each antler. Very rarely, an extra rear point (not a branch

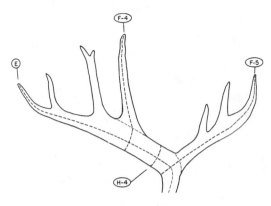

FIGURE 9-G

of the rear point) may develop on one or both antlers. In such a case, choose the more "normal" one to measure as the rear point. The other will receive credit only in the point count for the antler.

Measurement of the individual points F-4 and F-5 (second longest and longest top points) differs from other caribou point measurements in several ways. These two points are measured over their outer curve to the **lower edge** of the main beam, rather than to a base line established on the top edge of main beam. Commonly, these points are part of a noticeable palm formation, with a portion of their length "hidden" in the palm. For that reason, they are measured to the lower edge of beam to give proper credit. The first part of this measurement is in the usual manner, from the point tip to the top edge of main beam (where a base line would be drawn in the other antlered categories). Then, the measurement is continued at a right angle to the main beam axis to the lower edge of the beam, with the entire length being recorded. **Figure 9-G** demonstrates this technique. Note that the measurement is continued to the midpoint of the lower edge of palm, which is often keel-shaped. *A common error is to fail to remember to take the F-4 and F-5 point lengths to the bottom edge of the top palm.*

One additional consideration must be kept in mind when measuring the second longest top point (F- 4). F-4 **cannot** be a branch of the longest top point (F-5) It must arise upward from the top palm or the main beam as a separate point. This instruction is necessary as the longest top point may have an offshoot point that extends further from the main beam than the second longest top point. But, if this point branch was designated as the second longest point, it would create a false measurement for both G-2 (width of top palm) and H-4 (circumference at smallest place between two longest top points) by directing these lines of measurement to a point fork, rather than the true palm area.

FIGURE 9-H

The width of the brow palm (G-1) is measured in a straight line from the top edge to the lower edge at a right angle to the main axis of the brow palm. This measure-

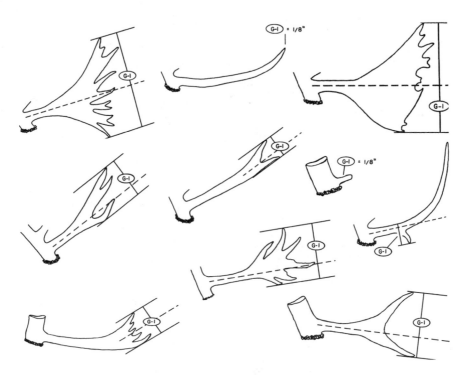

ment is best taken with calipers or a small pair of carpenter's squares. This measurement is one of the most complex on caribou since brow palms display a wide variety of configurations. Various brow palm formations, and the corresponding G-1 measurements, are illustrated in **figure 9-H**. You should find the one that most nearly matches the bull you are measuring as a pattern to follow. Within limits, the width of the brow palm should not duplicate its length nor should the width measurement be primarily one of measuring air space without palm material.

If the brow palm is not noticeably palmate, but it does show some flattening and/or enlargement indicative of palm formation at its tip, the width is recorded across the flattening. If the brow palm is a *single, spike point with no palmation enlargement at the tip*, a credit of 1/8 is entered for G-1 to identify the character of this point regardless of the actual point width.

Because of the great variation of caribou antlers, the brow palm width measurement is often more complicated than the score chart illustration. In order to take the width of the brow palm (G-1) measurements two parallel lines must be established.

FIGURE 9-I
VARIOUS
BROW PALM
FORMATIONS

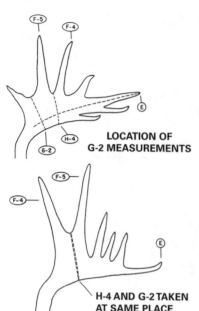

LOCATION OF
G-2 MEASUREMENTS

H-4 AND G-2 TAKEN
AT SAME PLACE

FIGURE 9-J

If the axis of the brow palm is markedly curved, and also shows palmation at the tip, the width of the brow palm is taken at a right angle to the tip (**figure 9-H**). This prevents the inflated measurement that would result if the measurement location were based primarily on the curvature of the axis of the brow palm, rather than its actual palmation.

A good method for establishing the two parallel lines is by the use of two carpenter's squares positioned parallel to the main axis of the brow palm. The width is then measured at right angles between these parallel lines. **Figure 9-I** illustrates various parallel lines and G-1 measurements.

Sometimes the bez points will show palmation similar to well-developed brow palms, and the question arises as to why a bez width is not recorded. The development of bez palmation is most common in woodland and Quebec-Labrador caribou and is less so in mountain and barren ground caribou. When the original committee chaired by Sam Webb was finalizing the scoring system for caribou, it considered this matter. They rejected the idea of crediting bez palmation, because of the great variation in the conformation of bez points.

The width of the top palm (G-2) is measured on the outside of the antler, from the midpoint (keel) of the lower edge of main beam to the midpoint (keel) of upper edge of palm between upward projecting points, at the widest part of the palm. Unlike brow palm width (G-1) which is a straight line measurement, the width of top palm is a curved line which begins and ends at midpoints of the palm edges and is taken in contact with the outside surface of the top palm. If the conformation dictates, it may be taken at the same place as the fourth circumference (H-4), if this is the widest area of palm. However, since it does not need to be between the longest and second longest top points, it can occur at other locations on the top palm (**figure 9-J**). The G-2 measurement must be taken in contact with antler surface and may not cross over open bay (open air). As noted, the G-2 measurement is taken between upward projecting points. Thus, points projecting downward from the bottom edge of the main beam are not considered when determining the location at which to take G-2, nor may a downward projecting point abnormally inflate this measurement.

Circumferences are measured by looping a ring-end tape around the beam at the appropriate location, with the zero mark up. Pull the tape together and gently move it along the beam until the smallest circumference measurement is obtained. If you use a clip-end tape to measure circumferences, overlap the tape at a full 10 inch increment to simplify the procedure. Be sure to subtract the amount of overlap before recording the measurement.

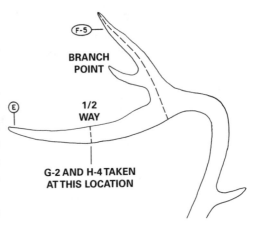

FIGURE 9-K

H-1 is taken between the brow palm and the bez. If the brow palm is completely missing the H-1 is taken between the burr and bez at the smallest value. As previously noted, the second and third circumferences are located by the presence of any development of the rear point (F-3). Should the rear point be totally absent, both circumferences would be taken at the same location, the smallest place between the bez and top palm points. The fourth circumference H-4 is taken at the smallest place between F-4 and F-5, the two longest upward projecting points of the top palm structure. In a fashion similar to that for other circumference measurements, the tape is pulled together until tight. If the top palm is cupped the tape will not be in contact with the antler material on the inner concave surface of the top palm when taking this measurement. As previously noted, the second longest top point cannot be a branch of the longest because it would artificially increase this fourth circumference.

In the unusual case where no second longest top point has developed **(figure 9-K)**, a zero is entered for the second top longest point value. If there is no second point, the G-2 width of the top palm and H-4 are both taken at a location that is one half the distance from the beam tip to the location where the length of the longest top point (F-5) crosses the main beam length measurement line.

The inside spread should be taken with a folding carpenter's rule, utilizing the extension to complete the measured line. Care must be exercised to properly position the rule for this measurement. The line of measurement should be at a right angle to the long axis of the skull. It must also be parallel to the skull cap. Thus, if one beam should be positioned higher than the other, it will be necessary to utilize a straightedge against the higher antler to properly locate the line. The actual measurement will reflect the greatest distance between the inside edges of the two main beams, making sure to keep the line oriented as noted above. The point of contact for this measurement should be on the inner surface of the top palm nearly opposite the location where the length of main beam was taken.

Rarely, one antler will curve inward in the normal fashion, while the other will flare outward. In such a case, subjective judgment must be exercised, choosing the point of measurement on the flaring antler where it begins to diverge from the "normal" curvature as found on the other antler.

Note that spread credit (Column 1 of the score chart) **cannot** exceed the length of the longer antler main beam. If the inside spread measurement does exceed the longer main beam, enter the longer main beam length (rather than the inside spread measurement) in Column 1 of the score chart for spread credit. An inside spread greater than the length of the longer antler is sometimes seen in Quebec-Labrador caribou trophies, but rarely in other classes.

The tip to tip spread and greatest spread are supplementary measurements and are not figured into the final score. They are recorded on the score chart as they do indicate the general conformation of the rack, and with the other measurements give a rather complete picture of antler formation for the trophy.

The tip to tip spread should also be taken by use of the carpenter's folding rule or steel tape. This measurement is simply from the center of the tip of one antler to the center of the tip of the other. Greatest spread is most easily taken by turning the rack upside down on a level surface. Then, position two perpendiculars, such as carpenter's levels held upright by large c-clamps or perfectly square-cut wooden blocks on either side of the rack. The measurement is then taken by yardstick or folding carpenter's rule between the perpendiculars. If perpendiculars are not available, a floor and wall can be used for one perpendicular with the second being improvised from a level or a straight, square-cut board. In no case should the human eye be relied upon for establishment of the second perpendicular line.

Field Judging Caribou

The Boone and Crockett Club recognizes five categories of *By Jay Lesser* caribou. These are the barren ground, Central Canada barren ground, mountain, Quebec-Labrador, and woodland caribou. The general conformation of the antlers is similar for all five categories, while the size of the antlers and the size of the ani-

MAXIMUM vs. MINIMUM
A Comparison of Two Records-Book Mountain Caribou

World's Record mountain caribou
Score: 453

TROPHY ANALYSIS
- 16x19 point frame
- Exceptional inside spread – over 45 inches
- Exceptional main beams – both over 48 inches
- Exceptional length for F-2s – averaging over 26 inches
- Exceptional length for F-5s – averaging over 24 inches
- Bonus rear points adding over 10 inches to final score

Minimum Entry mountain caribou
Score: 381-1/8

TROPHY ANALYSIS
- 16x19 point frame
- Above average F-2s – averaging 20 inches
- Above average main beams – both over 41 inches
- Average inside spread – nearly 30 inches
- Average length for F-5s – 16-1/8 and 19-4/8 inches
- Bonus rear points adding over 8 inches to final score

MAXIMUM vs. MINIMUM
A Comparison of Two Records-Book Woodland Caribou

World's Record woodland caribou
Score: 419-5/8

TROPHY ANALYSIS
- Exceptional main beams – 50-1/8 and 47-3/8 inches
- Exceptional inside spread – 42-2/8 inches
- Exceptional length of brow – averaging 19 inches
- Excellent length for F-2s – averaging 22 inches
- Excellent length for F-5s – averaging nearly 25 inches
- Bonus rear points adding over 10 inches to final score

Minimum Entry woodland caribou
Score: 270-1/8

TROPHY ANALYSIS
- 10x11 point frame
- Narrow inside spread – just over 32 inches
- Short main beams – both just over 32 inches
- Average length of brow – 12-6/8 and 13-7/8 inches
- Average length for F2s – both measuring around 14-6/8 inches
- Average length for F5s – 17-6/8 and 13-3/8 inches

mal that carries them varies. No other antlered game shows a greater variety in the development of antler points than the caribou and for this reason there is no such thing as an abnormal point on a caribou.

The definition of what constitutes a point on a caribou differs from the general definition used for all other antlered game. The Boone and Crockett Club defines a point on a caribou antler as any projection at least one-half inch long, and longer than it is wide at one-half inch or more measuring from the tip. The number of points that a caribou has is an important consideration when field judging them because the total number of points contributes directly to the score.

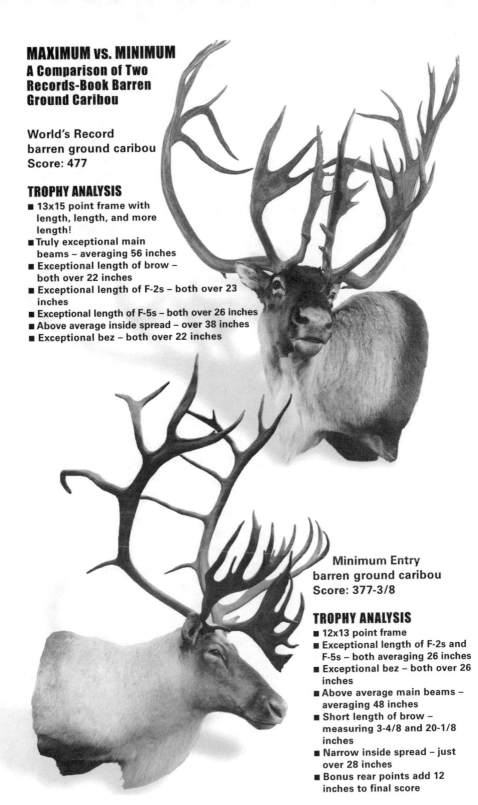

MAXIMUM vs. MINIMUM
A Comparison of Two Records-Book Barren Ground Caribou

World's Record
barren ground caribou
Score: 477

TROPHY ANALYSIS
- 13x15 point frame with length, length, and more length!
- Truly exceptional main beams – averaging 56 inches
- Exceptional length of brow – both over 22 inches
- Exceptional length of F-2s – both over 23 inches
- Exceptional length of F-5s – both over 26 inches
- Above average inside spread – over 38 inches
- Exceptional bez – both over 22 inches

Minimum Entry
barren ground caribou
Score: 377-3/8

TROPHY ANALYSIS
- 12x13 point frame
- Exceptional length of F-2s and F-5s – both averaging 26 inches
- Exceptional bez – both over 26 inches
- Above average main beams – averaging 48 inches
- Short length of brow – measuring 3-4/8 and 20-1/8 inches
- Narrow inside spread – just over 28 inches
- Bonus rear points add 12 inches to final score

Five Features to Look for in the Field
Length of the main beam

You can use the height of the animal to estimate the length of the main beam considering the average bull stands four to four-and-a-half feet high at the shoulder. However, it can be hard to accurately estimate the length because of the differences in the curve of the main beams of each individual bull's antlers. Those with straight beams appear to be very long, while those with deeply curved beams will appear shorter, but usually the latter will have a much longer actual beam length. When viewed from the side, bulls with a narrow spread will appear to have a longer main beam than those with a wide spread, but they seldom do. This is a good time to mention that the inside spread between the main beams contributes directly to the score and it too can be estimated by the shoulder height of the animal, but there is a catch here. If the inside spread exceeds the length of the longer main beam, spread credit is only equal to the length of the longer main beam. This isn't a normal occurrence with the western trophy categories, but it is fairly common to the Quebec-Labrador variety.

Brow palm

The brow palm, generally referred to as the "shovel," is the antler growth that projects horizontally out over the caribou's face. Most caribou bulls only have a well-developed shovel on one antler, with a spike or small shovel on the other. However, occasionally a bull will have "double shovels" (a well-developed shovel on each antler) and this will enhance the final score. Ideally the shovel(s) will project well out over the bridge of the caribou's nose and form a multi-pointed broad palm. The length of the shovel, the width of the palm, and the number of points on the shovel contribute directly to the final score. There are no deductions for asymmetry between the shovels.

Bez point

The next antler projection growing forward from the main beam just above the shovel is the bez (pronounced "bay"). There should be one on each antler with some hint of symmetry. The bez should have good length, and the more points growing off of them the better. Both of these features contribute to the score.

MAXIMUM vs. MINIMUM
A Comparison of Two Records-Book Central Canada Barren Ground Caribou

World's Record Central Canada barren ground caribou
Score: 433-4/8

TROPHY ANALYSIS

- 24x18 point frame with double shovel, plus length
- Exceptional main beams averaging nearly 49 inches
- Exceptional length of brow – over 18 inches
- Exceptional length of F-5s – averaging 24 inches
- Above average inside spread – over 40 inches
- Above average width of brow – averaging 12 inches
- Above average bez – averaging 22 inches

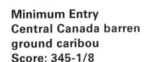

Minimum Entry Central Canada barren ground caribou
Score: 345-1/8

TROPHY ANALYSIS

- 11x13 point frame
- Truly exceptional main beams – both measuring over 55 inches
- Above average F-5s – averaging 16 inches
- Above average bez –averaging 18 inches
- Average inside spread – just under 40 inches
- Average length of brow – measuring 14-4/8 and 6-2/8 inches
- Weak brow width

Rear point

The rear point usually develops as an unbranched spike projecting backward from about the middle of the main beam. Although not all bulls have these points, their length, when present, adds to the score.

Top palm and top palm points

Top palm points, with occasional branch points, arise from the top of the antler main beam, with the beam often showing palmation at this location. Ideally, you are looking for lots of points on the top palm and well-developed palmation. The lengths of the two longest top palm points on each antler are a significant portion of the final score. Unlike any of the other antlered categories, top palm point lengths are taken from the tip of each point to the bottom edge of the palmation of the main beam. There is also a circumference measurement taken at the narrowest place between the two longest top palm points, as well as a width measurement at the widest place between top palm points. Thus, the top palm is measured four times (two points, width, and circumference). A well-developed top palm is a highly desirable attribute.

I would also mention there are three other circumference measurements taken on each main beam, making long, massive main beams another highly desirable attribute.

When hunting for a potential records-book caribou, try to find a bull that has as many of the features we have examined as possible and you just might get yourself a records-book animal. Very few bulls have all of these attributes, but the possibility of finding one is a part of the attraction of hunting the majestic caribou. ∎

MAXIMUM vs. MINIMUM
A Comparison of Two Records-Book Quebec-Labrador Caribou

World's Record
Quebec-Labrador
caribou
Score: 474-6/8

TROPHY ANALYSIS
- 22x30 point frame
- Off the chart inside spread – over 58 inches
- Extraordinary main beams – both over 60 inches
- Off the chart bez – both measuring over 24 inches
- Above average length and width of brow – averaging just under 18 inches and 12 inches, respectively
- Above average length of F5s – both measuring over 16 inches

Close to Minimum Entry
Quebec-Labrador caribou
Score: 372-6/8

TROPHY ANALYSIS
- 14x12 point frame
- Above average main beams – nearly 46 inches each
- Above average length of brow – averaging over 17 inches
- Above average length of F5s – averaging 15 inches
- Strong bez – both measuring over 20 inches
- Narrow inside spread – measuring just over 34 inches
- Bonus rear points adding over 13 inches to the final score

SCORECHART
Caribou

Records of
North American
Big Game

250 Station Drive
Missoula, MT 59801
(406) 542-1888

BOONE AND CROCKETT CLUB®
OFFICIAL SCORING SYSTEM FOR NORTH AMERICAN BIG GAME TROPHIES

CARIBOU

MINIMUM SCORES		
	AWARDS	ALL-TIME
mountain	360	390
woodland	265	295
barren ground	375	400
Central Canada		
barren ground	345	360
Quebec-Labrador	365	375

KIND OF CARIBOU (check one)
- ☐ mountain
- ☐ woodland
- ☐ barren ground
- ☐ Central Canada
-     barren ground
- ☐ Quebec-Labrador

Detail of Point
Measurement

SEE OTHER SIDE FOR INSTRUCTIONS			COLUMN 1	COLUMN 2	COLUMN 3	COLUMN 4
A. Tip to Tip Spread			Spread Credit	Right Antler	Left Antler	Difference
B. Greatest Spread						
C. Inside Spread of Main Beams		SPREAD CREDIT MAY EQUAL BUT NOT EXCEED LONGER MAIN BEAM				
D. Number of Points on Each Antler Excluding Brows						
Number of Points on Each Brow						
E. Length of Main Beam						
F-1. Length of Brow Palm or First Point						
F-2. Length of Bez or Second Point						
F-3. Length of Rear Point, If Present						
F-4. Length of Second Longest Top Point						
F-5. Length of Longest Top Point						
G-1. Width of Brow Palm						
G-2. Width of Top Palm						
H-1. Circumference at Smallest Place Between Brow and Bez Point						
H-2. Circumference at Smallest Place Between Bez and Rear Point						
H-3. Circumference at Smallest Place Between Rear Point and First Top Point						
H-4. Circumference at Smallest Place Between Two Longest Top Palm Points						
TOTALS						

ADD	Column 1		Exact Locality Where Killed:
	Column 2		Date Killed: Hunter:
	Column 3		Owner: Telephone #:
	Subtotal		Owner's Address:
SUBTRACT Column 4			Guide's Name and Address:
FINAL SCORE			Remarks: (Mention Any Abnormalities or Unique Qualities)

COPYRIGHT © 2000 BY BOONE AND CROCKETT CLUB®

I, _____, certify that I have measured this trophy on _____
　　　　　　PRINT NAME　　　　　　　　　　　　　　　　　　　　　　　　　　　　　　　　　　　　MM / DD / YYYYY

at _____
　　STREET ADDRESS　　　　　　　　　　　　　　　　　　　　　　　　　CITY　　　　　　　　　　　　STATE/PROVINCE

and that these measurements and data are, to the best of my knowledge and belief, made in accordance with the instructions given.

Witness: _____ Signature: _____ I.D. Number ☐☐☐☐
　　　　　　　　　　　　　　　　　　　　　　　　　　　　　B&C OFFICIAL MEASURER

INSTRUCTIONS FOR MEASURING CARIBOU

All measurements must be made with a 1/4-inch wide flexible steel tape to the nearest one-eighth of an inch. (Note: A flexible steel cable can be used to measure points and main beams only.) Enter fractional figures in eighths, without reduction. Official measurements cannot be taken until the antlers have air dried for at least 60 days after the animal was killed.

A. Tip to Tip Spread is measured between tips of main beams.

B. Greatest Spread is measured between perpendiculars at a right angle to the center line of the skull at widest part, whether across main beams or points.

C. Inside Spread of Main Beams is measured at a right angle to the center line of the skull at widest point between main beams. Enter this measurement again as the Spread Credit **if** it is less than or equal to the length of the longer main beam; if greater, enter longer main beam length for Spread Credit.

D. Number of Points on Each Antler: To be counted a point, a projection must be at least one-half inch long, with length exceeding width at one-half inch or more of length. Beam tip is counted as a point but not measured as a point. There are no "abnormal" points in caribou.

E. Length of Main Beam is measured from the center of the lowest outside edge of burr over the outer side to the most distant point of the main beam. The point of beginning is that point on the burr where the center line along the outer side of the beam intersects the burr, then following generally the line of the illustration.

F-1-2-3. Length of Points are measured from nearest edge of beam over outer curve to tip. Lay the tape along the outer curve of the beam so that the top edge of the tape coincides with the top edge of the beam on both sides of point to determine the baseline for point measurement. Record point lengths in appropriate blanks.

F-4-5. Length of Points are measured from the tip of the point to the top of the beam, then at a right angle to the bottom edge of beam. The Second Longest Top Point **cannot** be a point branch of the Longest Top Point.

G-1. Width of Brow is measured in a straight line from top edge to lower edge, as illustrated, with measurement line at a right angle to main axis of brow.

G-2. Width of Top Palm is measured from midpoint of lower edge of main beam to midpoint of a dip between points, at widest part of palm. The line of measurement begins and ends at midpoints of palm edges, which gives credit for palm thickness.

H-1-2-3-4. Circumferences are taken as illustrated for measurements. If brow point is missing, take H-1 at smallest point between burr and bez point. If rear point is missing, take H-2 and H-3 measurements at smallest place between bez and first top point. Do not depress the tape into any dips of the palm or main beam.

ENTRY AFFIDAVIT FOR ALL HUNTER-TAKEN TROPHIES

For the purpose of entry into the Boone and Crockett Club's® records, North American big game harvested by the use of the following methods or under the following conditions are ineligible:

   I.   Spotting or herding game from the air, followed by landing in its vicinity for the purpose of pursuit and shooting;

  II. Herding or chasing with the aid of any motorized equipment;

 III. Use of electronic communication devices, artificial lighting, or electronic light intensifying devices;

 IV. Confined by artificial barriers, including escape-proof fenced enclosures;

  V. Transplanted for the purpose of commercial shooting;

 VI. By the use of traps or pharmaceuticals;

VII. While swimming, helpless in deep snow, or helpless in any other natural or artificial medium;

VIII. On another hunter's license;

 IX. Not in full compliance with the game laws or regulations of the federal government or of any state, province, territory, or tribal council on reservations or tribal lands;

I certify that the trophy scored on this chart was not taken in violation of the conditions listed above. In signing this statement, I understand that if the information provided on this entry is found to be misrepresented or fraudulent in any respect, it will not be accepted into the Awards Program and 1) all of my prior entries are subject to deletion from future editions of **Records of North American Big Game** 2) future entries may not be accepted.

FAIR CHASE, as defined by the Boone and Crockett Club®, is the ethical, sportsmanlike and lawful pursuit and taking of any free-ranging wild, native North American big game animal in a manner that does not give the hunter an improper advantage over such game animals.

The Boone and Crockett Club® may exclude the entry of any animal that it deems to have been taken in an unethical manner or under conditions deemed inappropriate by the Club.

Date: _____ Signature of Hunter: _____
　　　　　　　　　　　　　　　　　　　(SIGNATURE MUST BE WITNESSED BY AN OFFICIAL MEASURER OR A NOTARY PUBLIC.)

Date: _____ Signature of Notary or Official Measurer: _____

MEASURING AND JUDGING
Sheep

The four categories of sheep eligible for records keeping are bighorn sheep, desert sheep, Stone's sheep, and Dall's sheep. Horn formation may be any of three basic types: the close curl, a close curl with flaring tips, or wide flaring horns. Bighorns generally show some degree of the close curl, while the close curl with flaring tips is often found in Stone's and Dall's sheep. The wide flaring conformation is less common in all varieties.

This common variation of horn conformation is a major reason greatest spread and tip to tip spread are supplementary data that are not figured into the score. Use of spread in the scoring would discriminate against close curl specimens. This would be particularly inappropriate in the bighorns, where a close curl and massive horns may combine to make a most impressive trophy.

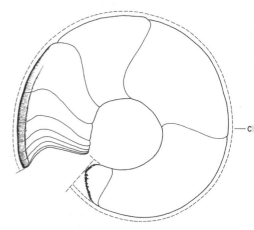

Only a 1/4-inch wide steel tape may be used for length and circumference measurements on sheep; a steel cable may not be substituted. At times the horns on sheep may be loose on their cores; it is permissible to remove the horns from their cores for measurement of the lengths and circumferences.

FIGURE 10-A

As in all horn measurements, location and accuracy in measuring the length of horn is vital to the subsequent measurements. As shown in **figure 10-A**, the length of horn measurement is started by hooking the clip-end of the measuring tape on the lowest front edge of the horn base where the crest of the horn begins. The line of measurement is then maintained along the horn surface to a point in line with the horn tip. Use a small carpenter's square (or a credit card) to determine the end of the measurement line by forming a perpendicular of the square and horn axis at that point. This technique is necessary because of broken and/or "broomed" horn tips often encountered in sheep, especially older bighorns.

The length of a sheep horn is correctly taken with the

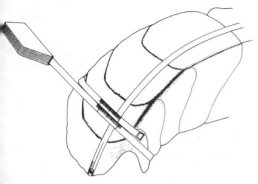

FIGURE 10-B

tape in contact with the high points along the horn, reflecting the greatest length of the entire horn. Be careful *not* to push the tape down into any depressions that result from the annual growth rings while taking this measurement. Mature rams, because they frequently strike their horns against those of other rams, tend to chip pieces from their horns. If the length measurement crosses such a location, the tape must be stretched across the gap in a natural fashion (and not pushed down into the gap giving an artificially longer measurement).

A mounted specimen presents a problem in location of the start of the line of measurement. Care must be exercised to begin the line at the above-mentioned edge of the hollow horn. This point is often covered with hair and cape and may be fused with the mounting media. Careful probing with a pen-knife point, using a bright light, is often necessary to properly locate this point.

Once the proper horn lengths are established, locations of the circumference measurements are determined by dividing the *longer* horn length measurement into quarters. The *Quarter Locations for Circumference Chart* in the back of this field guide provides these values. Record the locations of the three quarter locations in the blank area to the right of each circumference description on the score chart so they can easily be verified if there is any later question about the measurement. Mark the three quarter locations (D-2, D-3, and D-4, carefully on the original line of horn length measurement of each horn with a soft pencil.

Be sure to establish these quarters by measuring from each horn base to the tip. This is essential to give proper matching of quarters on both horns. If the quarters were located by measuring from the tip toward the base, the quarter locations would be placed nearer the base on the shorter horn than on the longer. This would probably make an artificial difference between the quarter measurements. When marking the quarters on the horn, be sure to hold the tape stationary along the original line followed in measuring the length of horn. Often a measurer will use masking tape to hold each of two clip-end tapes in place along the length measurement lines on each horn so that it is easier to mark the circumference locations.

Once the quarters have been properly located and marked with a pencil, and the calculations verified, measure each circumference by carefully arranging a ring-end measuring tape at a right angle to the horn axis at that point. At the zero point of the tape, the two ends should pass on opposite sides of the pencil mark, with the tape and the horn axis forming a right angle. Snug the tape around the horn before reading the result, again checking to be sure that the tape is correctly positioned on each side of the pencil mark. If you use a clip-end tape to measure circumferences, overlap the tape at a full 10" increment to simplify the procedure. Be sure to subtract the amount of overlap before recording the measurement.

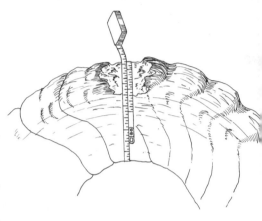

Take care in making the circumference of base measurement (D-1, of a mounted specimen to avoid including hair, plastic material added by the taxidermist, or a portion of the skull in this measurement. The D-1 measurement is taken perpendicular to the axis of the horn at the lowest

FIGURE 10-C

place where the tape remains in full contact with the horn base for its entire length and not across an open gap on the horn's inner or outer side. The measurement does not follow the irregular edge of the horn; such a line would result in an inflated value, which would be incorrect. **Figure 10-B** demonstrates the proper tape positioning.

If a chunk of horn is missing at the location where a quarter measurement is to be taken, no credit can be allowed for the missing piece. The circumference is measured in the usual manner by pulling the tape to its smallest value, perpendicular to the horn axis, at that point thus reflecting only the solid material still present **(figure 10-C)**. If it should happen that one horn is broomed to the extent that the horn material is completely missing at the D-4 circumference location, simply enter a zero value in the appropriate column of the score chart to reflect this missing value.

Since sheep often display broomed horns, there is no dif-

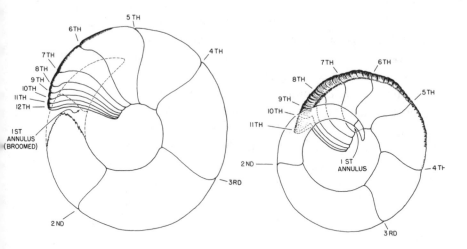

FIGURE 10-D

ference penalty for asymmetry in horn length. Along with the length and circumference values, also record the plug number for the sheep on the line provided in the upper right corner of the score chart.

The tip to tip measurement is simply from the center of the tip of one horn to the center of the tip of the other. It may be taken directly by use of the carpenter's folding rule or measuring tape unless brooming makes this impossible as the measured line passes through the skull or trophy mount. In such a case, it may be necessary to use large calipers or two levels to take this measurement.

Greatest spread is best taken by use of two perpendiculars, such as carpenter's levels held upright by large c-clamps. The measurement is then taken by a folding carpenter's rule or measuring tape between the perpendiculars. If perpendiculars are not available, a floor and wall can be used for one perpendicular with the second being improvised from a carpenter's level or a carpenter's square. In no case should the human eye be relied upon for establishment of the second perpendicular line.

The tip to tip spread and greatest spread are supplementary measurements and are not figured into the final score. They are recorded on the score chart as they do indicate the general conformation of the horns and with the other measurements give a rather complete picture of horn formation for the trophy.

Sheep and goat trophies offer the opportunity to age them by counting the horn annuli (rings) left as a mark of the cessation of horn growth during each winter **(figure 10-D)**. During the first winter the annulus is often only a swollen area in bighorns and is often totally absent in mountain goats. But, each winter after that a distinct annulus forms in both sheep and goats. The annuli should correspond on both horns of the same animal.

In sheep, the first annulus is generally within two to four inches of the tip of the unbroomed horn, with the second six to nine inches farther down the horn and the third three to five inches beyond the second, although there is great variation in the pattern of annuli formation in the various varieties of sheep. Almost all large bighorns and desert sheep will have broomed the first annulus and a very few severely broomed horns will have broomed the second annulus as well. Many Stone's and Dall's sheep will show unbroomed horns so that the number of annuli present is equal to the age in years. False annuli may appear on sheep horns, but they are usually not as deep as true annuli and do not extend completely around the horn. The annuli on desert sheep are less distinct than in other varieties but they can still be accurately counted.

Field Judging Sheep

In many respects, the field identification of a trophy-quality mountain sheep is easier than for most other North American big game. Normally, there are other rams in a bunch to provide a comparison between the trophy which initially looks best and those present of lesser quality. Nevertheless, if the rams are all within the same approximate age group, as frequently happens, one may easily be misled.

The fact is that a real trophy ram is instantly recognizable by anyone familiar with wild sheep. If one is inclined to hesitate as to whether the trophy is of record class, don't shoot. Inevitably it will fall short.

What, then, does one look for to identify a ram of probable trophy class. In the first instance, never make a judgment when the ram is facing away. Any mature ram will look much bigger than it actually is when viewed from behind. One must have a full frontal view to be sure. Even a broadside view is not adequate. Speaking of our four North American varieties, the lower curve of the horn of a trophy-quality ram will always drop below the line of the chin. The deeper the curl at this point, the more likely the horns are to meet or exceed the current all-time records book

MAXIMUM vs. MINIMUM
A Comparison of Two
Records-Book Bighorn Sheep

World's Record
bighorn sheep
Score: 208-3/8

TROPHY ANALYSIS
- Length plus mass
- Exceptional length –
  measuring 47-4/8 and
  46-5/8 inches
- Above average bases – both
  measuring 15-7/8 inches
- Carries mass well –
  1st Quarter 15-3/8 inches
  2nd Quarter 14-7/8 inches and
  3rd Quarter 12 inches
- Only 1 inch in symmetry deductions

Minimum Entry bighorn sheep
Score: 175

TROPHY ANALYSIS
- Excellent mass, but average length
- Length of horns measure 37-4/8
  and 34-4/8 inches
- Above average bases – both over
  15 inches
- Mass drops off dramatically –
  1st Quarter 14-7/8
  2nd Quarter 13-1/8
  3rd Quarter 8-5/8
- Only 4/8 inch symmetry
  deductions

MAXIMUM vs. MINIMUM
A Comparison of Two
Records-Book Desert Sheep

**World's Record desert sheep
Score: 205-1/8**

TROPHY ANALYSIS
- Strong in length and mass
- Exceptional length – both horns over 43 inches
- Exceptional bases – average just under 17 inches
- Carries mass well – 1st Quarter 16-4/8 2nd Quarter 15, and third quarter 10-6/8 inches
- Only 3/8 inch in symmetry deductions

**Minimum Entry desert sheep
Score: 165**

TROPHY ANALYSIS
- Better mass than length
- Above average bases – both over 14 inches
- Average length – around 34 inches
- Mass drops dramatically – 1st Quarter 13-4/8 2nd Quarter 12-2/8 3rd Quarter 8-7/8
- Only 4/8 inch in symmetry deductions

minimum entry score. One often sees rams with more than a full curl where the bottom line of the descending horn fails to approximate the bottom surface of the jawbone. Such trophies may readily measure on the curl from 36 to 39 inches. They are unlikely to measure 40 inches or better. In any event, it is very, very seldom that the weight of the horn on such a trophy will carry out far enough to produce good second and third quarter circumferences. Many are indeed beautiful, even magnificent trophies, but probably not records book size.

Obviously, the next criterion is the weight of the horn. For a given apparent length of horn, one that is already broomed will obviously carry more weight, and produce better circumferences for the second and third quarters, than will horns on which the lambing points (year one annuli) are still present. Good second and third quarter circumferences are vital to make the records books. A close check on the weight of the horns at the second and third quarters can generally only be done with a good side-view examination, but it is needed to properly identify a trophy ram.

These comments emphasize the need to take one's time in judging a ram. Sometimes circumstances really do not favor that deliberation. If the ram is bedded down, there is a far greater risk of error than if he is up and about and moving his head while grazing.

There are several other yardsticks that can be used in judging the length of horn. Parenthetically, in the aftermath of personal usage, they have not always justified a decision made to shoot a particular sheep.

Let us assume that a ram displays a full curl of the usual configuration found in the Stone's and Dall's sheep. If the bottom of the curl approximates the line of the lower jaw and rises to the level of the nostril, these horns are likely to run about 35 inches in length. If the same horns carry their lambing tips two or three inches above the eyes, you may be looking at a 37 or 38 inch horn. If in these instances the lambing tips have been well broomed-off, the first example represents a ram that might score around 145 points, while the second example might score 150-160. Neither would represent a records-book trophy.

With a bighorn, the curl described above would likely be as much as an inch shorter because many bighorns have fairly close curls. Again, as bighorns these would not make the records book. To make the records book a bighorn almost always requires a horn in which the bottom of the curl approximates the rear base of the lower jaw bone and the horn tips make a full curl, or more. The rest depends on weight from horn base to horn tip.

Turning now to desert sheep, we find a somewhat different horn configuration. Seldom do desert sheep show any argali-form characteristics, as frequently noted for our thin-horned sheep. In other words, the horns do not nip-in and then flare out at the tips. Many desert sheep also lack the close curl that is characteristic of the bighorns. Instead, their horns are more inclined to sweep out and down. It is not

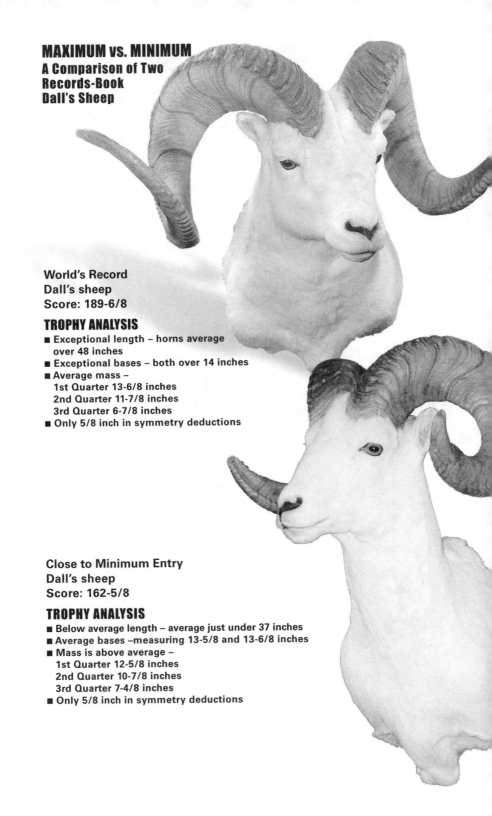

MAXIMUM vs. MINIMUM
A Comparison of Two Records-Book Dall's Sheep

World's Record
Dall's sheep
Score: 189-6/8

TROPHY ANALYSIS
- Exceptional length – horns average over 48 inches
- Exceptional bases – both over 14 inches
- Average mass –
  1st Quarter 13-6/8 inches
  2nd Quarter 11-7/8 inches
  3rd Quarter 6-7/8 inches
- Only 5/8 inch in symmetry deductions

Close to Minimum Entry
Dall's sheep
Score: 162-5/8

TROPHY ANALYSIS
- Below average length – average just under 37 inches
- Average bases –measuring 13-5/8 and 13-6/8 inches
- Mass is above average –
  1st Quarter 12-5/8 inches
  2nd Quarter 10-7/8 inches
  3rd Quarter 7-4/8 inches
- Only 5/8 inch in symmetry deductions

MAXIMUM vs. MINIMUM
A Comparison of Two Records-Book Stone' Sheep

World's Record
Stone's sheep
Score: 196-6/8

TROPHY ANALYSIS
- Extraordinary length
- Horns measure 50-1/8 and 51-5/8 inches – Only ram with both horns over 50 inches
- Exceptional bases – both 14-6/8 inches
- Mass carries well –
  1st Quarter 14-2/8 inches
  2nd Quarter 12-1/8 inches
  3rd Quarter 7 inches
- Only 5/8 inch for symmetry deductions

Close to Minimum Entry
Stone's sheep
Score: 165-6/8

TROPHY ANALYSIS
- Average length – horns averaging 40 inches
- Average bases – both 13-6/8 inches
- Mass drops off more than average
  1st Quarter 13 inches
  2nd Quarter 10-3/8 inches
  3rd Quarter 5-7/8 inches
- Only 3/8 inch for symmetry deductions

uncommon to find a desert ram with horns whose curl bottom is as much as two inches below the jawbone line. Frequently, such horns are not badly broomed. They may or may not carry their weight out to the tips. As a rule, a mature desert sheep can show a horn base circumference even larger than that of a bighorn of the same age. It is vital to get a good side view of such a ram to judge the massiveness of its horns through the second and third quarters. The criteria for judging the length of horn of the thin-horn sheep does not necessarily apply here. However, if you are looking head-on at a mature desert ram, with the bottom-of-curl lower than the base of the jawline and the tips of the horns approximating a full curl, you may well be looking at a records book sheep. When the tips are broomed such that you are looking at something between a strong 3/4 and 7/8 curl, you are probably looking at a length of horn of about 36 inches. A really heavy 36-inch curl on this particular sheep can readily make the records book minimum entry score.

Finally, a high-powered spotting scope will often enable one to roughly count the number of annular growth rings on the horns. While there are outstanding exceptions to this criterion, generally due to the very successful management programs in several states and provinces, a true trophy sheep will almost always prove to be from 10 to 13 years old. They seldom live longer than that. Therefore, should one find a solitary old ram on some high mountain pasture, an evident outcast of the herd, there is little doubt that it is of trophy quality. ■

SCORECHART
Sheep

250 Station Drive
Missoula, MT 59801
(406) 542-1888

BOONE AND CROCKETT CLUB®
OFFICIAL SCORING SYSTEM FOR NORTH AMERICAN BIG GAME TROPHIES

SHEEP

	MINIMUM SCORES	
	AWARDS	ALL-TIME
bighorn	175	180
desert	165	168
Dall's	160	170
Stone's	165	170

KIND OF SHEEP (check one)
- ☐ bighorn
- ☐ desert
- ☐ Dall's
- ☐ Stone's

PLUG NUMBER

_____

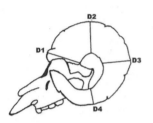

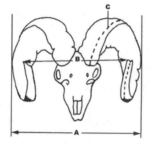

Measure to a
Point in Line
With Horn Tip

SEE OTHER SIDE FOR INSTRUCTIONS		COLUMN 1	COLUMN 2	COLUMN 3
A. Greatest Spread (Is Often Tip to Tip Spread)		Right Horn	Left Horn	Difference
B. Tip to Tip Spread				
C. Length of Horn				
D-1. Circumference of Base				
D-2. Circumference at First Quarter				
D-3. Circumference at Second Quarter				
D-4. Circumference at Third Quarter				
	TOTALS			

ADD	Column 1		Exact Locality Where Killed:	
	Column 2		Date Killed:	Hunter:
	Subtotal		Owner:	Telephone #:
SUBTRACT Column 3			Owner's Address:	
FINAL SCORE			Guide's Name and Address:	
			Remarks: (Mention Any Abnormalities or Unique Qualities)	

I, _____ , certify that I have measured this trophy on _____
      PRINT NAME   MM/DD/YYYYY

at _____
      STREET ADDRESS   CITY   STATE/PROVINCE

and that these measurements and data are, to the best of my knowledge and belief, made in accordance with the instructions given.

Witness: _____ Signature: _____ I.D. Number ☐☐☐☐

                                            B&C OFFICIAL MEASURER

INSTRUCTIONS FOR MEASURING SHEEP

All measurements must be made with a 1/4-inch wide flexible steel tape to the nearest one-eighth of an inch. Enter fractional figures in eighths, without reduction. Official measurements cannot be taken until horns have air dried for at least 60 days after the animal was killed.

- **A. Greatest Spread** is measured between perpendiculars at a right angle to the center line of the skull.
- **B. Tip to Tip Spread** is measured between tips of horns.
- **C. Length of Horn** is measured from the lowest point in front on outer curve to a point in line with tip. **Do not** press tape into depressions. The low point of the outer curve of the horn is considered to be the low point of the frontal portion of the horn, situated above and slightly medial to the eye socket (not the outside edge). Use a straight edge, perpendicular to horn axis, to end measurement on "broomed" horns.
- **D-1. Circumference of Base** is measured at a right angle to axis of horn. **Do not** follow irregular edge of horn; the line of measurement must be entirely on horn material.
- **D-2-3-4. Divide measurement C** of longer horn by four. Starting at base, mark **both** horns at these quarters (even though the other horn is shorter) and measure circumferences at these marks, with measurements taken at right angles to horn axis.

ENTRY AFFIDAVIT FOR ALL HUNTER-TAKEN TROPHIES

For the purpose of entry into the Boone and Crockett Club's® records, North American big game harvested by the use of the following methods or under the following conditions are ineligible:

- I. Spotting or herding game from the air, followed by landing in its vicinity for the purpose of pursuit and shooting;
- II. Herding or chasing with the aid of any motorized equipment;
- III. Use of electronic communication devices, artificial lighting, or electronic light intensifying devices;
- IV. Confined by artificial barriers, including escape-proof fenced enclosures;
- V. Transplanted for the purpose of commercial shooting;
- VI. By the use of traps or pharmaceuticals;
- VII. While swimming, helpless in deep snow, or helpless in any other natural or artificial medium;
- VIII. On another hunter's license;
- IX. Not in full compliance with the game laws or regulations of the federal government or of any state, province, territory, or tribal council on reservations or tribal lands;

I certify that the trophy scored on this chart was not taken in violation of the conditions listed above. In signing this statement, I understand that if the information provided on this entry is found to be misrepresented or fraudulent in any respect, it will not be accepted into the Awards Program and 1) all of my prior entries are subject to deletion from future editions of **Records of North American Big Game** 2) future entries may not be accepted.

FAIR CHASE, as defined by the Boone and Crockett Club®, is the ethical, sportsmanlike and lawful pursuit and taking of any free-ranging wild, native North American big game animal in a manner that does not give the hunter an improper advantage over such game animals.

The Boone and Crockett Club® may exclude the entry of any animal that it deems to have been taken in an unethical manner or under conditions deemed inappropriate by the Club.

Date: _____ Signature of Hunter:_____
(SIGNATURE MUST BE WITNESSED BY AN OFFICIAL MEASURER OR A NOTARY PUBLIC.)

Date: _____ Signature of Notary or Official Measurer:_____

MEASURING AND JUDGING
Pronghorn

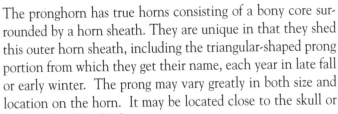

The pronghorn has true horns consisting of a bony core surrounded by a horn sheath. They are unique in that they shed this outer horn sheath, including the triangular-shaped prong portion from which they get their name, each year in late fall or early winter. The prong may vary greatly in both size and location on the horn. It may be located close to the skull or higher than the third quarter.

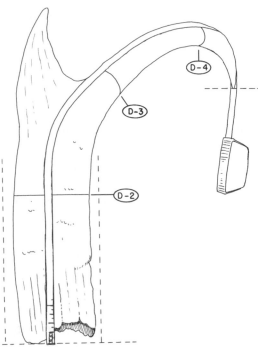

As prong measurements contribute significantly to the score, record-class heads will have well-developed prongs.

Only a 1/4-inch wide steel tape may be used for length and circumference measurements on pronghorn; a steel cable may not be substituted. At times the horns on pronghorn may be loose on their cores; it is permissible to remove the horns from their cores for measurement of the lengths and circumferences.

The first step in measuring pronghorns is the determination of the proper horn length measurement, which is vital to the subsequent measurements. Pronghorns show great variability in the degree of curvature and direction in which the horn tips point. In addition, the base of the horn is characteristically jagged or serrated. Therefore, the proper location for beginning the length of horn measurement is defined as the *lowest outside* edge of these serrations on the horn base. The **outside edge** of horn is defined as the area from the front center to the rear center of the base of the horn along its outer side.

As shown in **figure 11-A**, the start of the length of horn measurement is located with a straightedge held perpendicular to the horn axis touching the lowest point of horn on the

FIGURE 11-A

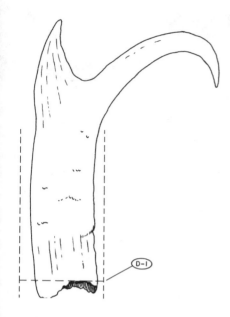

FIGURE 11-B

outside edge of the horn base. Often this point of contact is not at the center of the outside edge. Since the line of measurement is taken along the center of the outer side of the horn, it will be necessary to hook the clip-end tape on the bottom of the straightedge to begin the line of measurement. The line of measurement is then maintained along the horn surface to the tip. This line is along the outer curve of horn, which will vary in specimens according to the general curvature of their horns and the direction of the horn tips. If the horn tip is sharp, simply measure to its end. If it should be noticeably blunt, use a small carpenter's square (or a credit card) to determine the end of the measurement line by forming a perpendicular of the square and horn axis at that point.

Pronghorns commonly show small protuberances on the horn, occasionally developing into sizable ones. Should the length of horn measurement fall on these, simply measure across them so long as they do not noticeably affect the measurement. Should a large one inflate this measurement by pushing the measuring tape noticeably into the air, the tape should be *slightly* repositioned to keep the measured line close to the horn surface. Make note of any horn projections exceeding one-half inch in length that interfere with the length of horn measurement; explain how the measurement was taken in the REMARKS section, or in the blank space at the top of the score chart.

Measurement is best accomplished on unmounted trophies, since the hair grows above the horn base and necessitates the use of considerable care to locate the exact lowest edge of the serrated horn sheath for the start of the length-of-horn measurement. On a mounted specimen, the horn base is often covered with hair and cape and may be fused with the mounting media. Careful probing with a penknife point, using a bright light, is often necessary to properly find the proper starting point.

Once the proper horn lengths are established, locations of the circumference measurements are determined by dividing the **longer** horn length measurement into quarters. The *Quarter Locations for Circumference Chart* in the back of this manual provides these values. Record the values of the three quarter locations in the blank area to the right of each circumference description on the score chart so they can easily be verified if there is any later question about the measurement. Mark the three quarter locations (D-2, D-3, and D-4) carefully on the outer side of the horn on the original line of horn length measurement with a soft pencil **(figure 11-A)**.

Be sure to establish the quarter locations by measuring from each horn base to the tip. This is essential to get proper matching of quarters on both horns. If the quarters were located by measuring from the tip toward the base, the quarter locations would be placed nearer the base on the shorter horn than on the longer. This would probably make an artificial difference between the quarter measurements. When marking the quarters on the horn, be sure to hold the tape stationary along the original line followed in measuring the length of horn.

Take care in making the circumference of base measurement (D-1) of a mounted specimen to avoid including hair, plastic material added by the taxidermist, or a portion

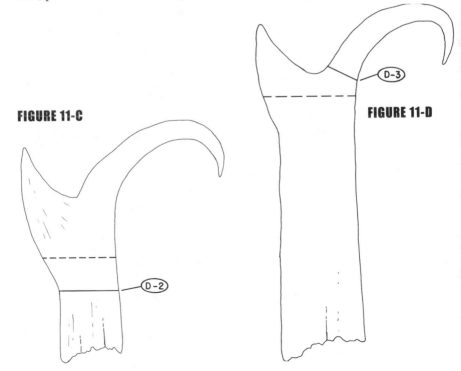

FIGURE 11-C

FIGURE 11-D

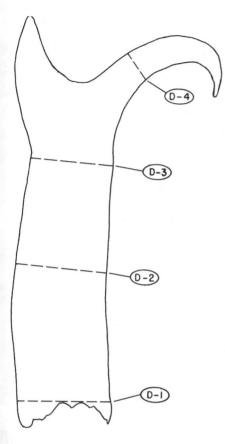

FIGURE 11-E
PROPER D-3
MEASUREMENT
WHEN SCORING
FOR THE BOONE
AND CROCKETT
CLUB

of the skull in this measurement. This measurement is taken at right angles to the base of the horn, *above* the serrations and entirely on horn sheath material, and not over air space. **Figure 11-B** shows the proper technique.

Once the quarters have been properly located and marked with a pencil, and the calculations verified, measure each circumference by carefully arranging a ring-end measuring tape at a right angle to the horn axis at that point. At the zero point of the tape, the two ends should pass on opposite sides of the pencil mark, with the tape and the horn axis forming a right angle. Snug the tape around the horn before reading the result, again checking to be sure that the tape is correctly positioned on each side of the pencil mark. If you use a clip-end tape to measure circumferences, overlap the tape a full 10 inch increment to simplify the procedure. Be sure to subtract the amount of overlap before recording the measurement. If it should happen that one horn is broken to the extent that the horn material is completely missing at the D-4 circumference location, simply enter a zero value in the appropriate column of the score chart to reflect this missing value.

The intent of the scoring system for pronghorns is that the first quarter circumference (D-2) is taken below the prong and the second quarter circumference (D-3) above the prong as **figure 11-A** illustrates. Therefore, should the swelling of the prong be at the marked location for a circumference measurement, simply either move the steel tape immediately below the prong for D-2 **(figure 11-C)** or up for D-3 **(figure 11-D)** to a point where the circumference can be measured without interference from the prong swelling. This avoids the artificial increase that would result if the swelling of the prong were included in the measurement.

Generally the D-3 circumference is taken above the prong. In a few, very rare cases the prong may be located so high that the D-3 quarter location falls below the prong swelling (figure 11-E). In such instances, the D-3 circumference is taken at the actual quarter location below the prong. (Note: A major difference between the Boone and Crockett records-keeping program and both the Pope & Young and Longhunter records-keeping programs is that the D-3 measurement below the prong is *only acceptable to Boone and Crockett*. The other two groups require that D-3 always be taken above the prong.)

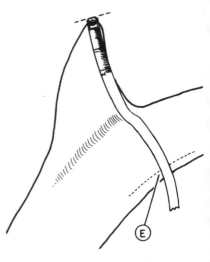

As noted earlier, bumps or projections may occur on the lower part of the horn. These may occur at circumference locations. If they are small and occur only on one horn, any increase in the circumference measurement is adjusted by the subtraction in Column 3 for lack of symmetry. If they are sizable and occur on both horns in such a location that the circumferences of both horns are unnaturally and significantly affected, the circumference measurements should be made around them if possible. In any case where such projections exceed one half inch in height and interfere with the circumference measurements, explain how the measurement was taken in the REMARKS section, or in the blank space at the top of the score chart.

FIGURE 11-F
LENGTH OF PRONG MEASUREMENT

The length of prong is measured from the tip of the prong along the upper edge of the prong on the outer side of the horn to the horn proper, then continued at a right angle to the horn axis to the back edge of the horn. Figure 11-F illustrates this measurement. The back of the horn is commonly rounded, making the exact location of the end of the measurement line difficult to establish. It is determined by placing a straightedge across the backs of both horns simultaneously. A lead pencil or chalk is used to mark the spot on each horn where the straightedge and horn material contact. These marks are then the ends of the measurement lines and may not fall on the exact center of the back of the horn.

The tip to tip measurement is simply from the center of the tip of one horn to the center of the tip of the other. It may be taken directly by the use of a carpenter's folding ruler or steel tape. It is a supplementary measurement and not figured in the final score.

The inside spread is measured at a right angle to the center line of the skull at the widest point between the main beam of the horns. This measurement is supplementary and not included in the final score computation *nor is there any deduction for excessive spread.* In order to be eligible for entry, both horns, when viewed from the front, should angle upward approximately 15 degrees or more from a horizontal plane projected across both horn bases. This eliminates heads with horns that project straight out or downward from inclusion in the records. Pronghorn antelope with split skulls are not eligible for entry into the records.

Field Judging Pronghorn

By
Eldon L. Buckner

The unique pronghorn, its population reduced to some 15,000 head in the early 1900s, is one of America's greatest conservation success stories. Now legally hunted in nearly every western state, it has become one of our most numerous game animals, second only to deer. For the pronghorn hunter, it is also one of the most difficult animals to judge in the field. Nearly always, the first-time successful pronghorn hunter finds the horns of his buck to be much smaller than they appeared to be when he made the shot.

The current B&C scoring system was adopted in 1950 and was first reflected in the 1952 B&C records book. There were 67 total pronghorn entries listed meeting the minimum score requirement of 70 points. In contrast, the latest 1999 book lists 1,443 entries with a score of 82 or more. Only 21 achieved that score in the 1952 book.

A pronghorn with heavy 14-inch horns and four-inch prongs will score about 70 points and is a trophy no one need be ashamed of. If, however, a trophy qualifying for the current B&C all-time records minimum of 82 is the hunter's goal, a buck with 15 to 16 inch horns, 6 to 7 inch bases, and 5 to 6 inch prongs must be found.

When guiding and hunting for pronghorn in several states over the past 36 years, I have used the following methods of evaluating the most critical features of trophy heads. Hunters who have attended the pronghorn hunting seminars where I have recommended these methods say they have worked well for them also.

Horn Length

Horns should appear to be much longer than the length of the

MAXIMUM vs. MINIMUM
A Comparison of Two
Records-Book Pronghorn

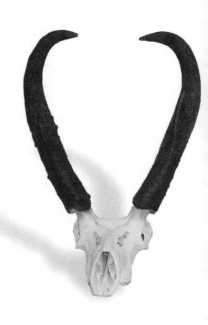

World's Record pronghorn
Score: 95

TROPHY ANALYSIS
- Above average horn length, plus very symmetrical – both 17-2/8 inches
- Average prong length – averaging just under 7 inches
- Exceptional mass – bases averaging nearly 7 inches and third quarter measurements averaging nearly 4 inches each

Minimum Entry pronghorn
Score: 80

TROPHY ANALYSIS
- No significant weaknesses
- Average horn length – both measuring over 16 inches each
- Average prong length – both over 5 inches
- Above average mass – bases both over 6 inches and third quarter measurements at 2-4/8 inches

pronghorn's head, measured from base of the ear to tip of nose. This distance averages around 13 inches. Also check the horns against ear length. If the horns appear to be 2-1/2 to 3 times the ear length, which averages 6 inches, they are probably long enough. Remember, horns that have pronounced, rounded curves inward with horn tips ending in downward hooks, may be half again as long as they appear to be, while straight horns with little hooks at the very tips will not yield much of a bonus.

Prongs

The prongs of most record-class buck will appear extremely large and will project from the horn at or above the level of the ear tips. Prongs are measured to the rear edge of the horn they project from, so a 6-inch prong will appear to extend about four inches from a heavy horn — or twice the width of the horn viewed from the side. A head with very high prongs may cause the third quarter circumference measurement to be taken below the prong instead of above it, which usually helps the score.

Horn Mass

As four circumference measurements are taken on each horn, it is obvious that heavy horns are a must for record-book pronghorn. The eyes of a pronghorn are located directly below the horn base, so they are a convenient feature to judge horn mass. As viewed from the side, the horn base should appear to be twice the width of the eye, which generally measures a little over 2 inches. This equates to horn base that measures 6 to 7 inches in circumference.

Pronghorn are usually found in open country and have exceptional vision. Therefore, good binoculars and a spotting scope are necessary to evaluate potential trophies at the distances required to avoid spooking them. Good optics and careful use of them will save the hunter many needless stalks when searching for a record-class buck.

A major factor in pronghorn trophy quality is seasonal weather. While not directly related to field evaluation, it may be a factor in where you choose to hunt. Pronghorn shed their outer horn sheaths in the fall, leaving a bony core upon which regrowth of horn material soon begins. A mild winter coupled with a warm, wet spring, and early summer providing abundant feed can result in much larger horns than will a severe winter and drought conditions the next summer. ∎

SCORECHART
Pronghorn

250 Station Drive
Missoula, MT 59801
(406) 542-1888

BOONE AND CROCKETT CLUB®
OFFICIAL SCORING SYSTEM FOR NORTH AMERICAN BIG GAME TROPHIES
PRONGHORN

MINIMUM SCORES	
AWARDS	ALL-TIME
80	82

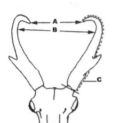

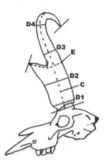

SEE OTHER SIDE FOR INSTRUCTIONS		COLUMN 1	COLUMN 2	COLUMN 3
A. Tip to Tip Spread		Right Horn	Left Horn	Difference
B. Inside Spread of Main Beams				
C. Length of Horn				
D-1. Circumference of Base				
D-2. Circumference at First Quarter				
D-3. Circumference at Second Quarter				
D-4. Circumference at Third Quarter				
E. Length of Prong				
TOTALS				

ADD	Column 1		Exact Locality Where Killed:	
	Column 2		Date Killed:	Hunter:
	Subtotal		Owner:	Telephone #:
SUBTRACT Column 3			Owner's Address:	
FINAL SCORE			Guide's Name and Address:	
			Remarks: (Mention Any Abnormalities or Unique Qualities)	

I, _____ , certify that I have measured this trophy on _____
PRINT NAME   MM/DD/YYYYY

at_____
STREET ADDRESS   CITY   STATE/PROVINCE

and that these measurements and data are, to the best of my knowledge and belief, made in accordance with the instructions given.

Witness:_____ Signature:_____ I.D. Number ☐☐☐☐
B&C OFFICIAL MEASURER

INSTRUCTIONS FOR MEASURING PRONGHORN

All measurements must be made with a 1/4-inch wide flexible steel tape to the nearest one-eighth of an inch. Enter fractional figures in eighths, without reduction. Official measurements cannot be taken until horns have air dried for at least 60 days after the animal was killed.

A. **Tip to Tip Spread** is measured between tips of horns.

B. **Inside Spread of Main Beams** is measured at a right angle to the center line of the skull, at widest point between main beams.

C. **Length of Horn** is measured on the outside curve on the general line illustrated. The line taken will vary with different heads, depending on the direction of their curvature. Measure along the center of the outer curve from tip of horn to a point in line with the lowest edge of the base, using a straight edge to establish the line end.

D-1. **Circumference of Base** is measured at a right angle to axis of horn. **Do not** follow irregular edge of horn; the line of measurement must be entirely on horn material.

D-2-3-4. **Divide measurement C** of longer horn by four. Starting at base, mark **both** horns at these quarters (even though the other horn is shorter) and measure circumferences at these marks. If the prong interferes with D-2, move the measurement down to just below the swelling of the prong. If D-3 falls in the swelling of the prong, move the measurement up to just above the prong.

E. **Length of Prong:** Measure from the tip of the prong **along the upper edge** of the outer side to the horn; then continue around the horn to a point at the rear of the horn where a straight edge across the back of both horns touches the horn, with the latter part being at a right angle to the long axis of horn.

ENTRY AFFIDAVIT FOR ALL HUNTER-TAKEN TROPHIES

For the purpose of entry into the Boone and Crockett Club's® records, North American big game harvested by the use of the following methods or under the following conditions are ineligible:

I. Spotting or herding game from the air, followed by landing in its vicinity for the purpose of pursuit and shooting;

II. Herding or chasing with the aid of any motorized equipment;

III. Use of electronic communication devices, artificial lighting, or electronic light intensifying devices;

IV. Confined by artificial barriers, including escape-proof fenced enclosures;

V. Transplanted for the purpose of commercial shooting;

VI. By the use of traps or pharmaceuticals;

VII. While swimming, helpless in deep snow, or helpless in any other natural or artificial medium;

VIII. On another hunter's license;

IX. Not in full compliance with the game laws or regulations of the federal government or of any state, province, territory, or tribal council on reservations or tribal lands;

I certify that the trophy scored on this chart was not taken in violation of the conditions listed above. In signing this statement, I understand that if the information provided on this entry is found to be misrepresented or fraudulent in any respect, it will not be accepted into the Awards Program and 1) all of my prior entries are subject to deletion from future editions of **Records of North American Big Game** 2) future entries may not be accepted.

FAIR CHASE, as defined by the Boone and Crockett Club®, is the ethical, sportsmanlike and lawful pursuit and taking of any free-ranging wild, native North American big game animal in a manner that does not give the hunter an improper advantage over such game animals.

The Boone and Crockett Club® may exclude the entry of any animal that it deems to have been taken in an unethical manner or under conditions deemed inappropriate by the Club.

Date:_____ Signature of Hunter:_____

(SIGNATURE MUST BE WITNESSED BY AN OFFICIAL MEASURER OR A NOTARY PUBLIC.)

Date:_____ Signature of Notary or Official Measurer:_____

MEASURING AND JUDGING
Rocky Mountain Goat

The horns of mountain goats, small in contrast to those of male mountain sheep, are coal black and their surfaces are shiny and smooth. Male and female goat horns are very similar in size and appearance, but those of females are more slender and tend to be more straight. Because of the smaller circumferences, few female goats are known with high enough scores to reach the present all-time records book minimum entry score of 50 points. Goats develop growth year annuli on their horns, but they are much more closely spaced than on male sheep and usually a distinct annulus does not develop during the first winter.

Only a 1/4-inch wide steel tape may be used for length and circumference measurements on goat; a steel cable may not be substituted. At times the horns on goat may be loose on their cores; it is permissible to remove the horns from their cores for measurement of the lengths and circumferences.

The first step in measuring goats is the determination of the proper horn length measurement, which is vital to the subsequent measurements. As **figure 12-A** shows, the measurement is started by hooking the measuring tape clip-end on the lowest front edge of the horn base. The line of measurement is then maintained along the outer curve of the horn surface to a point in line with the horn tip. Generally goat horns end in a sharp point that will form

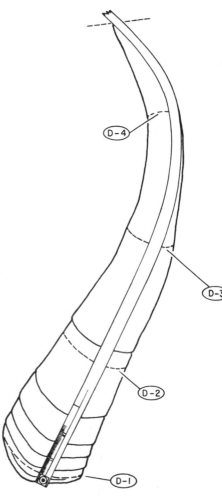

FIGURE 12-A
PROPER
HORN LENGTH
MEASUREMENT

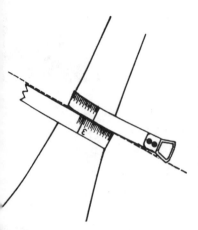

FIGURE 12-B
CIRCUMFERENCE
MEASUREMENT
TECHNIQUE

the end of the measurement line. But, if the tip should be broken off or blunted, use a small carpenter's square (or a credit card) to determine the end of the measurement line by forming a perpendicular of square and horn axis at that point.

A mounted specimen presents a problem in location of the start of the line of measurement. Care must be exercised to begin the line at the above mentioned edge of the horn. This point is often covered with hair and cape and may be fused with the mounting media (which may be colored black). Careful probing with a penknife point, using a bright light, is often necessary to properly locate the starting point.

Once the proper horn lengths are established, locations of the circumference measurements are determined by dividing the *longer* horn length measurement into quarters as shown in **figure 12-A**. The *Quarter Location for Circumference Chart* in the back of this manual provides these values. Record the locations of the three quarter locations in the blank area to the right of each circumference description on the score chart so they can easily be verified if there is any later question about the measurement. Mark the three quarter locations (D-2, D-3, and D-4) carefully on the original line of horn length measurement of each horn with a soft pencil. Since it is often difficult to see marks on the black horns, you may wish to use masking tape to mark these spots.

Be sure to establish these quarters by measuring from each horn base to the tip. This is essential to give proper matching of quarters on both horns. If the quarters were located by measuring from the tip toward the base, the quarter locations would be placed nearer the base on the shorter horn than on the longer. This would probably make an artificial difference between the quarter measurements. When marking the quarters on the horn, be sure to hold the tape stationary along the original line followed in measuring the length of horn.

Once the quarters have been properly located and marked by pencil, and the calculations verified, measure each circumference by carefully arranging a ring-end measuring tape at a right angle to the horn axis at that point. At the zero point of the tape, the two ends should pass on opposite sides of the pencil mark, with the tape and the horn axis forming a right angle **(figure 12-B)**. Snug the tape around the horn before reading the result, again checking to be sure that the tape is correctly positioned on each side of the pencil mark. If you use a clip-end tape to measure circumferences, overlap the tape at a full 10 inch increment to simplify the procedure. Be sure to subtract the amount of overlap before recording the measurement. If it should happen that one horn is broken to the extent that the horn material is completely missing at the D-4 circumference location, simply enter a zero value in the appropriate column of the score chart to reflect this missing value.

FIGURE 12-C

The circumference of base (D-1) is best measured before a taxidermist has mounted the trophy. The mountain goat has a doughnut-shaped, fleshy gland around the horn base that is most pronounced on the back side of the horn. In restoring the skin, the taxidermist is apt to cover the basal portion of the horn, which makes it very difficult to properly locate the basal circumference.

Therefore, be careful in making the circumference of base measurement of a mounted specimen to avoid including hair, plastic material added by the taxidermist, or a portion of the skull in this measurement. The D-1 measurement is taken at a right angle to the base of the horn, and not by following the basal edge of the horn. Following the irregular lower edge of the horn would result in an inflated value, which would be incorrect.

Goat horns may show natural damage on occasion due to the gland posterior to the horn base. The damage is usually minimal, but may extend as high as an inch or more up the back of the horn. Often the horn material is absent in this damaged area. When this happens, the basal circumference must be located at the top of the damaged area, so that the measuring tape is in complete contact with horn material. In extreme cases, the basal circumference may even be taken near the location of the first quarter circumference.

The supplementary data of tip to tip and greatest spread are recorded to show general conformation. They do not figure into the score. The tip to tip measurement is simply from the center of the tip of one horn to the center of the tip of the other. Normally, it is taken by use of the folding carpenter's rule or steel tape. Greatest spread can usually be taken with the same ruler or calipers. The greatest spread is simply the widest measurement available of the spread of the horns.

Sheep and goat trophies offer the opportunity to age them by counting the horn annuli (rings) left as a mark of the cessation of horn growth during each winter (figure 12-C). During the first winter the annulus is often only a swollen area in bighorn sheep and is often totally absent in mountain goats. But, each winter after that a distinct annulus forms in both sheep and goats. The annuli should correspond on both horns of the same animal. All sheep and goat trophies should be aged by the annuli present, and the number of annuli present on both horns should be recorded in the REMARKS section of the score chart.

Rocky Mountain goats do develop distinct horn annuli. But, usually no annulus develops during the first winter so that the specimen is one year older than the visible number of annuli. In an old goat, the annuli nearest the skull may be as close together as 1/8 inch, necessitating close examination for an accurate count. Knowing the age of your trophy billy, as determined by the annul rings, will certainly add additional satisfaction to a fine hunt. Of course, a goat trophy can be aged at any time, even after taxidermy, although mounting of the trophy may make determination of the most recent growth rings more difficult.

Field Judging Rocky Mountain Goats

Goats are usually harder to judge than rams. Nevertheless, there are certain criteria. In the first place, one has only to

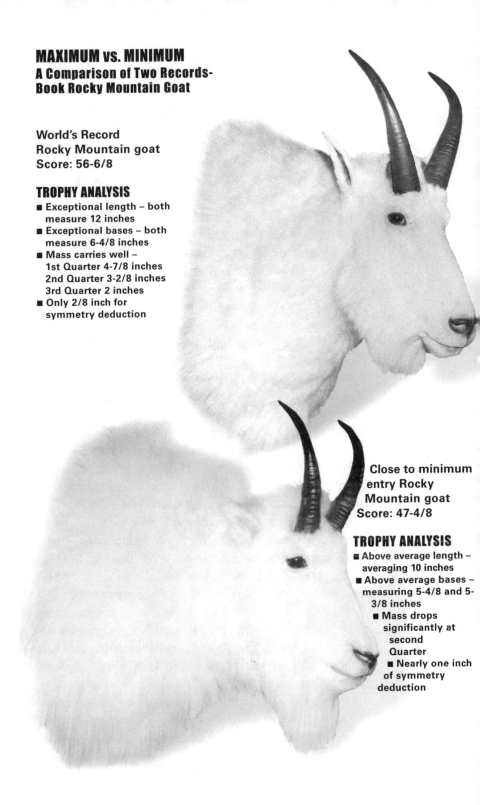

MAXIMUM vs. MINIMUM
A Comparison of Two Records-Book Rocky Mountain Goat

**World's Record
Rocky Mountain goat
Score: 56-6/8**

TROPHY ANALYSIS
- Exceptional length – both measure 12 inches
- Exceptional bases – both measure 6-4/8 inches
- Mass carries well –
  1st Quarter 4-7/8 inches
  2nd Quarter 3-2/8 inches
  3rd Quarter 2 inches
- Only 2/8 inch for symmetry deduction

**Close to minimum entry Rocky Mountain goat
Score: 47-4/8**

TROPHY ANALYSIS
- Above average length – averaging 10 inches
- Above average bases – measuring 5-4/8 and 5-3/8 inches
  - Mass drops significantly at second Quarter
  - Nearly one inch of symmetry deduction

glance at a billy goat in the proximity of a nanny to note the high humped shoulder, the shaggy pelt, and the chunkier overall profile. To bag a trophy North American mountain goat, one must almost certainly shoot a billy, although the horns of a nanny are sometimes longer than those of a billy of the same age. One's first necessity is then to make sure the quarry is a billy, not a nanny.

If the apparent horn length is visualized as straightened-out, and it then approximates the distance from the nostrils to the bottom of the eye, you are looking at a horn length of probably at least eight, but not over nine inches. If the same comparison yields an apparent length equivalent to the distance from the nostrils to the ear hole, you are un-questionably looking at a records-class billy, providing his horn tips are not broken and he appears to have a thick base on each horn.

Judging the base of a billy goat's horns is a fine art. The safest assumption is that if a billy meeting the above length-of-horn comparison is shot on the Pacific Coast, or the west slope of the Rockies, or in the Cassiars, it will have a tro-phy quality base. If shot east of the Rockies, it probably will not. Obviously there are exceptions.

Another useful gauge is the apparent length of the horns compared to the visible length of the ear. For trophy qual-ity, one normally must look for a horn that appears to be two and one-half times the visible length of the ear.

The use of a high-powered spotting scope is helpful in general evaluation, but certainly not in an attempt to count the number of annular growth rings on the horns. The rings are simply too small and spaced too close together to be counted at a distance. Bulk and pure size are then perhaps the final criteria. You are looking for a very old goat in ter-rain having mineralization to support better-than-average thickness of horns. This will almost never materialize in a breeding billy. Normally the trophy goat will be a loner. What makes this all the more difficult is that outside of the rutting season (late November) one seldom sees a mature billy other than alone or as one of a small group. Since a loner is not necessarily a big mature billy, an assessment of his size, bulk, and apparent horn length is essential to proper identification of a real trophy. ■

SCORECHART
Rocky Mountain Goat

Records of
North American
Big Game

250 Station Drive
Missoula, MT 59801
(406) 542-1888

BOONE AND CROCKETT CLUB®
OFFICIAL SCORING SYSTEM FOR NORTH AMERICAN BIG GAME TROPHIES

ROCKY MOUNTAIN GOAT

MINIMUM SCORES
AWARDS   ALL-TIME
47   50

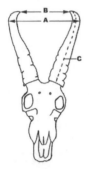

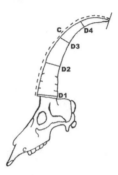

SEE OTHER SIDE FOR INSTRUCTIONS		COLUMN 1	COLUMN 2	COLUMN 3
A. Greatest Spread		Right Horn	Left Horn	Difference
B. Tip to Tip Spread				
C. Length of Horn				
D-1. Circumference of Base				
D-2. Circumference at First Quarter				
D-3. Circumference at Second Quarter				
D-4. Circumference at Third Quarter				
TOTALS				

ADD	Column 1		Exact Locality Where Killed:	
	Column 2		Date Killed:	Hunter:
Subtotal			Owner:	Telephone #:
SUBTRACT Column 3			Owner's Address:	
FINAL SCORE			Guide's Name and Address:	
			Remarks: (Mention Any Abnormalities or Unique Qualities)	

I, _____ , certify that I have measured this trophy on _____
PRINT NAME   MM/DD/YYYYY

at _____
STREET ADDRESS   CITY   STATE/PROVINCE

and that these measurements and data are, to the best of my knowledge and belief, made in accordance with the instructions given.

Witness: _____ Signature: _____ I.D. Number ☐☐☐☐☐
B&C OFFICIAL MEASURER

INSTRUCTIONS FOR MEASURING ROCKY MOUNTAIN GOAT

All measurements must be made with a 1/4-inch wide flexible steel tape to the nearest one-eighth of an inch. Wherever it is necessary to change direction of measurement, mark a control point and swing tape at this point. Enter fractional figures in eighths, without reduction. Official measurements cannot be taken until horns have air dried for at least 60 days after the animal was killed.

A. Greatest Spread is measured between perpendiculars at a right angle to the center line of the skull.
B. Tip to Tip spread is measured between tips of the horns.
C. Length of Horn is measured from the lowest point in front over outer curve to a point in line with tip.
D-1. Circumference of Base is measured at a right angle to axis of horn. Do not follow irregular edge of horn; the line of measurement must be entirely on horn material.
D-2-3-4. Divide measurement C of longer horn by four. Starting at base, mark both horns at these quarters (even though the other horn is shorter) and measure circumferences at these marks, with measurements taken at right angles to horn axis.

ENTRY AFFIDAVIT FOR ALL HUNTER-TAKEN TROPHIES

For the purpose of entry into the Boone and Crockett Club's® records, North American big game harvested by the use of the following methods or under the following conditions are ineligible:

  I.   Spotting or herding game from the air, followed by landing in its vicinity for the purpose of pursuit and shooting;
  II.   Herding or chasing with the aid of any motorized equipment;
  III. Use of electronic communication devices, artificial lighting, or electronic light intensifying devices;
  IV. Confined by artificial barriers, including escape-proof fenced enclosures;
  V.   Transplanted for the purpose of commercial shooting;
  VI. By the use of traps or pharmaceuticals;
  VII. While swimming, helpless in deep snow, or helpless in any other natural or artificial medium;
  VIII. On another hunter's license;
  IX. Not in full compliance with the game laws or regulations of the federal government or of any state, province, territory, or tribal council on reservations or tribal lands;

I certify that the trophy scored on this chart was not taken in violation of the conditions listed above. In signing this statement, I understand that if the information provided on this entry is found to be misrepresented or fraudulent in any respect, it will not be accepted into the Awards Program and 1) all of my prior entries are subject to deletion from future editions of **Records of North American Big Game** 2) future entries may not be accepted.

FAIR CHASE, as defined by the Boone and Crockett Club®, is the ethical, sportsmanlike and lawful pursuit and taking of any free-ranging wild, native North American big game animal in a manner that does not give the hunter an improper advantage over such game animals.

The Boone and Crockett Club® may exclude the entry of any animal that it deems to have been taken in an unethical manner or under conditions deemed inappropriate by the Club.

Date:_____ Signature of Hunter:_____
(SIGNATURE MUST BE WITNESSED BY AN OFFICIAL MEASURER OR A NOTARY PUBLIC.)

Date:_____ Signature of Notary or Official Measurer:_____

A BOONE AND CROCKETT CLUB FIELD GUIDE TO MEASURING AND JUDGING BIG GAME

MEASURING AND JUDGING
Bison

13

The bison is one of the most romantic of all the North American big-game trophies. They conjure up visions of the frontier days and a raw western prairie challenging the settlers and ranchers for their very existence. However, bison herds declined due to changes in habitat and increased human population limiting the number of free-ranging bison to relatively small, localized herds. In many areas bison are treated as domestic livestock. For these reasons, bison are fully eligible for entry into the records books and for possible awards *only* if they are taken in Alaska or Canada, where there are still truly wild and free-ranging herds in the original sense of such a definition. Bison shot in the lower 48 states are eligible for the all-time and Awards records books and for possible invitation to the final Awards Judging *only* if they are taken on a fair chase hunt in an area where they are recognized as wildlife (rather than as domestic livestock) and where a specific hunting license and/or big game tag is required for their taking.

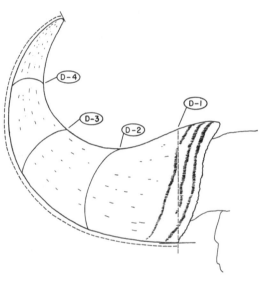

FIGURE 13-A

Only a 1/4-inch wide steel tape may be used for length and circumference measurements on bison; a steel cable may not be substituted. At times the horns on bison may be loose on their cores; it is permissible to remove the horns from their cores for measurement of the lengths and circumferences. Be sure to note the right and left horns as their shape is very similar

As shown in **figure 13-A**, the length measurement is started by hooking the measuring tape clip-end on the lowest outside base edge on the *underside* of the horn to reflect the longest horn length available. The line of measurement is then maintained along the outer horn surface to a point in line with the horn tip. If the horn tip ends in a sharp point, the measured line is simply read from the tape.

If the horn tip is broken or blunted, use a small carpenter's square (or a credit card) to determine the end of the measurement line by forming a perpendicular of the square and horn axis at that point.

A mounted specimen presents a problem in location of the start of the line of measurement. Care must be exercised to begin the line at the above mentioned edge of the hollow horn. This point is often covered with hair and cape and may be fused with the mounting media. Careful probing with a penknife point, using a bright light, is often necessary to properly locate this point.

Once the proper horn lengths are established, locations of the circumference measurements are determined by dividing the *longer* horn length measurement into quarters. The *Quarter Locations for Circumference Chart* in the back of this manual provides these values. Record the values of the three quarter locations in the blank area to the right of each circumference description on the score chart so they can be easily verified if there are any questions later about the measurement. Mark the three quarter locations (D-2, D-3, and D-4) carefully on the original line of horn length measurement of each horn with a soft pencil.

Be sure to establish these quarters by measuring from each horn base to the tip. This is essential to give proper matching of quarters on both horns. If the quarters were located by measuring from the tip toward the base, the quarter locations would be placed nearer the base on the shorter horn than on the longer. This would probably make an artificial difference between the quarter measurements. When marking the quarters on the horn, be sure to hold the tape stationary along the original line followed in measuring the length of horn.

Once the quarters have been properly located and marked by pencil, and the calculations verified, measure each circumference by carefully arranging a ring-end measuring tape at a right angle to the horn axis at that point. At the zero point of the tape, the two ends should pass on opposite sides of the pencil mark, with the tape and the horn axis forming a right angle. Snug the tape around the horn before reading the result, again checking to be sure that the tape is correctly positioned on each side of the pencil mark. If you use a clip-end tape to measure circumferences, overlap the tape at a full 10 inch increment to simplify the procedure. Be sure to subtract the amount of overlap before recording the measurement. If it should happen that one horn is broken to the extent that the horn material is completely missing at the D-4 circumference location, simply enter a zero value in the appropriate column of the score chart to reflect this missing value.

Take care in making the circumference of base measurement (D-1) of a mounted specimen to avoid including hair, plastic material added by the taxidermist, or a portion of the skull in this measurement. This measurement is taken at right angles to the base of the horn, and not by following the basal edge of the horn. The basal edge of the horn is usually irregular and lies at an angle with reference to the horn axis. This makes the proper measurement of D-1 a bit tricky. Very often it is an inflated, and thus incorrect, value. The key is to make the line of measurement perpendicular to the axis of the horn base. The measured line must be on horn material throughout the measurement, not on air space. **Figure 13-A** demonstrates this approach.

The tip to tip measurement is simply from the center of the tip of one horn to the center of the tip of the other. Normally, it is taken by using the carpenter's folding rule or a steel measuring tape.

Greatest spread is best taken by use of two perpendiculars, such as carpenter's levels held upright by large c-clamps or perfectly square-cut wooden blocks. The measurement is then taken by folding carpenter's rule between the perpendiculars. If perpendiculars are not available, a floor and wall can be used for one perpendicular, with the second being improvised from a carpenter's level or a straight, square-cut board. In no case should the human eye be relied upon for establishment of the second perpendicular line.

Note that tip to tip spread and greatest spread are supplementary measurements and are not figured into the final score. They are recorded on the score chart as they do indicate the general conformation of the horns and, with the other measurements, help to give a more complete picture of horn formation for the trophy.

Field Judging Bison

Evaluating the American bison (or buffalo as it is often commonly called) is not easy. Bison are not common enough for the average hunter to become familiar with their *immense* size. A good-sized bull is some six feet high at the top of the shoulder hump and will weigh about a ton on the hoof. The head is shaggy and usually with a beard reaching nearly to the ground. The huge shoulder hump adds to the effect of a really enormous animal. Thus, when confronted under field conditions with an average-sized bison, the hunter may well think it is a really big one. One therefore needs to observe enough bison to be able to tell the difference between an ordinary bull and a real trophy bull. Observation of bison at zoos, parks, or even on ranches and farms may be of great help.

One should always look at the size of the horns in comparison to the general body size of the bison. A set of large horns on a small-sized bull will appear relatively much larger than the same horns on a larger bodied bull. One needs to make sure that the trophy-sized horns apparently being offered by the bison in question are not just the illusion of large horns on a small body.

After you have looked at a number of bison, some general trends in horn development will be apparent that will aid trophy evaluation. In a young bull, the horns come out of the head and turn almost straight up. As the bull gets older, his horns will develop the characteristic gentle curve of the mature trophy, with the horn tips beginning to point toward each other. The horn bases increase considerably in size with age, whereas on a younger animal the horn will appear rather thin and nearly uniform along its length. On the mature trophy bull, the effect of the entire horn is that of a strongly tapering, half-moon curve.

As with all horned game, be sure to view both horns before making the decision to shoot. Often, one horn may be broomed or broken-off at the tip, materially lessening the score. ∎

MAXIMUM vs. MINIMUM
A Comparison of Two
Records-Book Bison

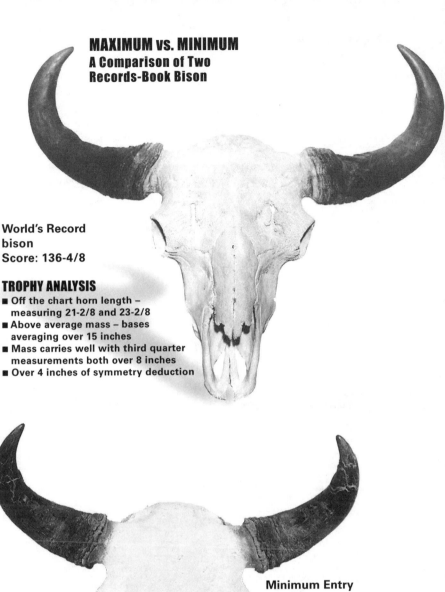

**World's Record
bison
Score: 136-4/8**

TROPHY ANALYSIS
- Off the chart horn length –
  measuring 21-2/8 and 23-2/8
- Above average mass – bases
  averaging over 15 inches
- Mass carries well with third quarter
  measurements both over 8 inches
- Over 4 inches of symmetry deduction

**Minimum Entry
bison
Score: 118**

TROPHY ANALYSIS
- Average horn length is compensated
  with above average mass – both
  bases measure 14-3/8 inches
- Mass drops considerably at third
  quarter measurement – both
  measure just under 6 inches
- Only 6/8 inch in symmetry
  deduction

SCORECHART
Bison

BOONE AND CROCKETT CLUB®
OFFICIAL SCORING SYSTEM FOR NORTH AMERICAN BIG GAME TROPHIES

BISON

MINIMUM SCORES	
AWARDS	ALL-TIME
115	115

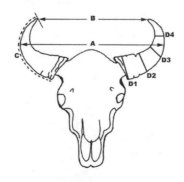

SEE OTHER SIDE FOR INSTRUCTIONS		COLUMN 1	COLUMN 2	COLUMN 3
A. Greatest Spread		Right Horn	Left Horn	Difference
B. Tip to Tip Spread				
C. Length of Horn				
D-1. Circumference of Base				
D-2. Circumference at First Quarter				
D-3. Circumference at Second Quarter				
D-4. Circumference at Third Quarter				
TOTALS				

ADD	Column 1		Exact Locality Where Killed:	
	Column 2		Date Killed:	Hunter:
	Subtotal		Owner:	Telephone #:
SUBTRACT Column 3			Owner's Address:	
FINAL SCORE			Guide's Name and Address:	
			Remarks: (Mention Any Abnormalities or Unique Qualities)	

I, _____ , certify that I have measured this trophy on _____
　　　　　　　PRINT NAME　　　　　　　　　　　　　　　　　　　　　　　　　　　　　　MM/DD/YYYY

at _____
　　STREET ADDRESS　　　　　　　　　　　　　　　　　　　CITY　　　　　　　　　　　　STATE/PROVINCE

and that these measurements and data are, to the best of my knowledge and belief, made in accordance with the instructions given.

Witness:_____ Signature:_____ I.D. Number [ ][ ][ ][ ]
　　　　　　　　　　　　　　　　　　　　　　B&C OFFICIAL MEASURER

INSTRUCTIONS FOR MEASURING BISON

All measurements must be made with a 1/4-inch wide flexible steel tape to the nearest one-eighth of an inch. Wherever it is necessary to change direction of measurement, mark a control point and swing tape at this point. Enter fractional figures in eighths, without reduction. Official measurements cannot be taken until horns have air dried for at least 60 days after the animal was killed.

- **A. Greatest Spread** is measured between perpendiculars at a right angle to the center line of the skull.
- **B. Tip to Tip Spread** is measured between tips of horns.
- **C. Length of Horn** is measured from the lowest point on underside over outer curve to a point in line with the tip. Use a straight edge, perpendicular to horn axis, to end the measurement, if necessary.
- **D-1. Circumference of Base** is measured at right angle to axis of horn. **Do not** follow the irregular edge of horn; the line of measurement must be entirely on horn material.
- **D-2-3-4. Divide measurement C** of **longer** horn by four. Starting at base, mark **both** horns at these quarters (even though the other horn is shorter) and measure the circumferences at these marks, with measurements taken at right angles to horn axis.

ENTRY AFFIDAVIT FOR ALL HUNTER-TAKEN TROPHIES

For the purpose of entry into the Boone and Crockett Club's® records, North American big game harvested by the use of the following methods or under the following conditions are ineligible:

I. Spotting or herding game from the air, followed by landing in its vicinity for the purpose of pursuit and shooting;
II. Herding or chasing with the aid of any motorized equipment;
III. Use of electronic communication devices, artificial lighting, or electronic light intensifying devices;
IV. Confined by artificial barriers, including escape-proof fenced enclosures;
V. Transplanted for the purpose of commercial shooting;
VI. By the use of traps or pharmaceuticals;
VII. While swimming, helpless in deep snow, or helpless in any other natural or artificial medium;
VIII. On another hunter's license;
IX. Not in full compliance with the game laws or regulations of the federal government or of any state, province, territory, or tribal council on reservations or tribal lands;

I certify that the trophy scored on this chart was not taken in violation of the conditions listed above. In signing this statement, I understand that if the information provided on this entry is found to be misrepresented or fraudulent in any respect, it will not be accepted into the Awards Program and 1) all of my prior entries are subject to deletion from future editions of **Records of North American Big Game** 2) future entries may not be accepted.

FAIR CHASE, as defined by the Boone and Crockett Club®, is the ethical, sportsmanlike and lawful pursuit and taking of any free-ranging wild, native North American big game animal in a manner that does not give the hunter an improper advantage over such game animals.

The Boone and Crockett Club® may exclude the entry of any animal that it deems to have been taken in an unethical manner or under conditions deemed inappropriate by the Club.

Date:_____ Signature of Hunter:_____
(SIGNATURE MUST BE WITNESSED BY AN OFFICIAL MEASURER OR A NOTARY PUBLIC.)

Date:_____ Signature of Notary or Official Measurer:_____

MEASURING AND JUDGING
Muskox

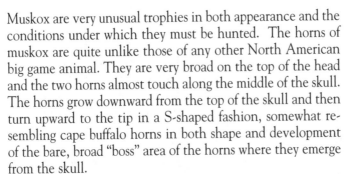

14

Muskox are very unusual trophies in both appearance and the conditions under which they must be hunted. The horns of muskox are quite unlike those of any other North American big game animal. They are very broad on the top of the head and the two horns almost touch along the middle of the skull. The horns grow downward from the top of the skull and then turn upward to the tip in a S-shaped fashion, somewhat resembling cape buffalo horns in both shape and development of the bare, broad "boss" area of the horns where they emerge from the skull.

Prior to measurement, muskox skulls should be cleaned by boiling and then removing all flesh and cartilage. It is important that all soft connective tissue be removed between the horns at the top of the skull. This is necessary so that, after the skull and horns have dried for 60 days after cleaning, the inside lower edge of the horn can be properly located to begin the horn length measurement.

As in all horn measurements, location and accuracy in measuring the lengths of the horns is vital to the subsequent measurements. The correct line of measurement is along the

FIGURE 14-A

FINDING THE D-1 MEASUREMENT USING TWO CARPENTER'S SQUARES

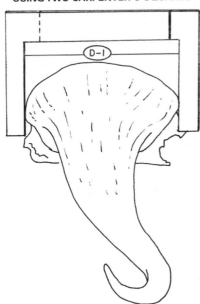

LOCATING THE CENTER POINT LINE USING THREE CARPENTER'S SQUARES

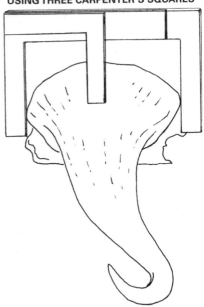

upper surface of the horn as it grows from the skull. As the curl reverses its direction, the measurement line remains in the same linear plane as begun, staying on the continuing upper surface which may gradually turn upside down in the curling tip.

Prior to making the length of horn measurement, one must first locate the center point of each boss (the enlarged and flattened skull portion of horn), since the length measurements pass over these points. To locate the center of the boss, the width of boss is determined. Unlike other horned game, the D-1 (and D-2) measurements are not circumferences but rather the straight-line widths of the bosses.

Calipers are often used to take these two measurements. Care must be taken to position the calipers properly at a right angle to the horn axis at the point of measurement. The caliper ends should be snug against the horn but not under tension. If the ends are under tension, the measurement line will "shrink" slightly when the calipers are removed and thus give an inaccurate measurement. When the calipers have been properly placed and closed correctly to reflect the greatest width of boss at the measurement point, they are carefully removed and placed against a folding carpenter's ruler or steel tape to determine the length of the measured line. This value is recorded as D-1.

Two carpenter's squares held together with small clamps can also be used. The arms of the two squares are held together and slowly moved inward until they contact the front and rear edge of the boss at its greatest width at right angles to horn axis.

The D-1 value is then divided by two and that value noted. The measurer then places a mark on the top of the boss corresponding to this half-width. One advantage of using the two carpenter's squares is that a third square can be set perpendicular to the other two to drop the center point line from the squares onto the boss. If calipers are initially used, you will still need a carpenter's square to find the actual center point. Due to the coloration of some horns, it may be easier to see this mark if a piece of masking tape is placed at the approximate center location and the mark placed on the tape. **Figure 14-A** illustrates the use of carpenter's squares for finding D-1 and the center point mark. Since the boss widths may vary from side to side, each will need to be taken separately and separate center marks made on each boss.

The length of horn measurement is begun at *the lowest point of horn material* at the center of the horn. It may be necessary to free the connective tissue between the horns at the center of the boss to locate the starting point of this measurement. This location is down between the faces of the boss. If the connective tissue has not separated from the horn material, then the line of measurement begins at the juncture of the connective material and horn. On horns where there is considerable separation of the connective tissue, the horn material may extend deeper toward the skull from the separation. The point of beginning is directly below the center point mark on the top of the boss.

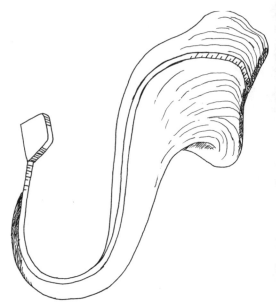

Once this starting point has been properly located, the measurement line then proceeds through the center of the boss, as noted above. Since the first two to three inches of the measurement are often between the faces of the two bosses, it is convenient to make a mark at the two (or three) inch location on tape placed on the boss and then continue measurement from that mark. As **figure 14-B** illustrates, the line of measurement is then maintained along the *upper* horn surface (even though "upper" may become the underside of the curve in the horn tip curl) to the point tip or to a point in line with the horn tip. If the horn tip should be broken or noticeably blunted, use a carpenter's square (or a credit card) to determine the end of the measurement line by forming a perpendicular of the square and horn axis at that point.

FIGURE 14-B
PROPER LINE OF
MEASUREMENT
FOR LENGTH OF
HORN

Nearly always, the horn shows very visible "grain" in its material, which offers an excellent line to follow in making the length of horn measurement. Simply pick out the groove which best corresponds to the half-width mark on the top of the boss beginning the line as noted above, then follow this grain to the horn tip. It is an excellent idea to use chalk or pencil to mark the measurement line before the actual measuring is done. You can then concentrate on following the marked line you have established, making an accurate measurement.

A mounted specimen presents a problem in locating the start of the line of measurement. On a mounted trophy (or even a poorly cleaned, bare skull), the horn base may be covered with hair, cartilage or mounting media. On such a specimen, it may not be possible to properly locate the beginning point of the measurement. Begin the measurement at the lowest point of horn material that is visible, which means the measurement will be somewhat shorter than the trophy is entitled to have. Therefore, it is certainly advisable to measure a muskox before it is mounted.

Once the proper horn lengths are established, locations of the quarters are determined by dividing the *longer* horn length measurement by four. The *Quarter Locations for Circumference Chart* in the back of this field guide provides these values. Record the values of the three quarter locations in the blank area to the right of each circumference description on the score chart so they can be easily verified if there is any later question about the measurement. Mark the three locations (D-2, D-3, and D-4) carefully on the original line of horn length measurement of each horn with a soft pencil.

Be sure to establish these quarters by measuring from each horn base to the tip. This is essential to give proper matching of quarters on both horns. If the quarters were located by measuring from the tip toward the base, the quarter locations would be placed nearer the base on the shorter horn than on the longer. This would probably make an artificial difference between the quarter measurements. When marking the quarters on the horn, be sure to hold the tape or cable in place along the original line followed in measuring the length of horn.

The D-2 measurement is taken in a similar fashion to the taking of D-1 in that it too is a straight-line width measurement. Calipers are generally used to take this measurement. Care must be taken to position the calipers properly at a right angle to the horn axis at the point of measurement. The calipers are held perpendicular to the horn surface at the first quarter mark and then closed to the edges of the main horn material (which usually overlays a portion of the boss). This measurement is of the horn width and **does not** include the flaring that may be present at the bottom of the horn edges.

The remaining two quarters (D-3 and 4) are measured as circumferences in the usual manner for horned game. Measure each one by carefully arranging a ring-end measuring tape at a right angle to the horn axis at that point. At the zero point of the tape, the two ends should pass on opposite sides of the pencil mark, with the tape and the horn axis forming a right angle. Snug the tape around the horn before reading the result, again checking to be sure that the tape is correctly positioned on each side of the pencil mark. If you use a clip-end tape to measure circumferences, overlap the tape at a full 10 inch increment to simplify the procedure. Be sure to subtract the amount of overlap before recording the measurement. If it should happen that one horn is broken to the extent that the horn material is completely missing at the D-4 circumference location, simply enter a zero value in the appropriate column of the score chart to reflect this missing value.

The tip to tip measurement is simply from the center of the tip of one horn to the center of the tip of the other. The sweeping curves of the muskox horns make it impossible on most specimens to take this measurement with a steel tape or carpenter's folding ruler. A large pair of calipers, required for taking the widths of boss and first quarter, will usually serve to take the tip to tip spread measurement.

Greatest spread is best taken by use of two perpendiculars, such as carpenter's levels held upright by large c-clamps or perfectly square-cut wooden blocks. The measurement is then taken by a folding carpenter's rule between the perpendiculars. If perpendiculars are not available, a floor and wall can be used for one perpendicular, with the second being improvised from a carpenter's level or a straight, square-cut board. In no case should the human eye be relied upon for establishment of the second perpendicular line.

Field Judging Muskox

In muskox, symmetry changes so much throughout the life of the animal that it is the number one consideration when evaluating them under field conditions. It takes about five years to produce a shootable muskox bull. Such a bull will have the horn bosses "closed-up" and the tips of the horns will have made the full half-circle that they are going to make. Probably about the animal's seventh or eighth year the maximum length of horn is attained. In Alaska muskox, this normally means about 25 to 27 inches around the curve.

After the animal's eighth year, the bosses, and the hairline going down the center of the bosses, begin to move and gravitate toward one side or the other (like a man parting his hair down the middle in his early years and then beginning to move the part left or right as he gets older). But, this can be very difficult to see at a distance. It is important, since a movement of the hairline of just a half-inch will add up to a one inch difference in horn length and a corresponding penalty. And, it will also make a difference in the quarter locations for width/circumference measurements, as well as a penalty for lack of symmetry between measurements.

You should also observe the general condition of the bosses. In the fifth, sixth, and seventh years, it will look like someone whitewashed the top of the bosses. The bosses are the widest, the hairline is in the middle, and the bull has achieved its maximum horn development about the seventh or eighth year. After that, there will be some loss of potential score. Before that time, some potential will not be realized because the edges of the boss are still soft, like a very rapidly growing sheep horn, and in the drying process will probably peel under, losing some material and therefore decreasing potential score.

As the animal grows, the horns grow with a wide flair, much like a cape buffalo. The horns drop down tighter and tighter against the head, until they begin to uncurl upward. As the horns drop down, the tips in effect are swung-out into the characteristic S-shaped curve of the mature horn.

In a good muskox, the horns will come back up above the eye, and the tips will have a little bit of black on them, usually an inch plus on a records book size bull. A line drawn right through the middle of the eyeball should show about 55 *percent* of the horn below and 45 *percent* above it on a 27-inch animal. If the line shows 52 *percent* by 48 *percent*, you have about a 26-inch animal. ∎

MAXIMUM vs. MINIMUM
A Comparison of Two Records-Book Muskox

World's Record muskox
Score: 127-2/8

TROPHY ANALYSIS
- Exceptional length – both measure over 29 inches
- Exceptional mass –
  2nd Quarter – both 11 inches
  3rd Quarter – 6 and 5-6/8 inches
- Above average boss width – both are 10-6/8 inches
- Only 1 inch of symmetry deduction

Close to Minimum
Entry muskox
Score: 109-4/8

TROPHY ANALYSIS
- Has the length, but a little thin
- Above average length – measuring 27 and 28-5/8 inches
- Average boss width – both over 9 inches
  - Over 3 inches of symmetry deduction

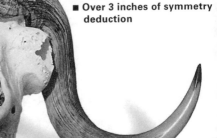

SCORECHART
Muskox

BOONE AND CROCKETT CLUB®
OFFICIAL SCORING SYSTEM FOR NORTH AMERICAN BIG GAME TROPHIES

MINIMUM SCORES
AWARDS   ALL-TIME
105   105

MUSKOX

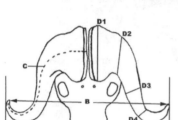

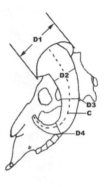

SEE OTHER SIDE FOR INSTRUCTIONS		COLUMN 1	COLUMN 2	COLUMN 3
A. Greatest Spread		Right Horn	Left Horn	Difference
B. Tip to Tip Spread				
C. Length of Horn				
D-1. Width of Boss				
D-2. Width at First Quarter				
D-3. Circumference at Second Quarter				
D-4. Circumference at Third Quarter				
	TOTALS			

ADD	Column 1		Exact Locality Where Killed:	
	Column 2		Date Killed:	Hunter:
	Subtotal		Owner:	Telephone #:
SUBTRACT Column 3			Owner's Address:	
FINAL SCORE			Guide's Name and Address:	
			Remarks: (Mention Any Abnormalities or Unique Qualities)	

I, _____ , certify that I have measured this trophy on _____
      PRINT NAME   MM/DD/YYYYY

at _____
  STREET ADDRESS   CITY   STATE/PROVINCE

and that these measurements and data are, to the best of my knowledge and belief, made in accordance with the instructions given.

Witness: _____ Signature: _____ I.D. Number ☐☐☐☐
                                                  B&C OFFICIAL MEASURER

INSTRUCTIONS FOR MEASURING MUSKOX

All measurements must be made with a 1/4-inch wide flexible steel tape and adjustable calipers to the nearest one-eighth of an inch. Enter fractional figures in eighths, without reduction. Official measurements cannot be taken until horns have air dried for at least 60 days after the animal was killed.

A. Greatest Spread is measured between perpendiculars at a right angle to the center line of the skull.

B. Tip to Tip Spread is measured between tips of horns.

C. Length of Horn is measured along center of upper horn surface, staying within curve of horn as illustrated, to a point in line with tip. Attempt to free the connective tissue between the horns at the center of the boss to determine the lowest point of horn material on each side. Hook the tape under the lowest point of the horn and measure the length of horn, with the measurement line maintained in the center of the upper surface of horn following the converging lines to the horn tip.

D-1. Width of Boss is measured with calipers at greatest width of the boss, with measurement line forming a right angle with horn axis. It is often helpful to measure D-1 before C, marking the midpoint of the boss as the correct path of C.

D-2-3-4. Divide measurement C of longer horn by four. Starting at base, mark **both** horns at these quarters (even though the other horn is shorter). Then, using calipers, measure width of boss at D-2, making sure the measurement is at a right angle to horn axis and in line with the D-2 mark. Circumferences are then measured at D-3 and D-4, with measurements being taken at right angles to horn axis.

ENTRY AFFIDAVIT FOR ALL HUNTER-TAKEN TROPHIES

For the purpose of entry into the Boone and Crockett Club's® records, North American big game harvested by the use of the following methods or under the following conditions are ineligible:

    I.   Spotting or herding game from the air, followed by landing in its vicinity for the purpose of pursuit and shooting;

    II.   Herding or chasing with the aid of any motorized equipment;

    III.   Use of electronic communication devices, artificial lighting, or electronic light intensifying devices;

    IV.   Confined by artificial barriers, including escape-proof fenced enclosures;

    V.   Transplanted for the purpose of commercial shooting;

    VI.   By the use of traps or pharmaceuticals;

    VII.   While swimming, helpless in deep snow, or helpless in any other natural or artificial medium;

    VIII.   On another hunter's license;

    IX.   Not in full compliance with the game laws or regulations of the federal government or of any state, province, territory, or tribal council on reservations or tribal lands;

I certify that the trophy scored on this chart was not taken in violation of the conditions listed above. In signing this statement, I understand that if the information provided on this entry is found to be misrepresented or fraudulent in any respect, it will not be accepted into the Awards Program and 1) all of my prior entries are subject to deletion from future editions of **Records of North American Big Game** 2) future entries may not be accepted.

FAIR CHASE, as defined by the Boone and Crockett Club®, is the ethical, sportsmanlike and lawful pursuit and taking of any free-ranging wild, native North American big game animal in a manner that does not give the hunter an improper advantage over such game animals.

The Boone and Crockett Club® may exclude the entry of any animal that it deems to have been taken in an unethical manner or under conditions deemed inappropriate by the Club.

Date:_____ Signature of Hunter:_____
                                  (SIGNATURE MUST BE WITNESSED BY AN OFFICIAL MEASURER OR A NOTARY PUBLIC.)

Date:_____ Signature of Notary or Official Measurer:_____

A BOONE AND CROCKETT CLUB FIELD GUIDE TO MEASURING AND JUDGING BIG GAME

MEASURING AND JUDGING
Walrus

15

The walrus is certainly a most unusual trophy. Hunting them under native conditions, with total reliance on the native guide and subject to Nature's whims of weather, can furnish unique hunting memories. The prominent ivory tusks are the trophy character measured. In life, they allow the walrus to dig into the harbor bottom after food and also function in ritual sparring for mates.

Though hunting seasons for walrus were closed for several years, the Club continued to receive a limited number of entries from picked-up skulls or old trophies that had not been previously entered. However, some permits are now being issued for Atlantic Walrus. Such trophies, when taken under conditions of fair chase and other Club guidelines, are eligible for entry. Two categories of listings appear for walrus—the larger Pacific Walrus and the generally smaller Atlantic Walrus.

Walrus tusks should always be removed from the animal (or mount), if possible, to properly take the measurements. Part of the tusk is inside the skull of the live animal and therefore inside the mounting medium in a mounted specimen. Only measurement of the loose tusks will ensure full credit for tusk length. Some taxidermists, unfortunately, mount tusks in such a way that they cannot readily be removed without the potential for damage.

If the tusks cannot be removed, then only the visible portion of the tusk can be measured. Naturally, the length of tusk will be shorter, by an unknown amount, when such a measurement is made on a mounted trophy. Please use the REMARKS section, or the blank space at the top of the score chart, to note such cases. Thus, the best time to measure walrus tusks is before the trophy is mounted.

If the tusks can be removed without undue problems, then an accurate measurement can be taken. If the tusks are removed for measurement, care must be taken to measure *only* tusk and not any mounting media that may still be adhering to the tusk. You should carefully check each tusk to determine if a taxidermist has added any fiberglass or other foreign material to lengthen or repair the tusk. Only the unrepaired portion of a tusk can be measured.

The walrus tusk is really just an uncurled horn insofar as measurement technique. The length of tusk measurement is therefore, similar to all horned game, of vital importance as it will establish the locations for the circumference measurements. A 1/4-inch wide steel tape must be used for the length and circumference measurements; a steel cable may not be substituted.

The length of tusk measurement is started by positioning the tusk so that the outer curve, which is therefore the longest plane of the tusk, is uppermost. Then begin the actual measurement from a point in line with the longest projecting edge of the root end of the tusk. Often the root end of the tusk is jagged and broken from being removed from the skull. It is also very thin, as the walls of the tusk continually taper to its base. Thus the base will have an uneven edge. (Essentially, square off the base when taking this measurement.)

As **figure 15-A** illustrates, the line of measurement is then maintained along the outer curve of the tusk to a point in line with the tusk tip. Use a small carpenter's square (or credit card) to determine the end of the measurement line by forming a perpendicular of the square and tusk axis at that point. This technique is necessary because blunted tusk tips are often encountered in walrus, especially older bulls.

Once the proper tusk lengths are established, locations of the circumference measurements are determined by dividing the *longer* tusk length by four. The *Quarter Locations for Circumference Chart* in the back of this field guide provides these values. Record these values of the three quarter locations in the blank area to the right of each circumference description on the score chart so they can be easily verified if there is any later question about the measurement. Mark the three quarter locations (D-2, D-3, and D-4) carefully on the outer curve along the original line of tusk length measurement of each tusk with a soft pencil.

Be sure to establish these quarters by measuring from each tusk base to the tip. This is essential to give proper matching of quarters on both tusks. If the quarters were located by measuring from the tip toward the base, the quarter locations would be placed nearer the base on the shorter tusk than on the longer. This would probably make an artificial difference between the quarter measurements. When marking the quarters on the tusk, be sure to hold the tape stationary along the original line followed in measuring the length of tusk.

Once the quarters have been properly located and marked with a pencil, and the calculations verified, measure each circumference by carefully arranging a ring-end measuring tape at a right angle to the tusk axis at that point. At the zero point of the tape, the two ends should pass on opposite sides of the pencil mark, with the tape and the tusk axis forming a right angle. Snug the tape around the tusk before reading the result, again checking to be sure that the tape is correctly positioned on each side of the pencil mark. If you use a clip-end tape to measure circumferences, overlap the tape at a full 10 inch increment to simplify the procedure. Be sure to subtract the amount of overlap before recording the measurement. If it should happen that one tusk is broken to the extent that the tusk material is completely missing at the D-4 circumference location, simply enter a zero value in the appropriate column of the score chart to reflect this missing value.

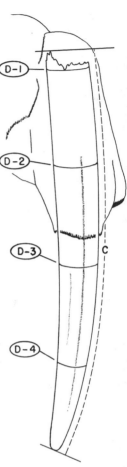

Special care must be taken in measuring the circumference of base (D-1). This measurement must be taken at a right angle to the tusk axis. As previously mentioned, the base of the tusk is often splintered and serrated due to its thin construction. The circumference of base measurement must be made entirely on tusk material, not over air space. Therefore, the measurement location may be slightly lower on the tusk in order to maintain full contact of the tape with tusk. **Figure 15-A** displays this measurement.

Obviously, if the tusks are removed at the time of measurement the usual tip to tip spread and greatest spread measurements cannot be made. They can be made while the tusks are either in the skull or in the mount. As usual in horned game, these measurements are supplementary data that do not figure into the final score for the trophy, but do help indicate the conformation of the trophy. They are taken in much the same fashion as for horned game, with tip to tip spread being simply the distance from the tip of one tusk to the tip of the other, and greatest spread displaying the greatest distance measurable from the outer edge of one tusk to the outer edge of the other, at a right angle to the skull axis.

FIGURE 15-A

Field Judging Walrus

Big bull walrus vary from about 3,200 to 4,400 pounds in good condition. A walrus will have about eight inches of tusk imbedded in the skull. The width of the whisker covered nose — varies from 11 to 14 inches. If you mentally draw a parallel-sided, rectangular box around the tusks, with the bottom of

the gum line as the box top, the bottom of the tusks as the box bottom, and the outer edges of the tusks being the sides of the box, you can readily estimate the tusk lengths. If the length of the imaginary box is double its width, the tusks are probably 28 to 30 inches. If the length of the rectangle you form is 1.6 or 1.8 times its width, you're probably looking at an animal with 26-inch tusks. Multiply the length by four and you ye got the approximate score. This method works well so long as you compensate for light tusks or tusks that are badly worn-off. For example, 29-30 inches on our imaginary box translates to a score of 120.11 there is a very light tusk with a nice sharp point, or one of the tusks is lighter than the other, you're probably going to be a couple points shy of four times the length, say about 116 to 118. If the tusks are heavy, with the tips rubbed-off, the score may go as high as 130. ∎

World's Record
Pacific walrus
Score: 147-4/8

TROPHY ANALYSIS
- Not the longest tusks in the book, but above average length – averaging over 37 inches
- Carries mass well with third quarter measurements over 7 inches

SCORECHART
Walrus

MINIMUM SCORES		WALRUS	KIND OF WALRUS (check one)
	AWARDS	ALL-TIME	
Atlantic	95	95	☐ Atlantic
Pacific	100	100	☐ Pacific

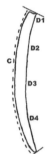

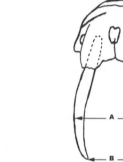

SEE OTHER SIDE FOR INSTRUCTIONS		COLUMN 1	COLUMN 2	COLUMN 3
A. Greatest Spread (If possible)		Right Tusk	Left Tusk	Difference
B. Tip to Tip Spread (If possible)				
C. Entire Length of Loose Tusk				
D-1. Circumference of Base				
D-2. Circumference at First Quarter				
D-3. Circumference at Second Quarter				
D-4. Circumference at Third Quarter				
TOTALS				

ADD	Column 1		Exact Locality Where Killed:	
	Column 2		Date Killed:	Hunter:
	Subtotal		Owner:	Telephone #:
SUBTRACT Column 3			Owner's Address:	
FINAL SCORE			Guide's Name and Address:	
			Remarks: (Mention Any Abnormalities or Unique Qualities)	

I, _____ , certify that I have measured this trophy on _____
   PRINT NAME   MM/DD/YYYYY

at _____
   STREET ADDRESS   CITY   STATE/PROVINCE

and that these measurements and data are, to the best of my knowledge and belief, made in accordance with the instructions given.

Witness: _____ Signature: _____ I.D. Number ☐☐☐☐
                                         B&C OFFICIAL MEASURER

INSTRUCTIONS FOR MEASURING WALRUS

All measurements must be made with a 1/4-inch wide flexible steel tape to the nearest one-eighth of an inch. Enter fractional figures in eighths, without reduction. Tusks **should** be removed from mounted specimens for measuring. Official measurements cannot be taken until tusks have air dried for at least 60 days after the animal was killed.

    A. Greatest spread is measured between perpendiculars at a right angle to the center line of the skull.

    B. Tip to Tip Spread is measured between tips of tusks.

    C. Entire Length of Loose Tusk is measured over outer curve from a point in line with the greatest projecting edge of the base to a point in line with tip.

    D-1. Circumference of Base is measured at a right angle to axis of tusk. **Do not** follow irregular edge of tusk; the line of measurement must be entirely on tusk material.

    D-2-3-4. Divide length of longer tusk by four. Starting at base, mark **both** tusks at these quarters (even though the other tusk is shorter) and measure circumferences at these marks.

ENTRY AFFIDAVIT FOR ALL HUNTER-TAKEN TROPHIES

For the purpose of entry into the Boone and Crockett Club's® records, North American big game harvested by the use of the following methods or under the following conditions are ineligible:

    I.   Spotting or herding game from the air, followed by landing in its vicinity for the purpose of pursuit and shooting;

    II. Herding or chasing with the aid of any motorized equipment;

    III. Use of electronic communication devices, artificial lighting, or electronic light intensifying devices;

    IV. Confined by artificial barriers, including escape-proof fenced enclosures;

    V. Transplanted for the purpose of commercial shooting;

    VI. By the use of traps or pharmaceuticals;

    VII. While swimming, helpless in deep snow, or helpless in any other natural or artificial medium;

    VIII. On another hunter's license;

    IX. Not in full compliance with the game laws or regulations of the federal government or of any state, province, territory, or tribal council on reservations or tribal lands;

I certify that the trophy scored on this chart was not taken in violation of the conditions listed above. In signing this statement, I understand that if the information provided on this entry is found to be misrepresented or fraudulent in any respect, it will not be accepted into the Awards Program and 1) all of my prior entries are subject to deletion from future editions of **Records of North American Big Game** 2) future entries may not be accepted.

FAIR CHASE, as defined by the Boone and Crockett Club®, is the ethical, sportsmanlike and lawful pursuit and taking of any free-ranging wild, native North American big game animal in a manner that does not give the hunter an improper advantage over such game animals.

The Boone and Crockett Club® may exclude the entry of any animal that it deems to have been taken in an unethical manner or under conditions deemed inappropriate by the Club.

Date:_____ Signature of Hunter:_____
                                           (SIGNATURE MUST BE WITNESSED BY AN OFFICIAL MEASURER OR A NOTARY PUBLIC.)

Date:_____ Signature of Notary or Official Measurer:_____

AN INSIGHT INTO SPORT OPTICS

By John E. Ruitta

While the development and continuous improvement of the rifle is of great importance to the hunter, the development of modern sporting optics – the binocular, the spotting scope, and the riflescope – are of equal importance. Without the benefits offered by modern optics, the practice of hunting would still be quite primitive; it would be far more dangerous, more animals would be wounded, and game management would be nearly impossible without the aid of optics in population assessment surveys. Therefore it is of great importance that every hunter give careful thought and consideration to the proper selection and use of sporting optics. The subjects of this book also speak volumes of the need for quality optics. Success rates for selectively hunting, and the field judging of a mature animal rise exponentially when using quality optics.

The idea for the first telescope dates back to nearly 1600. Hans Lippershey, an eyeglass lens manufacturer in Holland, discovered that holding two lenses, one in front of the other away from the eye, produced a larger image of a distant object. From Lippershey's discovery came what was to be the telescope, the basis of all sporting optics.

The development of the first binocular was nearly simultaneous to the development of the telescope. Lippershey applied for a patent for a "binocular instrument" in 1608. Being a designer of eyeglasses, he realized the benefits of using both eyes rather than only one to view a distant object through a magnifying lens system. However, as there was no way either to focus the image or align the two halves so that they produced a single image, the headaches caused to the first users must have been terrible. Also, the only way at that time to make the magnification level higher was to make the instrument larger, making the early binoculars too large and heavy for any practical use. The invention was put aside for almost 250 years until someone improved upon its design.

That someone was Ignatio Porro, who in 1854 invented a design for an optical system that used prisms to overcome the problem of making a higher magnification instrument small enough to be practical and allow it to be focused. The modern porro prism binocular (as Porro's design became known) is very similar to Porro's original idea, although refinement of materials, lens production, and manufacturing techniques have brought it to a level that would have amazed him.

Naturally, the development of the improvements in telescopes eventually led to the development of the riflescope. While it is true that simple riflescopes predate the Civil War, the earliest design of the modern riflescope was created in Europe shortly after 1900. Still crude by today's standards, these scopes were difficult to make and very expensive. Consequently, most hunters could not afford them. Hence, these first examples of the modern scope had little influence on the practice of hunting; most hunters still continued to use conventional sights. However this would soon change.

By the early 1930s, less costly riflescopes became available in the U.S. These new scopes used adjustable mount systems and limited internal reticle adjustments. Yet there remained considerable widespread doubt that riflescopes were actually necessary for hunting. They were not waterproof, were prone to fogging, and the early internal adjustments were often unreliable. Overcoming these problems was key if a truly useful riflescope was ever to be produced.

Marcus Leupold, the son of Fred Leupold, the founder of Leupold & Stevens, and an avid hunter, was determined to create a riflescope that was waterproof and resistant to fogging. Immediately following World War II, Marcus began developing one of the first riflescopes deemed to be accurate, reliable, and waterproof. His pioneering attitude and far-sighted thinking removed all doubts about the usefulness of riflescopes. Leupold's advances in riflescope design created a cultural change among sportsmen. Today, it is indeed rare to find someone who does not recognize the advantages of the telescopic sight over conventional iron sights.

The use of modern sports optics provides a number of benefits, for the user, for other hunters, for the animal, and for the practice of hunting itself. For the user, the binocular and spotting scope offer better discrimination of the size, sex, and condition of the animal, while the riflescope offers the benefit of a more accurate target picture and, thus better shot placement. Better selection and shot placement reduce the number of mistakenly shot, as well as of wounded, animals, which in turn benefits game management and the image of hunters. Limitations on eyesight are reduced or eliminated, as is eye strain as the eye no longer must change its focus repeatedly while viewing the target. A more accurate sight picture is a benefit to other hunters in the field as it reduces the possibility of mistaken identity and the sometimes tragic consequences of it.

Thus with all these advantages, it is easy to see how the riflescope has changed hunting as we know it today. However, it is surprising to discover just how little many hunters know about optics. Great care is often taken in the selection of a firearm, including customizations for individual fit and shooting style. Equal care is taken with ammunition selection, whether store bought or hand loaded. Yet many hunters do not make the same effort in the assessment and selection of their optics. Quite often, this is not from inattention; it simply comes from the belief that the subject of optics is too complex to learn. The following pages will prove that impression to be incorrect, and will allow a hunter to bring just as much insight and understanding to the selection of a riflescope as is brought to the selection of all other hunting equipment.

The Optical Triangle:
The Foundation of Modern Optics

All optical devices rely on their optical system. Optical system design is limited by the laws of physics. To make a superior optical instrument, optical engineers must take advantage of every possible advance in materials and combine them together in such a way that they push the limits of these laws. To do this, they must create an optical system that balances three crucial features – magnification, field of view, and eye relief – within the Optical Triangle

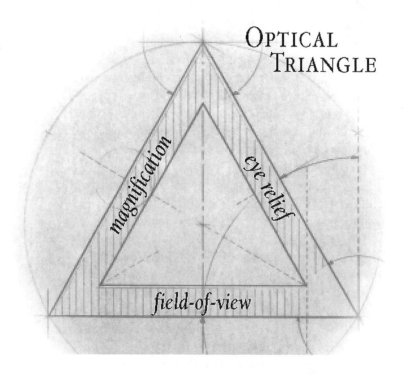

OPTICAL TRIANGLE

magnification

eye relief

field-of-view

In the Optical Triangle, each side represents the limits of one of the three features common to all optical systems – magnification, field of view, and eye relief. Magnification is, of course, how much the optic magnifies the object. Field of view is simply how much area is shown to the user in the image, typically measured by how many feet are visible from one edge of the image to the other at a distance of 100 yards. Eye relief is the distance measuring how far away from the eyepiece the user's eye can be and still achieve a full sight picture. While these three features may not seem linked together, in truth, they are inseparable.

The space inside the triangle represents all the possible combinations of these three features. Every optical system design can be placed somewhere in this triangle by virtue of its amounts of magnification, field of view, and eye relief. If you begin in the center of the triangle and move closer to one side, you will see that you are moving away from another. As each side represents one feature, this means that as one feature increases, one feature decreases. Moving from one position to another within the triangle demonstrates how the elements of a scope's design are a delicate balance between features.

The optical engineer must make the determination as to just where to strike a balance that will offer the best possible combination of features without making the optic difficult to use. For instance, if eye relief is sacrificed to get a better field of view, someone wearing eyeglasses may not be able to use the device. Trade-offs include safety considerations as well, especially in the case of eye relief in riflescopes.

Field of View and Magnification

Of the three critical factors in optical design described by the Optical Triangle, field of view is perhaps the most important to the hunter. A wide field of view allows an animal to be brought into view quickly. In the case of binoculars and spotting scopes, large areas can be scanned quickly to discover possible harvestable game. In riflescopes, field of view is a key factor in determining how quickly a the point of aim can be aligned on the target. A narrow field of view in a riflescope can place the hunter at a severe, or in the case of such dangerous game as bear or African buffalo, dangerous, disadvantage.

As the Optical Triangle clearly shows, changes in magnification level affect field of view. It is a general principle that the higher the magnification, the narrower the field of view. For example, assume that the field of view at 6x is 36 feet at 100 yards. If the animal viewed is 6 feet long, then at 6x you would divide the size of the object by the field of view (6÷36=.16 or about 1/6th), so the animal would fill 1/6th of the field of view at 100 yards. At 10x, for example, assume the field of view is 20 feet at 100 yards. For the same animal viewed at 10x, using the same equation (6÷20=.3 or about 1/3rd), would fill 1/3rd of the field of view. Clearly, if getting the animal into view quickly is important, a magnification level that causes the animal to fill less of the field of view will allow for easier and more rapid viewing.

The difference in field of view between magnification levels is why so many hunters choose variable magnification level riflescopes scopes such as 3.5-10x40mm or 4.5-14x40mm models that allow for lower magnification

– wider field of view settings when needed. It is also why open plains hunters opt for higher magnification binoculars than those hunting in the forest. The key is to know the expectations of the terrain and conditions when choosing the right optics for the hunt.

That's why it's important to know when to use which optical tool in the field. Each has its own strengths and weaknesses. Binoculars with their 8x, 10x, and occasionally 12x magnification settings can be very useful in surveying areas or in assessing not-to-distant animals as possible targets. Spotting scopes are most often higher in magnification and as such are the best choice for long distance viewing. However, an important item to remember is that increased magnification magnifies not only the item you wish to view, it also magnifies everything else, such as moisture in the air, heat waves, smoke, etc. That's why most hunters seldom use more magnification than 40 to 45x spotting scopes; higher magnification than this is rarely usable in the field because of atmospheric condition.

Then of course, there are riflescopes. Riflescopes are intended for aligning the point of aim on the target. It is never a good idea to scan the terrain with one as this could result in the rifle being pointed at another person. Variable magnification scopes are very useful for general purpose scopes as they allow for the scope to be set at a low magnification setting for target acquisition then adjusted up for fine shot placement. In the case of dangerous game where the action is fast and the distances close, fixed low magnification scopes with their extraordinarily large field of view are preferred.

The Importance of Being Waterproof

One of the great ironies of modern binoculars, spotting scopes, and riflescopes is that despite all the new technological developments in materials, designs, and manufacturing techniques, a tiny amount of water, even water vapor, inside an instrument can render all these developments meaningless. Many people simply take it for granted that all scopes are waterproof these days. They're not. Yet a scope or binocular fogging is one of the worst equipment malfunctions that can happen on a hunting trip; it is literally a "hunt stopper." Marcus Leupold learned this

Ocular Lens

It works with the objective and erector lenses to magnify the image, and then projects it, with the reticle to the eye.

Reticle Housing

The reticle is the central aiming point.

Power Selector Ring

This adjusts magnification on variable power scopes.

Erector Lenses

This system rights the image.

Windage and Elevation Adjustments

Located together on the turret, these adjustments allow you to sight-in the firearm or make field adjustments.

Parallax Elimination Adjustment

Found only on select scopes. On some scopes they take the form of adjustable objectives and others they are in the form of a third dial on the turret.

Objective Lens

It provides image definition and magnification.

firsthand – which is why his company, Leupold & Stevens, invented the first waterproof riflescope.

Some hunters think that they do not need to be concerned about waterproof products. They use their optics in places that they are not likely to fall into a river or get terribly wet. Even so, they should still be concerned as being waterproof can give a scope or binoculars other benefits as well, such as fog resistance.

Not all waterproof sports optics are resistant to fogging. To make them both waterproof and resistant to fogging, they must not only be capable of keeping water out, they must be filled with and retain nitrogen inside as well. If air is left inside the water vapor in that trapped air can condense into fog when the temperature changes. That's why truly waterproof instruments are filled with nitrogen, which cannot form water molecules. However, this leaves the manufacturer with an additional challenge, not only keeping out the water and the air, but also keeping in the nitrogen.

For the best results, precision manufacturing and assembly is a necessity. All sports optics have some external joints, such as adjustment dials and eyepiece shells. The key is to keep the tolerances tight. A precisely designed, manufactured, and assembled joint fits closely and is easier to seal effectively. The final question that should always be asked is "Is the manufacturer willing to guarantee the product to be waterproof?"

Summary

Clearly, the development of modern sports optics has revolutionized the way hunting is practiced. The benefits of more successful harvests as well as increased safety and reduced animal wounding themselves justify their use. The decision then is to determine which one to use. Magnification is useful to determine animal selection, as well as discrimination of detail and precision shot placement, however it can be a hindrance if speed in sight alignment is hindered by the constriction of field of view that accompanies higher magnification levels.

The waterproof properties of a scope can indicate other crucial factors in the scope, such as its resistance to fogging and the retention of anti-fogging gasses such as nitrogen.

Strong waterproof guarantees and testing also denote scopes with tight fitted joints that can only be the result of careful attention in manufacturing and assembly, which in turn often denote durability and hence reliability.

Careful consideration of these things when selecting sports optics will be of great benefit, as they can greatly increase the chances that the scope selected will give decades of good service and aid in successful harvests. Neglect of these factors can result in ill-chosen products that may likely fail in the field, resulting in missed or wounded animals, and lost opportunities. As such, good optics are worth ten times their price while poor ones are frightfully expensive and are never a bargain even if obtained for free. ■

A BOONE AND CROCKETT CLUB FIELD GUIDE TO MEASURING AND JUDGING BIG GAME

BASIC TIPS
For Field Judging

17

The serious trophy hunter should thoroughly study the score chart for each category he intends to hunt. He should observe and measure as many mature trophies as possible. In hunting camps he can score every trophy brought in by other hunters so as to continuously sharpen his skill at estimating trophy size. In national parks, in zoos, or in other protected areas, he should make a practice of estimating the scores of the mature males.

The serious trophy hunter should check the records books for the areas that have historically and consistently produced record trophies in the category(s) in which he is interested. He should also look for outfitter(s) in those areas with the best reputation and who have produced records-class trophies. Check the references furnished by the outfitter by both mail and telephone to ascertain both hunter satisfaction and also compliance with the rules of Fair Chase. This should go a long way toward giving the basic essentials for an enjoyable hunt with a reasonable expectation of success.

There is great variation in the ability of big-game guides to judge trophies. Those who have worked for years in areas that have yielded records-book animals may become highly skilled in judging the quality of animals in the field. Less experienced guides, like hunters in general, are more likely to overestimate the size of the trophy characters when the animal is about to take off for distant parts. The hunter really needs to develop enough expertise to be responsible for the decision of whether or not the animal is of trophy quality. Probably the majority of trophies listed in the records books were not surely known to be records book size before the hunter pulled the trigger.

A number of trophy categories are defined geographically and are based, in part, upon subspecific characteristics. (Examples: mule and blacktail deer, caribou, moose.) *Be sure* you are aware of these boundaries, and that you are applying the proper field-evaluation techniques. Obviously, applying Wyoming moose evaluation tips while in Canada moose territory would result in almost every bull encountered seeming to be record-class.

Be sure to get yourself in top shape physically *before* your hunting trips. There's never enough time on a trip and you don't want to waste it. You won't be nearly as effective if you are out-of-shape and your guide may well decide that you just can't make it to the far reaches where the big ones usually hang out. ∎

18

GENERAL PROCEDURES
Of the Records Program

Entry Procedures

Once the trophy has been measured there are a series of steps that need to be completed to insure the efficient and accurate processing of the trophy entry.

Score Chart

The most obvious and basic item needed to enter a trophy is **a fully completed, current, original score chart, signed and dated by an Official Measurer appointed by the Boone and Crockett Club.** Photocopies of score charts, as well as incomplete score charts, are unacceptable. Entries submitted on Pope and Young Club score charts, or on outdated score charts, such as those distributed by the Club when it was still headquartered in Virginia (or for that matter, at the Carnegie Museum in Pittsburgh, PA, in the early 1970s), are also unacceptable. When an entry is not submitted on the correct (and properly completed) score chart, all other processing steps must wait until a correct and accurate original score chart is received.

Entry Affidavit Notarization

Another item of importance that must be submitted with each hunter-taken trophy is an original Entry Affidavit properly signed and witnessed. The correct Entry Affidavit is on the back of all current score charts.

The hunter's signature on the Entry Affidavit needs to be notarized by a notary public, or witnessed by an Official Measurer. Once a trophy has been measured that makes the minimum score, the Official Measurer should give the trophy owner an opportunity to read the Entry Affidavit on the back of the score chart. Once the hunter is satisfied that he/she understands and meets all aspects of the Entry Affidavit, he/she should sign it in the presence of the Official Measurer who should then witness the hunter's signature by signing and dating it in the spaces provided on the score chart.

Please note that the Official Measurer's signature witnessing an Entry Affidavit on the back of the score chart is in addition to the Official Measurer's signature on the score chart verifying his/her measurement. The Official Measurer must actually be present and see the hunter sign the Entry Affidavit before the measurer signs it, or the Entry Affidavit is unacceptable.

The notary public is still required in cases where trophy owners have no direct contact with an Official Measurer. For example, measurers frequently do not meet trophy owners when they are scoring trophies for big buck contests, or when a friend, taxidermist, or other individual delivers a trophy to a measurer for the hunter. Canadian trophy owners only can also have their signature witnessed by an employee of a fish and game department, in lieu of the notary's or Official Measurer's signature.

Entry Fee

A check or money order for $25 in U.S. funds must accompany each entry to cover the entry fee. If the entry fee is not included with the entry materials, or if the incorrect amount is tendered, the trophy owner is notified that the entry fee is needed and processing is held up until the correct amount is received.

Photograph Requirements

All bear and cat entries must be accompanied with clearly focused, close-up photo prints (black and white or color) of the front, left side, right side, and top of the clean, dry skull. All trophies with antlers, horns, or tusks must be accompanied with clearly focused, close-up photo prints of the front, left side, and right side of the trophy, preferably with a plain background. Slides are unacceptable.

Field photograph submissions are highly desired, but not required for trophy acceptance. We accept any submissions and publish photos showing the hunter with the animal in the landscape where the hunt occurred, excluding vehicles or structures. Please note that not all field photos will be published.

Digital photographs, which were previously unacceptable for many reasons, are now acceptable in place of regular print photographs. The primary reason is technology to make and reproduce high quality digital photographs needed to guarantee and protect the integrity of the Club's archives is now adequate to meet our needs. Many digital photographs we receive are printed with poor resolution (less than 1,200 dots per inch) and/

or are printed on plain copy paper. Such photographs are unacceptable because they cannot be reproduced in B&C publications and are highly susceptible to damage. Digital photographs submitted for acceptance into the Club's Awards Programs, must comply with the following criteria:

A) Camera quality – the resolution level of the image must be 2 mega-pixels and above.

B) Printer – digital photographs must be printed at 1,200 DPI or better.

C) Paper – digital photographs must be printed on glossy, photo-grade paper.

The Club needs high quality photographs that will last forever with each trophy entry. The photographs, especially field photographs, if available, need to be high quality to be reproduced in books and magazines.

Hunter, Guide and Hunt Information Form

Each entry that was taken by a hunter must also include a completed Hunter, Guide and Hunt (HGH) form, *even if the services of a guide were not employed on the hunt.* The hunter simply needs to complete the parts of the HGH form that apply to his particular trophy. The HGH form, and all other required forms, are available from the Official Measurer (or from the Records Office). A copy of this form is included in the Reference Section that follows.

Entry Requirements

For entry submission, the score chart original, signed and dated by the Official Measurer, must be sent to the Boone and Crockett Club, 250 Station Drive, Missoula, MT 59801, along with:

■ The $25.00 registration fee

■ Clearly focused photographs of trophy front, left and right sides (for cat and bear entries - front, left and right sides, and top of clean, dry skull)

■ A completed Hunter, Guide, and Hunt Information Form*

■ A notarized signature of the Entry Affidavit*

■ A copy of the hunting license/big game tags used to take the trophy*

*Does not apply for trophies of unknown origin or picked-up.

Hunting License and/or Tags

A copy of the appropriate hunting license (and/or tags, if applicable) must accompany each entry that was taken by a hunter. If a copy of the license and/or tags is no longer available, the Club will accept a statement from an appropriate Game and Fish Department official who will certify that a license (and any required tags) was possessed by the hunter at the time the trophy was taken. If the Game and Fish Department no longer has records at its disposal to verify the purchase of a license, a written statement, on official letterhead, from Game and Fish personnel stating the fact that the license information is no longer available is acceptable.

The last three items listed above, the Entry Affidavit, Hunter Guide and Hunt Information form and the hunting license copy, are only required for trophies that are known to have been taken by hunters. Trophy owners submitting picked up trophies, trophies of unknown origin, or trophies taken by deceased hunters are not required to submit these items to complete the entry.

Incidentally, up to four people can be listed in the records book as the hunter for a single trophy. However, in order to list more than one person, each hunter must submit a signed and witnessed fair chase statement, as well as a copy of his or her hunting license/tag, for the trophy being entered. There are no special requirements to list more than one owner.

Acceptance Certificates

The new trophy acceptance certificate **(figure 17-A)** has been presented (free of charge) to all trophy owners receiving acceptance notifications since January 15, 1996. Trophy owners who would like a copy of this certificate for a trophy accepted prior to this date, or to replace a damaged certificate, can order one by sending $10 (U.S. funds, postage included), along with a copy of their original acceptance certificate, to the Club's headquarters. If the original certificate is not available, include your full name and address with your order, as well as your trophy's category, score, and date of acceptance (or entry period).

Trophy Recognition Plaques

The Records Committee approved and designed a trophy recognition plaque **(figure 17-B)** for trophy owners with trophies accepted in any of the Club's Awards Programs. The plaque, which is optional, is a very handsome shadowbox consisting of an 8x10 inch black walnut frame with a black velvet background. The name of the trophy owner, category, score and location of kill, date of kill and entry period are engraved on a raised, black metal plate in gold letters along with a rendition of the Club's logo. Anyone who owns a trophy listed in any of the Boone and Crockett Club's records books can order a trophy recognition plaque for their trophy room or office directly from the Club's headquarters. Just contact the Club's office for current pricing and ordering information.

Invitation to Awards Programs

The Boone and Crockett Club receives and processes entries in three year entry periods called Awards Programs. At the end of each recording period scores are finalized and an Awards Program book (e.g. *Boone and Crockett Club's 24th Big Game Awards*) featuring and listing only the trophies accepted during that Awards Program is published. As part of this process the Boone and Crockett Club conducts an Awards Banquet during which the Boone and Crockett Club medal is given to top-ranking trophies. The top five or so trophies in each category are invited to a central location where they are remeasured by a select panel of judges. This judging amounts to a verification of scores of the top few trophies received during the previous three year Awards Program. Only those trophies that receive an invitation to the Final Awards Judging are **eligible** for an Award. Furthermore, only those trophies that are sent in to the Final Awards Judging, and there certified for an Award by the Judges' Panel, are eligible to receive an Award.

The specific invitation criteria are:

1. All potential World's Records receive an invitation because only the Judges' Panel can declare a trophy a new World's Record. Any potential World's Record that is not so remeasured and certified by the Judge's Panel can never take its rightful place at the top of the list. It will be asterisked and will remain unranked at the bottom of its category until it is seen by a Judges' Panel or dropped from the Records.

2. All trophies that potentially rank in the all-time **top ten** of their category, as determined by the listings in the most recent edition of **Records of North American Big Game**, and any Awards books, also receive an invitation. In an entirely new category with no previously published listing, the top ten entries of that category will be invited.

3. Trophies of "unknown origin," "picked up" trophies, and trophies that are owned by someone other than

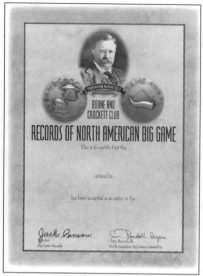

Figure 17-A

the hunter are *not normally invited* unless they rank in the all-time top ten since they *are not eligible for Place Awards* (i.e. First Place, Second Place, etc.) Place Awards are reserved for *hunter-owned* trophies.

4. Bison trophies below the all-time top 10 are not invited from the lower 48 states. Only those trophies taken in Alaska and Canada from free-ranging herds are eligible for Place Awards. Bison trophies from the lower 48 states are eligible only for *Certificates of Merit* if they are sent to panel.

5. In the case of a tie for fifth place all trophies at that score are invited.

6. Fewer than five trophies can be invited if the overall quality, based on entry scores, is too low.

Panel Judging

The panel judging serves as a verification process. Certain allowances for shrinkage are made. Trophies retain their original entry score if, during the panel measurement process, the scores obtained fall within preset limits of the original measurement. If the judges' score is higher, then a new, higher score is recorded as the trophy obviously did not shrink. Should a trophy's score fall below the preset ranges then too a new, but lower score will be used.

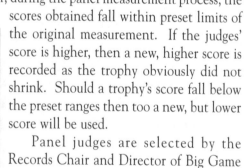

Panel judges are selected by the Records Chair and Director of Big Game Records. These individuals are assisted by several consultants who have been present at several previous panel judging sessions. The Judges' Panel is coordinated by a Chairman of Judges selected by the Records Committee. Club policy is that a measurer may serve as a Panel Judge a maximum of three times.

Figure 17-B

Teams of judges, assisted by consultants, are assigned to measure each trophy submitted to the panel judging.

Each trophy is measured a minimum of two times by independent teams. If differences arise, they are resolved by the consultants and Chairman of Judges. Often this may result in a third remeasurement of the trophy. Judges are selected based on service to the Club, experience, and geographic location. Typically at least two judges from Canadian provinces are present on each panel. Upon verification by the Chairman of Judges and the Records Office, the panel scores are final.

Special Judges Panel
The Boone and Crockett Club's Records Committee created the Special Judges Panel with the express purpose of verifying and announcing potential new World's Records as they are submitted during any triennial Awards Program. A Special Judges Panel will be convened on an "as needed" basis whenever a potential new World's Record trophy is entered. It is important to note, however, that the Club will not require trophy owners with potential World's Records to submit their trophy to a Special Judges Panel. Trophy owners still have the option of sending their trophy to be re-scored and verified by a Final Awards Program Judges Panel at a regularly scheduled triennial Awards Program, as in the past, if they so desire.

A Special Judges Panel consists of the chair of the Records Committee and an unspecified number of official measurers with preference being given to Official Measurers with experience on previous Final Awards Program Judges Panels. One member of the Special Judges Panel is designated as chair of the panel.

Each potential World's Record trophy submitted to the Special Judges Panel is re-scored by two teams of two measurers each. Any discrepancies in scores between the two teams and the entry score are resolved by the different teams of measurers first, and then by the chair of the Special Judges Panel and the chair of the Records Committee.

The score arrived at by the Special Judges Panel is final, whether or not a trophy is verified as a new World's Record. Trophies submitted for verification are still expected to be submitted for display in the next Awards Program trophy exhibit. Trophies that are re-scored by the Special Judges Panel are only eligible for Boone and Crockett Club medallions and certificates, including the coveted Sagamore Hill Award, if they are sent in for inclusion in the next Awards Program trophy exhibit.

Figure 17-C

Awards Criteria

The Judges' Panel assigns the following awards to the trophies sent for final awards judging:

Sagamore Hill Award
World's Record Certification
Place Awards
Honorable Mention Awards
Certificates of Merit

The Judges' Panel may, with concurrence of the Club's officers, award the coveted Sagamore Hill Medal **(figure 17-C)** if they feel that there is one big game trophy truly worthy of such singular recognition. Since the Club initiated the Big-Game Competitions (later called Awards) in 1947, the prized Sagamore Hill Award has been given at only 16 of the first 24 Awards Programs. The award is based both on the quality of the trophy and the fair chase, quality aspects of the hunt. To be considered for the Sagamore Hill Award, the trophy must still be owned by the hunter. The Sagamore Hill Award is given in memory of Theodore Roosevelt (the Club's founder), and his sons Theodore Roosevelt, Jr., and Kermit Roosevelt.

Figure 17-D

Typical awards **(figure 17-D)** normally consist of up to five place awards (1st, 2nd, 3rd, 4th, and 5th), Honorable Mention, and Certificate of Merit. The awards themselves are not necessarily assigned to trophies in order of their final scores. There are some very basic criteria that are followed when assigning awards.

First of all, to be eligible for a Place Award (1st, 2nd, etc.) or Honorable Mention a trophy must have been hunter-taken and still owned by the hunter.

Honorable Mentions are given to trophies if the final score of an invited, hunter-taken trophy drops significantly from its entry score, putting it below the level of other trophies accepted in the Awards Program that could have been invited to the Final Awards Judges' Panel.

Certificates of Merit are awarded to trophies entered in the Awards Program by someone other than the hunter. Certificates of Merit are also awarded to bison trophies from the lower 48 states that are sent in for remeasurement by the Final Awards Judges' Panel.

In addition, those trophies that are indeed sent to the Final Awards Judging and certified there for a Place Award and/or Certificate will be featured with a full-page photograph and a story of the hunt in the Boone and Crockett Club's next Big Game Awards book. ■

Sagamore Hill Award Winners

1948 - ROBERT C. REEVE
Alaska brown bear
1949 - E.C. HAASE
Rocky Mountain goat
1950 - R.C. BENTZEN
typical American elk
1951 - GEORGE H. LESSER
woodland caribou
1953 - EDISON A. PILLMORE
typical mule deer
1957 - FRANK COOK
Dall's sheep
1959 - FRED C. MERCER
typical American elk
1961 - HARRY L. SWANK, JR.
Dall's sheep
1963 - NORMAN BLANK
Stone's sheep
1965 - MELVIN J. JOHNSON
typical whitetail
1973 - DOUG BURRIS, JR.
typical mule deer
1976 - GARRY BEAUBIEN
mountain caribou
1986 - MICHAEL J. O'HACO, JR.
pronghorn
1989 - GENE C. ALFORD
cougar
1992 - CHARLES E. ERICKSON, JR.
non-typical Coues' whitetail
2001 - GERNOT WOBER
Rocky Mountain goat

GENERAL POLICIES
Of the Records Program

Age Data

If known, the Club would like to obtain the age of each trophy entry **if** the age was determined by a competent authority. The age data will be useful in managing big-game populations for trophy animals, as well as supporting the case for trophy hunting. Complete details for providing this information are given on the back of each Hunter, Guide and Hunt Information form that must be submitted with each hunter-taken entry.

Altered Trophies

Trophies that have been tampered with to gain an advantage obviously are not eligible for entry into the records books. Examples of trophy tampering include the deliberate removal of abnormal points from typical racks to increase a trophy's score and/or the addition of antler or horn material. If any points are deliberately removed from antlers of any trophy by breaking or sawing them off, that trophy is not eligible for entry in the Awards Programs and/or records books. Deliberate modification of horns by adding to horn length or artificially increasing circumference measurements is also grounds for disqualification of a trophy.

Antler Buyers

The Records Committee has discussed the role played by Official Measurers in dealing with antler buying and selling. When acting as an Official Measurer, the individual is a representative of the Boone and Crockett Club and not of local clubs or individuals. Increased activity in the buying and selling of antlers has led to the potential for problems to arise as a result of these transactions as it relates to the role of an Official Measurer. As a general guideline, Official Measurers score trophies for the hunter or the owner not for someone else.

Baiting

Trophies taken with the aid of bait are eligible for entry in the Club's Awards Programs and listing in the records books so long as the practice is legal in the state or province where the trophy was taken.

Cable Usage
A flexible steel cable is approved for measuring lengths of antlers and points only. It is not approved for taking circumference measurements or for measuring horn lengths. The only exception is that a cable may be used to determine horn length on muskox.

Charging For Measuring
Official measurers volunteer their time and talents to officially score trophies for the Club's Awards Programs. This service is provided to the public free-of-charge, regardless of whether or not a trophy meets the minimum scores established by the Club. Measurers who reportedly charge are simply asked to refrain from such activity or to resign from their positions.

There are many reasons why this policy was implemented. However, the most significant reason is the fact that the Club does not want measurers put in a position that compromises their integrity in any way.

Clean Skulls – Bears, Cats and Muskox
All bear, cat and muskox skulls must be cleaned of all adherent flesh, fat and membrane before they can be officially measured. There is a popular misconception among trophy owners, and even some measurers, that only the "contact points" of bear and cat skulls must be cleaned to perform an official measurement. This is incorrect, as all skulls must be completely cleaned before they can be officially measured. A properly cleaned skull is ready for public display.

Prior to measurement, muskox skulls should be cleaned by boiling and then removing all flesh and cartilage. It is important that all soft connective tissue be removed between the horns at the top of the skull. This is necessary so that, after the skull and horns have dried for 60-days after cleaning, the inside lower edge of the horn can be properly located to begin the horn length measurement.

Damaged and/or Repaired Trophies
Prior to January 1, 1980, the Club did not accept any re-

paired trophies for the records books. After that date, however, the Records Committee agreed to accept repaired trophies for the records books on a case by case basis. Trophies that have been repaired can be accepted by the Records Committee if the owner or the Official Measurer identifies the repair, and if the repair is made with original horn or antler material. The Committee still reserves the right to reject any repaired trophy, at the Committee's discretion.

When scoring any trophies that have been repaired, **no** portion of the repaired material can be included in any measurement nor can any allowance be made for lost material. For example, measurements of repaired points or main beams can only be taken to the point of the break.

When measuring horns, no allowances can be made for missing horn material. For example, there are frequently large chunks of horn material missing in the area where the D-2 circumferences are taken on desert sheep. This damage probably occurs when sheep are sparring with each other. If a D-2 circumference falls on the damaged area, the circumference is still taken through the damaged area by wrapping the tape snugly around the horn.

Cat and bear skulls are also prone to being damaged. Some damage occurs naturally when bears are sparring with each other. More frequently, however, skulls are damaged when trophies are shot in the head. In any event, measurement of damaged skulls must include only the intact, unrepaired portions of the skull.

Older deer racks often have a varnish coating. It seems that varnishing trophies must have been a common practice in the "good old days," since it seems it is generally only older racks that surface with varnish on them. Because all velvet must be removed from antlers before they can be measured, people may assume all varnish must be removed from antlers before they can be officially measured. This is **not** so. Basically, the antlers can be scored, so long as the varnish doesn't have any effect on the final score. However, if there are pockets or spots of thick varnish that affect any measurements, the varnish must be removed before the trophy can be officially measured.

Depredation Permits
Trophies taken with depredation permits under fair chase

hunting conditions are eligible for entry in the Club's Awards Programs and records books. The acceptability of trophies taken with depredation permits, however, is determined on a case by case basis. Hunters submitting a trophy taken with a depredation permit must include a brief narrative that includes the details of the hunt with the other entry materials.

Drying Period
Official measurements cannot be taken until the antlers, horns, skulls or tusks have air dried at normal room temperature for least 60 days after the animal was killed. If the trophy has been frozen prior to cleaning, as is often the case with skulls, the 60-day drying period begins once the cleaning process is complete. The drying process for trophies that have been boiled or freeze-dried starts the day they are removed from the boiling pot or freeze-drier, respectively.

In the case of picked up trophies, the 60-day drying period also applies. If it is clear from the condition of the antlers, horns, skulls or tusks that the trophy has dried for more than 60 days, one does not have to wait another 60 days from when it was found to measure it. However, it is necessary to enter the approximate date the animal died on the line provided for the date of kill on the score chart. Trophy owners may be asked to provide a brief history for "picked up" trophies or trophies of unknown origin to substantiate the approximate date of death.

Entry Disqualification
As keeper of the *Records of North American Big Game*, the Club has the inherent responsibility to maintain the integrity of the records. On occasion the validity of some entries is questioned. The Records Committee treats such questions as serious matters. If, upon completion of the Club's investigation, it is found that the trophy was inappropriately entered, the matter is taken to the Records Committee. The typical action by the committee in such cases is to remove that trophy and **all others that that particular trophy owner has entered** into the records books and to preclude any future entries from that hunter or trophy owner, as the case may be.

Fake Antlers and Horns

At its December 1989 meeting, the Boone and Crockett Club's Records of North American Big Game Committee established specific guidelines to aid in detecting the attempt of an unscrupulous individual to enter a fake set of antlers or horns in the Club's Awards Programs. Should there be any doubt in the Official Measurer's mind about the authenticity of a set of antlers or horns, the following verification process should be carefully followed.

Verification for the antler set, or horn pair, is by means of drilling a 1/16-inch diameter hole on the backside (away from the trophy front where it would be easily noticeable) of the right antler or horn, near the base. The hole should be drilled just deep enough to go through the outer surface and into the under-surface, providing a sample to be examined for proof of natural material. The measurer will place the material drilled-out of the hole in a plastic bag, then submitting it along with the completed and signed score chart directly to the Records Office. (Obviously, it will be necessary for the measurer to obtain permission of the trophy owner before drilling the hole.)

If the Records Office determines that the material removed from the antler or horn is artificial, or if the trophy owner denies permission for the Official Measurer to drill the antler or horn, the trophy in question will be disqualified from entry into the Awards Programs. Please note that the decision of final acceptability in such a case will be made by the Records Office, to ensure equality and also to make sure that measurements are available in the office files. This will ensure that the office is aware of the existence of the fake set, and the individuals attempting such deception.

If there should be any doubt about previously measured and/or accepted trophies in this matter, or questions on the part of the Official Measurers regarding procedures and intent, please contact the Records Office at once. This procedure took effect on January 1, 1990, for all horned and antlered trophies presented by their owners for an official measurement.

Horn Preparation

Shrinkage of horns (pronghorns, goats, etc.) has been a concern of many trophy owners over the years. It is acceptable to remove horns from the skull, clean them, and then have them reset with a bonding substance as **long as the horns are not altered in the process.** Thus, a bonding substance can be used but its presence cannot enhance the horn's basal circumference. Alteration of the basal circumference is grounds for disqualification of the trophy.

Intergrades of Mule/Whitetail Deer

In some locations it is possible for mule deer to interbreed with Coues' deer or other whitetails. In such cases, antlers must be measured for the species with the higher minimum score.

Location of Kill

Every effort is made by the Club to ensure that the location of kill data for trophies listed in the records books and *Fair Chase* magazine are accurate and correct. Space is provided on both the score chart and the Hunter, Guide and Hunt Information form to include this data for each entry.

Please keep in mind that we are looking for the following information when completing the blanks provided for the location of kill information. For trophies taken in the lower 48 states, we need the county and state (e.g. Lawrence Co., PA) where the trophy was taken (or found). If the county is unknown, we need to know the state where it was taken. A standard road atlas is used to ensure the correct spelling of counties in the lower 48 states.

For trophies taken in Canada and Alaska, we need the name of the nearest geographic feature (e.g. Post River, AK; Glacier Lake, BC; Cataract Creek, AB) that can be found on a map or in a geographic atlas of place names for that state or province. The Club has a small library of geographic atlases and topographic maps used to ensure that the name of a geographic location is a nationally accepted name (not simply a local name) and that it is properly spelled.

At times we have problems collecting geographic information from Canadian and Alaskan hunters. For example, a whitetail buck taken in an agricultural area in the prairie provinces may be a hundred miles from the nearest geographic feature. However, while we shy away from using the names of towns, since most animals are not actually killed in a town—only near it, we will use towns if no other location of kill information is available.

If there is more than one geographic feature that could be listed for a trophy, we prefer to list the feature closest to the site of kill. For example, Divide Lake is a better location of kill for a mountain caribou than the Mackenzie Mountains that covers thousands of square miles. Similarly, it is not very useful to list a location of kill for a whitetail deer as Lake Winnipeg since it stretches for hundreds of miles through the heart of Manitoba. For trophies taken in Mexico we simply need to know the state it was taken in.

If the location of kill or find is not known, the location should be listed as "unknown." Of course, an unknown location of kill is unacceptable for trophies separated from subspecies by boundaries. For example, an elk trophy from Washington State cannot be accepted in the Roosevelt's elk category with an unknown location of kill since we must be able to verify that it came from an area where Roosevelt's elk are located.

It is rare that we ask an individual to pinpoint the exact location of kill for his or her trophy on a map. However, we may need this information for categories of big game separated by boundaries. If we receive this information from a trophy owner, the information remains confidential and is never divulged to anyone for any reason.

When completing the location of kill information on the score chart and HGH form please be as accurate as possible. This will continue to add scientific validity to the records listings and ensure that the location is correctly spelled.

Method of Harvest
The Boone and Crockett Club accepts hunter-taken trophies harvested with: firearms, including muzzle loaders, pistols, shotguns, etc.; archery tackle, including compound bows and traditional archery equipment; crossbows; etc. All hunter-taken trophies are eligible for entry into the Club's Awards Programs and records books, so long as the equipment is legal in the state or province where the animal is harvested. (Pope and Young Club only accepts trophies taken with a bow.)

The Boone and Crockett Club also accepts trophies that are picked up (e.g. winter kills, road kills, etc.) and trophies of unknown origin (e.g. garage sales, taxidermists, attics, etc.). Trophies accepted with unknown locations of harvest are eligible only if they are for a category without a boundary.

Multiple Hunters Listed

Up to four people can be listed in the records book as the hunter for a single trophy. However, in order to list more than one person, each hunter must submit a signed and witnessed Entry Affidavit, as well as a copy of his or her hunting license/tag, for the trophy being entered. There are no special requirements to list more than one owner.

Party Hunting

"Party hunting" is a practice whereby one hunter tags an animal he or she has killed with the tag of another person in his or her hunting party. This practice is illegal in most states and provinces. Party hunting, which has been a fair chase concern of the Club for many years, is a legal practice in at least three states, Wisconsin, Minnesota and Iowa, and one Canadian province, Ontario. The Club has adopted a policy concerning the acceptability of trophies taken while "party hunting" where such a practice is legal.

The Club will **only** accept the first deer killed by the hunter during that season and then only if the hunter uses his or her tag on that deer. If a hunter uses someone else's tag on the deer he or she intends to submit for entry or if the hunter has taken other deer in that state or province during the same season and used another hunter's tag on those deer, he or she may not enter these trophies into the Club's Awards Program.

This policy does not apply to trophies taken in states/provinces that issue hunters multiple tags for the same species. Nor does it apply in states/provinces that issue a single license to multiple hunters. For example, Minnesota moose licenses are issued to a party of up to four hunters. The license is filled when any one of the hunters gets a moose. In such cases, all hunters can be listed in the book as hunters and/or owners.

Proxy Hunting

Trophies taken with a "proxy hunting license," issued by a state, province or tribal council, that permits an individual to take an animal for another person are **not** eligible for entry in the Club's Awards Programs and/or listing in the records books.

Rack and Tusk Weights

The Club would like to record the rack or tusk weights (in pounds and ounces) for elk, moose, caribou, and walrus. These weights can be used to make comparisons between various North American big-game species, as well as comparisons with their counterparts in other parts of the world. Complete details for providing this information are given on the back of each Hunter, Guide, and Hunt Information form that must be submitted with each hunter-taken entry.

Score Shopping

The Records Committee clearly does not condone "shopping for higher scores." To prevent this, **every** measurer should ask **each** trophy owner requesting his or her services if the trophy was previously officially measured. If it has been officially measured, the measurer should refuse to repeat the process.

The Records Committee has ruled that trophies of anyone caught "shopping for a higher score" will be accepted at the **lowest score** arrived at by the different measurers who scored it. As a way to better identify the situation, Official Measurers receive a supply of trophy report cards to fill out and return to the Club office for each trophy measured. This will enable immediate identification of any subsequent measurements of a trophy.

There are many reasons why the Club discourages trophy owners from shopping for higher scores. Foremost among them, the Club feels all of its Official Measurers are equally trained and qualified to measure trophies for all categories of North American big game recognized by the Club.

Also, all Official Measurers are volunteers who donate their time to score trophies for the Awards Programs. They receive no compensation for scoring trophies, and there is no point in wasting their time rescoring a trophy already officially scored by another qualified individual.

The most common excuses from individuals who shop for higher scores are, "I'm certain the Official Measurer made a mistake." Or, "My trophy should have scored higher."

We're all human, and mistakes can occur. An Official Measurer can make an occasional "interpretative error" or "mistake" with a difficult trophy. However, when a trophy owner suspects a "mistake" has been made, he or she should first talk it over with the Official Measurer.

If, after the trophy owner discusses his or her concerns with the Official Measurer, he or she still has questions about the scoring, the owner should correspond with the records office. The Club will then review the score chart and entry materials to see if there is a reason to have the trophy re-checked or rescored. If the concerns cannot be resolved in the Records Office, they will be forwarded to the Records Committee for review and a final interpretation.

Under no circumstances should the trophy owner ever ask a different measurer to rescore his trophy without prior approval from the records office as only the Records Office can approve a remeasurement.

Scoring Live Animals

Official measurers should never score the antlers or horns of live animals restrained by any method, including, but not limited to, squeeze chutes or drugs.

Shed Antlers/Split Skulls

Shed antlers, as well as any set of antlers with a split skull plate, are not eligible for entry in the Club's Awards Programs and/or records books, regardless of how well they have been restored to their original condition. This is because the inside spread, which is an integral part of the final score of antlered trophies, cannot be accurately determined if the skull plate is absent or split. If an official measurer suspects that a set of antlers he or she is measuring is either shed antlers or a split skull, he or she should contact the Club's headquarters for instructions on x-raying that trophy. This policy applies to trophy specimens of deer, caribou, moose and elk, as well as pronghorn.

Stags not Eligible for Entry

Stag is a word that is commonly used to refer to a healthy, mature, adult male caribou. Stag is a word that is also used to identify a male animal that is castrated after maturity.

Such stags, which occasionally occur in the wild in the antlered categories, are not eligible for entry in the Boone and Crockett Club's Awards Programs and/or records books because their antlers continuously grow, never lose their velvet and are never shed.

Subsistence Licenses
In general, trophies taken with a subsistence license/permit are acceptable for entry in the Awards Programs and listing in the Club's records books so long as they meet all the Club's entry requirements, including all aspects of fair chase.

Three-Antlered Deer
Deer with three (or more) antlers are not eligible for entry in the Club's records archives or for listing in the records books. The Club's scoring system was designed to recognize massiveness and symmetry. Numerous measurements are taken to account for massiveness of a trophy. Symmetry is taken care of by comparing the measurements of one antler with the same measurements on the opposite antler and deducting the differences. The system was not designed to record measurements of a third antler.

This policy applies to a third antler that is completely separated from either of the other antlers with flesh and hide and has its own pedicel and is shed separately from the other two antlers each fall. In some cases the third antler may actually arise from one of the two normal pedicels, but it is shed separately from the other two normal antlers. This policy does not apply to normal points that branch off one of the antlers near the burr. Several of these trophies have been entered in the non-typical categories.

Three-antlered trophies are certainly unique and noteworthy. However, the Records Committee ruled many years ago that such trophies are considered "freaks" and are not eligible for entry in the records program. The fact that a three-antlered deer is not eligible for entry in the records archives does not diminish such a trophy in any way. The scoring system was simply not designed to handle such trophies.

Trophies Taken on Reservations
Trophies taken on tribal/communal lands in line with sound game management practices, taken in full compliance with

tribal/communal laws or regulations regarding such hunting, and with possession of the usual state/provincial hunting license where applicable, and taken in full compliance with the Boone and Crockett Club's rules of Fair Chase, will be fully accepted as entries for both awards and publication in the records books.

Trophies Taken Prior to 1887
Many trophies are not officially measured until several years after they were taken. Essentially, there is no time limit for submitting trophies that exceed the all-time minimum scores for entry in the records books. Trophies taken prior to 1887, the year the Club was founded, are considered on a case-by-case basis. The date they are received, however, determines which Awards Entry Period they are entered in and the minimum scores for entry.

Trophy Rank During an Awards Program
Many people wish to know how well their trophy ranks among those entered during a current three year Awards Program. The Club does not, however, announce the potential rankings of any trophies accepted during an Awards Program until the listings are published in either the all-time or Awards records books.

Velvet Antlers
The Boone and Crockett Club does not accept antlers in "velvet" for entry into the Awards Programs and/or records books unless the velvet is removed before official measurements are made. Remnants of velvet are permissible as long as they do not affect any measurements.

Zoo/Captive Animals
Antlers, horns, skulls and tusks of zoo-raised and/or captive animals are not eligible for entry into the Awards Programs and/or listing in the Club's records books.

MEASURING PROCEDURES
A Comparison of B&C and P&Y Systems

By Randy Byers

Many of you measure for several records-keeping groups including the Pope & Young Club. In the early formative days of the Pope & Young Club, founder Glenn St. Charles (a Boone & Crockett Club member) obtained permission from the Boone and Crockett Club to use their copyrighted system to serve as the basis for the measuring system for the *Bowhunting Big Game Records of North America*. The Pope and Young Club has employed it since. Thus, a caribou scoring 416-2/8 is measured in the same fashion and will have the same score if it is entered in both programs. As Pope & Young Club evolved, however, certain differences in the application of the system also came about. So what are the differences in these two measuring systems?

First, the obvious ones. The Pope & Young Club records only list trophies taken with a bow and arrow which meet the P&Y Club's equipment standards. The Boone and Crockett Club records are open to animals harvested by any legal means, picked up trophies and trophies of unknown origin. Thus, a whitetail taken by a hunter using a crossbow or a compound bow with 75% let off would be eligible for entry in the Boone and Crockett Club program, while not eligible for entry in Pope & Young Club program, assuming that trophy met the minimum score for Boone and Crockett Club entry. This brings us to the next obvious difference. Each organization has established its own minimum scores and reviews and adjusts them independently. For example, the Pope & Young Club's minimum score for typical mule deer is 145; for Boone and Crockett Club, it is 180 for the Awards Book and 190 for the All-time Book.

The Boone and Crockett Club accepts walrus entries while the Pope & Young Club does not. In similar fashion, the Boone and Crockett Club accepts entries for non-typical Sitka blacktail deer while Pope and Young Club does not. The Boone and Crockett Club recently added tule elk from California as a separate, new category for elk. The Records Committee of the Pope & Young Club is currently evaluating whether or not to take similar action but it does not seem likely to occur at this time. All other entry categories are the same in both groups. One other key difference in this area is that the P&Y

Club accepts velvet entries for all antlered categories. These are listed at the end of each category listing and appear in only one record book.

In addition to scores for tule elk (Pope & Young treats them as American elk), there are some differences in the application of the system that may lead to different scores for the same trophy. One occurs on pronghorn. The vast majority of pronghorns have the D-3 circumference measurement taken above the prong. On rare occasion, the location of the D-3 measurement may fall below the swelling of the prong. The Boone and Crockett Club *rule* is that it is permissible to take the D-3 measurement below the prong. The Pope & Young Club *rule* is that in such cases the D-3 measurement is taken immediately above the prong. The primary reason for this difference in *rules* was that some younger, high prong antelope qualify for the lower Pope & Young Club minimums. These younger bucks have less developed prongs and it is not uncommon for the D-3 location to fall below the prong. The P&Y *rule* was implemented to keep these obviously smaller bucks from receiving higher scores than bucks that have more fully developed horns.

Another, and again uncommon, situation where differences may happen is the measurement of deer which have developed a third, separate antler beam. Usually these third beams are short and often unbranched spikes. However, on occasion fully branched beams appear. In the Boone and Crockett Club program, these deer are treated as freaks and, as such, are not eligible for entry. In Pope & Young system, these third beams and any points that project from them are measured as abnormal points and either added to or deducted from the final score depending on whether the buck is entered in the non-typical or typical categories.

While the actual entry procedures in both programs are similar, there are again some differences. Each organization has its own hunter entry affidavit. Thus, an entry of a trophy into both systems would require the hunter to complete two separate entry affidavit statements and two separate hunt information forms. For antlered and horned trophies, the entry photo requirements are the same–one of each side plus one front view and an optional (but desired) photo at the kill site. For the entry of bear and cougar, the Boone and Crockett Club requires one additional photo– one from each side plus a top view and a frontal view. A B&C entry requires a photocopy of the licenses and tag for hunter taken trophies; a P&Y entry does not. Entries into Boone and Crockett Club program must be measured by an official B&C measurer and on a copyrighted B&C Club score form. The Pope and Young Club accepts entries from either P&Y official measurers or B&C official measurers using either the P&Y or B&C copyrighted score forms. Neither Club accepts modified score forms.

Both groups collect entries into recording periods. The 25th Awards Program for the Boone and Crockett Club is currently underway ending on Dec. 31, 2003. Boone and Crockett Club Recording Periods are three years in duration. The Pope & Young Club uses two year Recording Periods. The end of the P&Y's 24th Recording Period will be Dec. 31, 2004.

Clarifications (changes) to the procedures for measuring trophy-class animals typically are reviewed and approved or disapproved by the Records Committees of both organizations. Most differences in procedures between the application of the measuring system by the two groups have been resolved in recent years. Working together, the two organizations have developed the recognized measurement standard by which North American big trophies are evaluated. ∎

A BOONE AND CROCKETT CLUB FIELD GUIDE TO MEASURING AND JUDGING BIG GAME

HUNTER, GUIDE, AND HUNT
Information Form - Front

Records of
North American
Big Game

250 Station Drive
Missoula, MT 59801
(406) 542-1888

BOONE AND CROCKETT CLUB®
HUNTER, GUIDE, AND HUNT INFORMATION SHEET
(TO BE COMPLETED BY HUNTER)

Trophy Category: _____ Score: _____

Hunter's Name: _____

    Mailing Address:_____
                                                           (ZIP/POSTAL CODE)

Guide's Name: _____

    Mailing Address:_____
                                                           (ZIP/POSTAL CODE)

Taxidermist's Name:_____

    Mailing Address:_____
                                                           (ZIP/POSTAL CODE)

Location of Hunt:_____
                    (LOCALITY IN RELATION TO MOUNTAIN, LAKE, TOWN, OR MAP COORDINATES)

_____
(COUNTY)   (STATE/PROVINCE)   (COUNTRY)

Date of Arrival:_____ Date of Departure: _____
                    (MONTH/DAY/YEAR)   (MONTH/DAY/YEAR)

Mode of Transportation: _____ _____
                                      (IN)   (OUT)

Were motor-powered vehicles used?_____ If so, specify type and purpose:_____

_____

                                              ☐ a.m.

Kill date:_____; Time:_____ ☐ p.m.; At a distance of: _____
              (MONTH/DAY/YEAR)   (YARDS)

Gun caliber:_____ Bullet type/weight:_____
                    (OR TYPE AND PULL OF BOW)   (OR BROADHEAD TYPE/ARROW WEIGHT)

Check term(s) best describing weather at the time of kill:

☐ sunny/clear   ☐ Lightly raining   ☐ lightly snowing
☐ moderate overcast   ☐ heavily raining   ☐ heavily snowing
☐ heavy overcast   ☐ wind_____mph   _____ inches of snow on ground

Other Information: _____

_____

_____

_____   _____
(DATE)   (SIGNATURE OF HUNTER)

(PLEASE COMPLETE OTHER SIDE, IF APPLICABLE)

HUNTER, GUIDE, AND HUNT

Information Form - Back

ADDITIONAL INFORMATION REQUEST

In an effort to expand the value of the records data, we desire to obtain age data for all trophies. We also wish to obtain rack weights of unmounted caribou, moose, and elk, and tusk weights for walrus. Adding age data to the other measurements for trophies should help substantiate the contention that most trophy-sized animals are well past prime breeding age. Weights of racks for caribou, moose and elk will aid in correlation of our records keeping with those systems used in Europe for their representatives of these animals. **Please note that this is only a request for information;** lack of this information for your trophy will not affect its entry status.

A. AGE DATA: If your trophy was aged by a wildlife biologist of the state or province you took it in, please attach a copy of the age determination. If age has not been determined, we would appreciate you forwarding the appropriate material indicated below, **if still available.** Should the requested material no longer be available, please indicate this on the line provided below.

      1) An incisor or small cheek tooth for all bears and cats.
      2) Any one of the small teeth for walrus.
      3) One-half of the lower jaw with all teeth intact for all others.

Comments by hunter: _____

_____

_____

_____

B. RACK/TUSK WEIGHTS: The rack and attached skull weight for all **unmounted** caribou, moose, and elk should be taken in pounds and ounces and recorded below. Please use the codes below to indicate the amount of attached skull (circle the one that most closely describes the rack). For walrus tusks, the weight of each loose tusk should be taken, to the nearest ounce. If your rack or tusks are mounted, please check the box to the right. ☐ MOUNTED RACK/TUSKS

RACK WEIGHT: _____   TUSK WEIGHT: _____ _____
               (LBS./OZ.)   (LBS./OZ.)   (LBS./OZ.)

RACK CODE DESCRIPTION	CODE
Rack cut from skull **ABOVE** the eye socket, resulting in a small amount of attached skull.	SMALL
Rack cut from skull **THROUGH** or below the eye socket, resulting in a moderate amount of attached skull.	DEEP
Rack with **INTACT** skull, less lower jaw.	SKULL

MINIMUM ENTRY SCORES
For North American Big Game

CATEGORY	AWARDS	ALL-TIME
black bear	20	21
grizzly bear	23	24
Alaska brown bear	26	28
polar bear*	27	27
jaguar*	14-$^8/_{16}$	14-$^8/_{16}$
cougar	14-$^8/_{16}$	15
Atlantic walrus	95	95
Pacific walrus	100	100
American typical elk	360	375
American non-typical elk	385	385
tule elk	270	285
Roosevelt's elk	275	290
typical mule deer	180	190
non-typical mule deer	215	230
typical Columbia blacktail	125	135
non-typical Columbia blacktail	155	155
typical Sitka blacktail deer	100	108
non-typical Sitka blacktail	118	118
typical whitetail deer	160	170
non-typical whitetail deer	185	195
typical Coues' deer	100	110
non-typical Coues' deer	105	120
Canada moose	185	195
Alaska-Yukon moose	210	224
Wyoming moose	140	155
mountain caribou	360	390
woodland caribou	265	295
barren ground caribou	375	400
Central Canada barren ground caribou	345	360
Quebec-Labrador caribou	365	375
pronghorn	80	82
bison**	115	115
Rocky Mountain goat	47	50
muskox	105	105
bighorn sheep	175	180
desert sheep	165	168
Dall's sheep	160	170
Stone's sheep	165	170

* Must be taken and/or possessed in full compliance with the Marine Mammals Act, Endangered Species Act and/or other federal and state game laws.

** FROM LOWER 48 STATES, ELIGIBLE ONLY IF RECOGNIZED BY STATE AS GAME ANIMAL, WITH HUNTING SEASON AND LICENSE SPECIFIED.

A BOONE AND CROCKETT CLUB FIELD GUIDE TO MEASURING AND JUDGING BIG GAME

QUARTER LOCATIONS
For Horn Circumference Measurements
From 8 to $19^7/_8$

LONGER HORN	1st QTR D-2	2nd QTR D-3	3rd QTR D-4	LONGER HORN	1st QTR D-2	2nd QTR D-3	3rd QTR D-4
8	2	4	6	14	$3^4/_8$	7	$10^4/_8$
$8^1/_8$	$2^1/_{32}$	$4^1/_{16}$	$6^3/_{32}$	$14^1/_8$	$3^{17}/_{32}$	$7^1/_{16}$	$10^{19}/_{32}$
$8^2/_8$	$2^1/_{16}$	$4^1/_8$	$6^3/_{16}$	$14^2/_8$	$3^9/_{16}$	$7^1/_8$	$10^{11}/_{16}$
$8^3/_8$	$2^3/_{32}$	$4^3/_{16}$	$6^9/_{32}$	$14^3/_8$	$3^{19}/_{32}$	$7^3/_{16}$	$10^{25}/_{32}$
$8^4/_8$	$2^1/_8$	$4^2/_8$	$6^3/_8$	$14^4/_8$	$3^5/_8$	$7^2/_8$	$10^7/_8$
$8^5/_8$	$2^5/_{32}$	$4^5/_{16}$	$6^{15}/_{32}$	$14^5/_8$	$3^{21}/_{32}$	$7^5/_{16}$	$10^{31}/_{32}$
$8^6/_8$	$2^3/_{16}$	$4^3/_8$	$6^9/_{16}$	$14^6/_8$	$3^{11}/_{16}$	$7^3/_8$	$11^1/_{16}$
$8^7/_8$	$2^7/_{32}$	$4^7/_{16}$	$6^{21}/_{32}$	$14^7/_8$	$3^{23}/_{32}$	$7^7/_{16}$	$11^5/_{32}$
9	$2^2/_8$	$4^4/_8$	$6^6/_8$	15	$3^6/_8$	$7^4/_8$	$11^2/_8$
$9^1/_8$	$2^9/_{32}$	$4^9/_{16}$	$6^{27}/_{32}$	$15^1/_8$	$3^{25}/_{32}$	$7^9/_{16}$	$11^{11}/_{32}$
$9^2/_8$	$2^5/_{16}$	$4^5/_8$	$6^{15}/_{16}$	$15^2/_8$	$3^{13}/_{16}$	$7^5/_8$	$11^7/_{16}$
$9^3/_8$	$2^{11}/_{32}$	$4^{11}/_{16}$	$7^1/_{32}$	$15^3/_8$	$3^{27}/_{32}$	$7^{11}/_{16}$	$11^{17}/_{32}$
$9^4/_8$	$2^3/_8$	$4^6/_8$	$7^1/_8$	$15^4/_8$	$3^7/_8$	$7^6/_8$	$11^5/_8$
$9^5/_8$	$2^{13}/_{32}$	$4^{13}/_{16}$	$7^7/_{32}$	$15^5/_8$	$3^{29}/_{32}$	$7^{13}/_{16}$	$11^{23}/_{32}$
$9^6/_8$	$2^7/_{16}$	$4^7/_8$	$7^5/_{16}$	$15^6/_8$	$3^{15}/_{16}$	$7^7/_8$	$11^{13}/_{16}$
$9^7/_8$	$2^{15}/_{32}$	$4^{15}/_{16}$	$7^{13}/_{32}$	$15^7/_8$	$3^{31}/_{32}$	$7^{15}/_{16}$	$11^{29}/_{32}$
10	$2^4/_8$	5	$7^4/_8$	16	4	8	12
$10^1/_8$	$2^{17}/_{32}$	$5^1/_{16}$	$7^{19}/_{32}$	$16^1/_8$	$4^1/_{32}$	$8^1/_{16}$	$12^3/_{32}$
$10^2/_8$	$2^9/_{16}$	$5^1/_8$	$7^{11}/_{16}$	$16^2/_8$	$4^1/_{16}$	$8^1/_8$	$12^3/_{16}$
$10^3/_8$	$2^{19}/_{32}$	$5^3/_{16}$	$7^{25}/_{32}$	$16^3/_8$	$4^3/_{32}$	$8^3/_{16}$	$12^9/_{32}$
$10^4/_8$	$2^5/_8$	$5^2/_8$	$7^7/_8$	$16^4/_8$	$4^1/_8$	$8^2/_8$	$12^3/_8$
$10^5/_8$	$2^{21}/_{32}$	$5^5/_{16}$	$7^{31}/_{32}$	$16^5/_8$	$4^5/_{32}$	$8^5/_{16}$	$12^{15}/_{32}$
$10^6/_8$	$2^{11}/_{16}$	$5^3/_8$	$8^1/_{16}$	$16^6/_8$	$4^3/_{16}$	$8^3/_8$	$12^9/_{16}$
$10^7/_8$	$2^{23}/_{32}$	$5^7/_{16}$	$8^5/_{32}$	$16^7/_8$	$4^7/_{32}$	$8^7/_{16}$	$12^{21}/_{32}$
11	$2^6/_8$	$5^4/_8$	$8^2/_8$	17	$4^2/_8$	$8^4/_8$	$12^6/_8$
$11^1/_8$	$2^{25}/_{32}$	$5^9/_{16}$	$8^{11}/_{32}$	$17^1/_8$	$4^9/_{32}$	$8^9/_{16}$	$12^{27}/_{32}$
$11^2/_8$	$2^{13}/_{16}$	$5^5/_8$	$8^7/_{16}$	$17^2/_8$	$4^5/_{16}$	$8^5/_8$	$12^{15}/_{16}$
$11^3/_8$	$2^{27}/_{32}$	$5^{11}/_{16}$	$8^{17}/_{32}$	$17^3/_8$	$4^{11}/_{32}$	$8^{11}/_{16}$	$13^1/_{32}$
$11^4/_8$	$2^7/_8$	$5^6/_8$	$8^5/_8$	$17^4/_8$	$4^3/_8$	$8^6/_8$	$13^1/_8$
$11^5/_8$	$2^{29}/_{32}$	$5^{13}/_{16}$	$8^{23}/_{32}$	$17^5/_8$	$4^{13}/_{32}$	$8^{13}/_{16}$	$13^7/_{32}$
$11^6/_8$	$2^{15}/_{16}$	$5^7/_8$	$8^{13}/_{16}$	$17^6/_8$	$4^7/_{16}$	$8^7/_8$	$13^5/_{16}$
$11^7/_8$	$2^{31}/_{32}$	$5^{15}/_{16}$	$8^{29}/_{32}$	$17^7/_8$	$4^{15}/_{32}$	$8^{15}/_{16}$	$13^{13}/_{32}$
12	3	6	9	18	$4^4/_8$	9	$13^4/_8$
$12^1/_8$	$3^1/_{32}$	$6^1/_{16}$	$9^3/_{32}$	$18^1/_8$	$4^{17}/_{32}$	$9^1/_{16}$	$13^{19}/_{32}$
$12^2/_8$	$3^1/_{16}$	$6^1/_8$	$9^3/_{16}$	$18^2/_8$	$4^9/_{16}$	$9^1/_8$	$13^{11}/_{16}$
$12^3/_8$	$3^3/_{32}$	$6^3/_{16}$	$9^9/_{32}$	$18^3/_8$	$4^{19}/_{32}$	$9^3/_{16}$	$13^{25}/_{32}$
$12^4/_8$	$3^1/_8$	$6^2/_8$	$9^3/_8$	$18^4/_8$	$4^5/_8$	$9^2/_8$	$13^7/_8$
$12^5/_8$	$3^5/_{32}$	$6^5/_{16}$	$9^{15}/_{32}$	$18^5/_8$	$4^{21}/_{32}$	$9^5/_{16}$	$13^{31}/_{32}$
$12^6/_8$	$3^3/_{16}$	$6^3/_8$	$9^9/_{16}$	$18^6/_8$	$4^{11}/_{16}$	$9^3/_8$	$14^1/_{16}$
$12^7/_8$	$3^7/_{32}$	$6^7/_{16}$	$9^{21}/_{32}$	$18^7/_8$	$4^{23}/_{32}$	$9^7/_{16}$	$14^5/_{32}$
13	$3^2/_8$	$6^4/_8$	$9^6/_8$	19	$4^6/_8$	$9^4/_8$	$14^2/_8$
$13^1/_8$	$3^9/_{32}$	$6^9/_{16}$	$9^{27}/_{32}$	$19^1/_8$	$4^{25}/_{32}$	$9^9/_{16}$	$14^{11}/_{32}$
$13^2/_8$	$3^5/_{16}$	$6^5/_8$	$9^{15}/_{16}$	$19^2/_8$	$4^{13}/_{16}$	$9^5/_8$	$14^7/_{16}$
$13^3/_8$	$3^{11}/_{32}$	$6^{11}/_{16}$	$10^1/_{32}$	$19^3/_8$	$4^{27}/_{32}$	$9^{11}/_{16}$	$14^{17}/_{32}$
$13^4/_8$	$3^3/_8$	$6^6/_8$	$10^1/_8$	$19^4/_8$	$4^7/_8$	$9^6/_8$	$14^5/_8$
$13^5/_8$	$3^{13}/_{32}$	$6^{13}/_{16}$	$10^7/_{32}$	$19^5/_8$	$4^{29}/_{32}$	$9^{13}/_{16}$	$14^{23}/_{32}$
$13^6/_8$	$3^7/_{16}$	$6^7/_8$	$10^5/_{16}$	$19^6/_8$	$4^{15}/_{16}$	$9^7/_8$	$14^{13}/_{16}$
$13^7/_8$	$3^{15}/_{32}$	$6^{15}/_{16}$	$10^{13}/_{32}$	$19^7/_8$	$4^{31}/_{32}$	$9^{15}/_{16}$	$14^{29}/_{32}$

QUARTER LOCATIONS
For Horn Circumference Measurements
From 20 to $31^7/_8$

LONGER HORN	1st QTR D-2	2nd QTR D-3	3rd QTR D-4	LONGER HORN	1st QTR D-2	2nd QTR D-3	3rd QTR D-4
20	5	10	15	26	$6^4/_8$	13	$19^4/_8$
$20^1/_8$	$5^1/_{32}$	$10^1/_{16}$	$15^3/_{32}$	$26^1/_8$	$6^{17}/_{32}$	$13^1/_{16}$	$19^{19}/_{32}$
$20^2/_8$	$5^1/_{16}$	$10^1/_8$	$15^3/_{16}$	$26^2/_8$	$6^9/_{16}$	$13^1/_8$	$19^{11}/_{16}$
$20^3/_8$	$5^3/_{32}$	$10^3/_{16}$	$15^9/_{32}$	$26^3/_8$	$6^{19}/_{32}$	$13^3/_{16}$	$19^{25}/_{32}$
$20^4/_8$	$5^1/_8$	$10^2/_8$	$15^3/_8$	$26^4/_8$	$6^5/_8$	$13^2/_8$	$19^7/_8$
$20^5/_8$	$5^5/_{32}$	$10^5/_{16}$	$15^{15}/_{32}$	$26^5/_8$	$6^{21}/_{32}$	$13^5/_{16}$	$19^{31}/_{32}$
$20^6/_8$	$5^3/_{16}$	$10^3/_8$	$15^9/_{16}$	$26^6/_8$	$6^{11}/_{16}$	$13^3/_8$	$20^1/_{16}$
$20^7/_8$	$5^7/_{32}$	$10^7/_{16}$	$15^{21}/_{32}$	$26^7/_8$	$6^{23}/_{32}$	$13^7/_{16}$	$20^5/_{32}$
21	$5^2/_8$	$10^4/_8$	$15^6/_8$	27	$6^6/_8$	$13^4/_8$	$20^2/_8$
$21^1/_8$	$5^9/_{32}$	$10^9/_{16}$	$15^{27}/_{32}$	$27^1/_8$	$6^{25}/_{32}$	$13^9/_{16}$	$20^{11}/_{32}$
$21^2/_8$	$5^5/_{16}$	$10^5/_8$	$15^{15}/_{16}$	$27^2/_8$	$6^{13}/_{16}$	$13^5/_8$	$20^7/_{16}$
$21^3/_8$	$5^{11}/_{32}$	$10^{11}/_{16}$	$16^1/_{32}$	$27^3/_8$	$6^{27}/_{32}$	$13^{11}/_{16}$	$20^{17}/_{32}$
$21^4/_8$	$5^3/_8$	$10^6/_8$	$16^1/_8$	$27^4/_8$	$6^7/_8$	$13^6/_8$	$20^5/_8$
$21^5/_8$	$5^{13}/_{32}$	$10^{13}/_{16}$	$16^7/_{32}$	$27^5/_8$	$6^{29}/_{32}$	$13^{13}/_{16}$	$20^{23}/_{32}$
$21^6/_8$	$5^7/_{16}$	$10^7/_8$	$16^5/_{16}$	$27^6/_8$	$6^{15}/_{16}$	$13^7/_8$	$20^{13}/_{16}$
$21^7/_8$	$5^{15}/_{32}$	$10^{15}/_{16}$	$16^{13}/_{32}$	$27^7/_8$	$6^{31}/_{32}$	$13^{15}/_{16}$	$20^{29}/_{32}$
22	$5^4/_8$	11	$16^4/_8$	28	7	14	21
$22^1/_8$	$5^{17}/_{32}$	$11^1/_{16}$	$16^{19}/_{32}$	$28^1/_8$	$7^1/_{32}$	$14^1/_{16}$	$21^3/_{32}$
$22^2/_8$	$5^9/_{16}$	$11^1/_8$	$16^{11}/_{16}$	$28^2/_8$	$7^1/_{16}$	$14^1/_8$	$21^3/_{16}$
$22^3/_8$	$5^{19}/_{32}$	$11^3/_{16}$	$16^{25}/_{32}$	$28^3/_8$	$7^3/_{32}$	$14^3/_{16}$	$21^9/_{32}$
$22^4/_8$	$5^5/_8$	$11^2/_8$	$16^7/_8$	$28^4/_8$	$7^1/_8$	$14^2/_8$	$21^3/_8$
$22^5/_8$	$5^{21}/_{32}$	$11^5/_{16}$	$16^{31}/_{32}$	$28^5/_8$	$7^5/_{32}$	$14^5/_{16}$	$21^{15}/_{32}$
$22^6/_8$	$5^{11}/_{16}$	$11^3/_8$	$17^1/_{16}$	$28^6/_8$	$7^3/_{16}$	$14^3/_8$	$21^9/_{16}$
$22^7/_8$	$5^{23}/_{32}$	$11^7/_{16}$	$17^5/_{32}$	$28^7/_8$	$7^7/_{32}$	$14^7/_{16}$	$21^{21}/_{32}$
23	$5^6/_8$	$11^4/_8$	$17^2/_8$	29	$7^2/_8$	$14^4/_8$	$21^6/_8$
$23^1/_8$	$5^{25}/_{32}$	$11^9/_{16}$	$17^{11}/_{32}$	$29^1/_8$	$7^9/_{32}$	$14^9/_{16}$	$21^{27}/_{32}$
$23^2/_8$	$5^{13}/_{16}$	$11^5/_8$	$17^7/_{16}$	$29^2/_8$	$7^5/_{16}$	$14^5/_8$	$21^{15}/_{16}$
$23^3/_8$	$5^{27}/_{32}$	$11^{11}/_{16}$	$17^{17}/_{32}$	$29^3/_8$	$7^{11}/_{32}$	$14^{11}/_{16}$	$22^1/_{32}$
$23^4/_8$	$5^7/_8$	$11^6/_8$	$17^5/_8$	$29^4/_8$	$7^3/_8$	$14^6/_8$	$22^1/_8$
$23^5/_8$	$5^{29}/_{32}$	$11^{13}/_{16}$	$17^{23}/_{32}$	$29^5/_8$	$7^{13}/_{32}$	$14^{13}/_{16}$	$22^7/_{32}$
$23^6/_8$	$5^{15}/_{16}$	$11^7/_8$	$17^{13}/_{16}$	$29^6/_8$	$7^7/_{16}$	$14^7/_8$	$22^5/_{16}$
$23^7/_8$	$5^{31}/_{32}$	$11^{15}/_{16}$	$17^{29}/_{32}$	$29^7/_8$	$7^{15}/_{32}$	$14^{15}/_{16}$	$22^{13}/_{32}$
24	6	12	18	30	$7^4/_8$	15	$22^4/_8$
$24^1/_8$	$6^1/_{32}$	$12^1/_{16}$	$18^3/_{32}$	$30^1/_8$	$7^{17}/_{32}$	$15^1/_{16}$	$22^{19}/_{32}$
$24^2/_8$	$6^1/_{16}$	$12^1/_8$	$18^3/_{16}$	$30^2/_8$	$7^9/_{16}$	$15^1/_8$	$22^{11}/_{16}$
$24^3/_8$	$6^3/_{32}$	$12^3/_{16}$	$18^9/_{32}$	$30^3/_8$	$7^{19}/_{32}$	$15^3/_{16}$	$22^{25}/_{32}$
$24^4/_8$	$6^1/_8$	$12^2/_8$	$18^3/_8$	$30^4/_8$	$7^5/_8$	$15^2/_8$	$22^7/_8$
$24^5/_8$	$6^5/_{32}$	$12^5/_{16}$	$18^{15}/_{32}$	$30^5/_8$	$7^{21}/_{32}$	$15^5/_{16}$	$22^{31}/_{32}$
$24^6/_8$	$6^3/_{16}$	$12^3/_8$	$18^9/_{16}$	$30^6/_8$	$7^{11}/_{16}$	$15^3/_8$	$23^1/_{16}$
$24^7/_8$	$6^7/_{32}$	$12^7/_{16}$	$18^{21}/_{32}$	$30^7/_8$	$7^{23}/_{32}$	$15^7/_{16}$	$23^5/_{32}$
25	$6^2/_8$	$12^4/_8$	$18^6/_8$	31	$7^6/_8$	$15^4/_8$	$23^2/_8$
$25^1/_8$	$6^9/_{32}$	$12^9/_{16}$	$18^{27}/_{32}$	$31^1/_8$	$7^{25}/_{32}$	$15^9/_{16}$	$23^{11}/_{32}$
$25^2/_8$	$6^5/_{16}$	$12^5/_8$	$18^{15}/_{16}$	$31^2/_8$	$7^{13}/_{16}$	$15^5/_8$	$23^7/_{16}$
$25^3/_8$	$6^{11}/_{32}$	$12^{11}/_{16}$	$19^1/_{32}$	$31^3/_8$	$7^{27}/_{32}$	$15^{11}/_{16}$	$23^{17}/_{32}$
$25^4/_8$	$6^3/_8$	$12^6/_8$	$19^1/_8$	$31^4/_8$	$7^7/_8$	$15^6/_8$	$23^5/_8$
$25^5/_8$	$6^{13}/_{32}$	$12^{13}/_{16}$	$19^7/_{32}$	$31^5/_8$	$7^{29}/_{32}$	$15^{13}/_{16}$	$23^{23}/_{32}$
$25^6/_8$	$6^7/_{16}$	$12^7/_8$	$19^5/_{16}$	$31^6/_8$	$7^{15}/_{16}$	$15^7/_8$	$23^{13}/_{16}$
$25^7/_8$	$6^{15}/_{32}$	$12^{15}/_{16}$	$19^{13}/_{32}$	$31^7/_8$	$7^{31}/_{32}$	$15^{15}/_{16}$	$23^{29}/_{32}$

QUARTER LOCATIONS
For Horn Circumference Measurements
From 32 to 43$^7/_8$

LONGER HORN	1st QTR D-2	2nd QTR D-3	3rd QTR D-4	LONGER HORN	1st QTR D-2	2nd QTR D-3	3rd QTR D-4
32	8	16	24	38	9 4/8	19	28 4/8
32 1/8	8 1/32	16 1/16	24 3/32	38 1/8	9 17/32	19 1/16	28 19/32
32 2/8	8 1/16	16 1/8	24 3/16	38 2/8	9 9/16	19 1/8	28 11/16
32 3/8	8 3/32	16 3/16	24 9/32	38 3/8	9 19/32	19 3/16	28 25/32
32 4/8	8 1/8	16 2/8	24 3/8	38 4/8	9 5/8	19 2/8	28 7/8
32 5/8	8 5/32	16 5/16	24 15/32	38 5/8	9 21/32	19 5/16	28 31/32
32 6/8	8 3/16	16 3/8	24 9/16	38 6/8	9 11/16	19 3/8	29 1/16
32 7/8	8 7/32	16 7/16	24 21/32	38 7/8	9 23/32	19 7/16	29 5/32
33	8 2/8	16 4/8	24 6/8	39	9 6/8	19 4/8	29 2/8
33 1/8	8 9/32	16 9/16	24 27/32	39 1/8	9 25/32	19 9/16	29 11/32
33 2/8	8 5/16	16 5/8	24 15/16	39 2/8	9 13/16	19 5/8	29 7/16
33 3/8	8 11/32	16 11/16	25 1/32	39 3/8	9 27/32	19 11/16	29 17/32
33 4/8	8 3/8	16 6/8	25 1/8	39 4/8	9 7/8	19 6/8	29 5/8
33 5/8	8 13/32	16 13/16	25 7/32	39 5/8	9 29/32	19 13/16	29 23/32
33 6/8	8 7/16	16 7/8	25 5/16	39 6/8	9 15/16	19 7/8	29 13/16
33 7/8	8 15/32	16 15/16	25 13/32	39 7/8	9 31/32	19 15/16	29 29/32
34	8 4/8	17	25 4/8	40	10	20	30
34 1/8	8 17/32	17 1/16	25 19/32	40 1/8	10 1/32	20 1/16	30 3/32
34 2/8	8 9/16	17 1/8	25 11/16	40 2/8	10 1/16	20 1/8	30 3/16
34 3/8	8 19/32	17 3/16	25 25/32	40 3/8	10 3/32	20 3/16	30 9/32
34 4/8	8 5/8	17 2/8	25 7/8	40 4/8	10 1/8	20 2/8	30 3/8
34 5/8	8 21/32	17 5/16	25 31/32	40 5/8	10 5/32	20 5/16	30 15/32
34 6/8	8 11/16	17 3/8	26 1/16	40 6/8	10 3/16	20 3/8	30 9/16
34 7/8	8 23/32	17 7/16	26 5/32	40 7/8	10 7/32	20 7/16	30 21/32
35	8 6/8	17 4/8	26 2/8	41	10 2/8	20 4/8	30 6/8
35 1/8	8 25/32	17 9/16	26 11/32	41 1/8	10 9/32	20 9/16	30 27/32
35 2/8	8 13/16	17 5/8	26 7/16	41 2/8	10 5/16	20 5/8	30 15/16
35 3/8	8 27/32	17 11/16	26 17/32	41 3/8	10 11/32	20 11/16	31 1/32
35 4/8	8 7/8	17 6/8	26 5/8	41 4/8	10 3/8	20 6/8	31 1/8
35 5/8	8 29/32	17 13/16	26 23/32	41 5/8	10 13/32	20 13/16	31 7/32
35 6/8	8 15/16	17 7/8	26 13/16	41 6/8	10 7/16	20 7/8	31 5/16
35 7/8	8 31/32	17 15/16	26 29/32	41 7/8	10 15/32	20 15/16	31 13/32
36	9	18	27	42	10 4/8	21	31 4/8
36 1/8	9 1/32	18 1/16	27 3/32	42 1/8	10 17/32	21 1/16	31 19/32
36 2/8	9 1/16	18 1/8	27 3/16	42 2/8	10 9/16	21 1/8	31 11/16
36 3/8	9 3/32	18 3/16	27 9/32	42 3/8	10 19/32	21 3/16	31 25/32
36 4/8	9 1/8	18 2/8	27 3/8	42 4/8	10 5/8	21 2/8	31 7/8
36 5/8	9 5/32	18 5/16	27 15/32	42 5/8	10 21/32	21 5/16	31 31/32
36 6/8	9 3/16	18 3/8	27 9/16	42 6/8	10 11/16	21 3/8	32 1/16
36 7/8	9 7/32	18 7/16	27 21/32	42 7/8	10 23/32	21 7/16	32 5/32
37	9 2/8	18 4/8	27 6/8	43	10 6/8	21 4/8	32 2/8
37 1/8	9 9/32	18 9/16	27 27/32	43 1/8	10 25/32	21 9/16	32 11/32
37 2/8	9 5/16	18 5/8	27 15/16	43 2/8	10 13/16	21 5/8	32 7/16
37 3/8	9 11/32	18 11/16	28 1/32	43 3/8	10 27/32	21 11/16	32 17/32
37 4/8	9 3/8	18 6/8	28 1/8	43 4/8	10 7/8	21 6/8	32 5/8
37 5/8	9 13/32	18 13/16	28 7/32	43 5/8	10 29/32	21 13/16	32 23/32
37 6/8	9 7/16	18 7/8	28 5/16	43 6/8	10 15/16	21 7/8	32 13/16
37 7/8	9 15/32	18 15/16	28 13/32	43 7/8	10 31/32	21 15/16	32 29/32

QUARTER LOCATIONS
For Horn Circumference Measurements
From 44 to 50$^7/_8$

LONGER HORN	1st QTR D-2	2nd QTR D-3	3rd QTR D-4	LONGER HORN	1st QTR D-2	2nd QTR D-3	3rd QTR D-4
44	11	22	33	50	12$^4/_8$	25	37$^4/_8$
44$^1/_8$	11$^1/_{32}$	22$^1/_{16}$	33$^3/_{32}$	50$^1/_8$	12$^{17}/_{32}$	25$^1/_{16}$	37$^{19}/_{32}$
44$^2/_8$	11$^1/_{16}$	22$^1/_8$	33$^3/_{16}$	50$^2/_8$	12$^9/_{16}$	25$^1/_8$	37$^{11}/_{16}$
44$^3/_8$	11$^3/_{32}$	22$^3/_{16}$	33$^9/_{32}$	50$^3/_8$	12$^{19}/_{32}$	25$^3/_{16}$	37$^{25}/_{32}$
44$^4/_8$	11$^1/_8$	22$^2/_8$	33$^3/_8$	50$^4/_8$	12$^5/_8$	25$^2/_8$	37$^7/_8$
44$^5/_8$	11$^5/_{32}$	22$^5/_{16}$	33$^{15}/_{32}$	50$^5/_8$	12$^{21}/_{32}$	25$^5/_{16}$	37$^{31}/_{32}$
44$^6/_8$	11$^3/_{16}$	22$^3/_8$	33$^9/_{16}$	50$^6/_8$	12$^{11}/_{16}$	25$^3/_8$	38$^1/_{16}$
44$^7/_8$	11$^7/_{32}$	22$^7/_{16}$	33$^{21}/_{32}$	50$^7/_8$	12$^{23}/_{32}$	25$^7/_{16}$	38$^5/_{32}$
45	11$^2/_8$	22$^4/_8$	33$^6/_8$				
45$^1/_8$	11$^9/_{32}$	22$^9/_{16}$	33$^{27}/_{32}$				
45$^2/_8$	11$^5/_{16}$	22$^5/_8$	33$^{15}/_{16}$				
45$^3/_8$	11$^{11}/_{32}$	22$^{11}/_{16}$	34$^1/_{32}$				
45$^4/_8$	11$^3/_8$	22$^6/_8$	34$^1/_8$				
45$^5/_8$	11$^{13}/_{32}$	22$^{13}/_{16}$	34$^7/_{32}$				
45$^6/_8$	11$^7/_{16}$	22$^7/_8$	34$^5/_{16}$				
45$^7/_8$	11$^{15}/_{32}$	22$^{15}/_{16}$	34$^{13}/_{32}$				
46	11$^4/_8$	23	34$^4/_8$				
46$^1/_8$	11$^{17}/_{32}$	23$^1/_{16}$	34$^{19}/_{32}$				
46$^2/_8$	11$^9/_{16}$	23$^1/_8$	34$^{11}/_{16}$				
46$^3/_8$	11$^{19}/_{32}$	23$^3/_{16}$	34$^{25}/_{32}$				
46$^4/_8$	11$^5/_8$	23$^2/_8$	34$^7/_8$				
46$^5/_8$	11$^{21}/_{32}$	23$^5/_{16}$	34$^{31}/_{32}$				
46$^6/_8$	11$^{11}/_{16}$	23$^3/_8$	35$^1/_{16}$				
46$^7/_8$	11$^{23}/_{32}$	23$^7/_{16}$	35$^5/_{32}$				
47	11$^6/_8$	23$^4/_8$	35$^2/_8$				
47$^1/_8$	11$^{25}/_{32}$	23$^9/_{16}$	35$^{11}/_{32}$				
47$^2/_8$	11$^{13}/_{16}$	23$^5/_8$	35$^7/_{16}$				
47$^3/_8$	11$^{27}/_{32}$	23$^{11}/_{16}$	35$^{17}/_{32}$				
47$^4/_8$	11$^7/_8$	23$^6/_8$	35$^5/_8$				
47$^5/_8$	11$^{29}/_{32}$	23$^{13}/_{16}$	35$^{23}/_{32}$				
47$^6/_8$	11$^{15}/_{16}$	23$^7/_8$	35$^{13}/_{16}$				
47$^7/_8$	11$^{31}/_{32}$	23$^{15}/_{16}$	35$^{29}/_{32}$				
48	12	24	36				
48$^1/_8$	12$^1/_{32}$	24$^1/_{16}$	36$^3/_{32}$				
48$^2/_8$	12$^1/_{16}$	24$^1/_8$	36$^3/_{16}$				
48$^3/_8$	12$^3/_{32}$	24$^3/_{16}$	36$^9/_{32}$				
48$^4/_8$	12$^1/_8$	24$^2/_8$	36$^3/_8$				
48$^5/_8$	12$^5/_{32}$	24$^5/_{16}$	36$^{15}/_{32}$				
48$^6/_8$	12$^3/_{16}$	24$^3/_8$	36$^9/_{16}$				
48$^7/_8$	12$^7/_{32}$	24$^7/_{16}$	36$^{21}/_{32}$				
49	12$^2/_8$	24$^4/_8$	36$^6/_8$				
49$^1/_8$	12$^9/_{32}$	24$^9/_{16}$	36$^{27}/_{32}$				
49$^2/_8$	12$^5/_{16}$	24$^5/_8$	36$^{15}/_{16}$				
49$^3/_8$	12$^{11}/_{32}$	24$^{11}/_{16}$	37$^1/_{32}$				
49$^4/_8$	12$^3/_8$	24$^6/_8$	37$^1/_8$				
49$^5/_8$	12$^{13}/_{32}$	24$^{13}/_{16}$	37$^7/_{32}$				
49$^6/_8$	12$^7/_{16}$	24$^7/_8$	37$^5/_{16}$				
49$^7/_8$	12$^{15}/_{32}$	24$^{15}/_{16}$	37$^{13}/_{32}$				

B&C ASSOCIATES PROGRAM
Go the Distance... Join B&C Today!

Since you're obviously committed to learning more about scoring and sharpening your field judging skills we would like to ask you to go one step further – join the Boone and Crockett Club's Associates program.

We could write a separate book on the over 100-year history of the Boone and Crockett Club's efforts to promote hunting, fair chase ethics, conservation, and sound wildlife and habitat management backed by science. The truth is, there is a lot more to B&C than scoring and records books and if we are to continue to preserve our hunting heritage, we need your support.

You'll receive the satisfaction of belonging to the one organization of hunters who have done whatever is necessary, plus...

Fair Chase magazine – the official publication of the Boone and Crockett Club. Published quarterly, *Fair Chase* is an immeasurable source of hunting, conservation, and ethical issues concerning today's sportsmen. Each issue contains the latest record book entries, hunting stories written by Associates, trophy owners and today's most respected outdoor writers, as well as current information on what is happening in big game management, hunting, and conservation.

Discounts – A 20 percent discount on Boone and Crockett Club books, Boone and Crockett sportswear, plus other unique Club merchandise.

Priority – Associates are notified of the location and dates for the triennial Boone and Crockett Club Big Game Awards Trophy Display and Awards Banquet and other special events.

Exclusive Web Access – Associates receive exclusive access to the Associate's On-Line Community. Here you can learn everything you need to know to research and plan your next big game hunting adventure

Recognition Items – Associates receive a wallet-size identification card, a full-color certificate suitable for framing, and a B&C window decal.

It's Easy
You can join on-line at www.booneandcrockettclub.com, send check or money order to: Boone and Crockett Club, 250 Station Drive, Missoula, MT 59801, or call toll free (888)840-4868 to order with credit card. Your membership is only $25 for one year, $45 for two years, or $100 for five years.

B&C LIFETIME ASSOCIATE

In 1994, Boone and Crockett began a Lifetime Associates Program for those individuals who wanted to increase their support of the Club. Lifetime Associates receive the following benefits: A lifetime subscription to Fair Chase magazine, a long-sleeve shooting shirt exclusively embroidered for Lifetime Associates, and a brown cap with leather bill, Lifetime Associates plaque, special invitations to Club events, wallet card and window decal, 20 percent discount on merchandise, and a significant tax deduction of $850 (the Boone and Crockett Club is a 501(c)(3) organization).

The cost for the Lifetime Associates program is $1,000. We offer the following payment plans: 1) One payment, check or credit card for $1,000; 2) Four quarterly charges to your credit card of $250.00; or 3) Twelve monthly charges to your credit card of $83.34.

To sign up for our Lifetime Associates Program call toll-free (888)840-4868.

FIELD EVALUATION OF TROPHIES
Acknowledgments

The field judging material in this book is a combination of original thoughts, based upon years afield, and those generally accepted criteria for judging trophies under field conditions. In no way is this the only means by which to judge trophies, nor are these necessarily the final words upon the subject. However, it is unlikely that any better cross-section of experts on trophy evaluation has ever been assembled than those contributing to this section. The contributors have spent a collective total of several centuries afield after trophy game.

John H. Batten – the late dean of sheep hunters today, authored several major trophy hunting books including *The Best of Sheep Hunting* and *Skyline Pursuits*. He was a long-time member of the Records of North American Big Game Committee, and a long-time Official Measurer and Final Awards Judge.

Craig Boddington – a professional member and long-time editorial contributor to the Boone and Crockett Club, Boddington has written numerous hunting and gun books. He has served in the U.S. Marine Corps for nearly 30 years.

Eldon "Buck" Buckner – Former Forest Service wildlife staff, pronghorn hunter, guide, outdoor writer, shooting instructor, and Official Measurer for over 35 years, and current chairman of the Club's Records of North American Big Game Committee.

Lynn Castle – well-known Alaska guide and writer, with a number of his own trophies placed in the records books, as well as many for clients.

Frank Cook – the late hunter for the all-time number two Dall's sheep and a long-time member of the Records of North American Big Game Committee. He was a veteran Official Measurer and Final Awards Judge many times.

Jay Lesser – Custom gun builder. Well-known Wyoming outfitter. Board member of the Wyoming Outfitters and Guides Association for three terms. Outdoor writer for several large gun and hunting publications.

Wm. Harold Nesbitt – Former Executive Director of the Boone and Crockett Club, Editor and/or Co-editor of several records book(s), an Official Measurer, and former Secretary of the Records of North American Big Game Committee.

Glenn St. Charles – Founder and Senior Member of the Pope and Young Club, a long-time Official Measurer and Final Awards Judge, and member of the Records of North American Big Game Committee.

Jim Shockey – Well-known Canadian outfitter for huge black bears and whitetails. Outdoor writer and the first person to take the "Ultimate Slam," 30 North American animals with a muzzleloader, all qualifying for the muzzleloader record book.

Dr. Robert E. Speegle – renowned world-wide hunter, Weatherby Award Winner, and former member of the Records of North American Big Game Committee.

Dr. Philip L. Wright former Chairman of the Records of North American Big Game Committee, well-known mammalogist, co-editor for the all-time records book, and frequent Final Awards Judge. The late Dr. Wright was one of the original Official Measurers appointed by the Club when the current records-keeping system was adopted in 1950.

With each category, photos of both the current World's Record and a minimum score specimen have been included. With this visual representation of both the greatest expression of trophy character known, as well as the minimum expression required for entry in the Club's Awards Program, it is anticipated that the reader will have a much better idea of what to look for in a trophy animal. ∎

FIELD NOTES

FIELD NOTES

A BOONE AND CROCKETT CLUB FIELD GUIDE TO MEASURING AND JUDGING BIG GAME

FIELD NOTES

FIELD NOTES

FIELD NOTES

FIELD NOTES

FIELD NOTES

FIELD NOTES

FIELD NOTES

FIELD NOTES

FIELD NOTES

FIELD NOTES

FIELD NOTES

FIELD NOTES

FIELD NOTES

FIELD NOTES

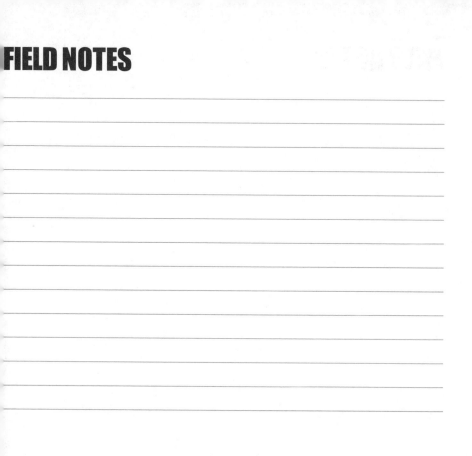

FIELD NOTES

FIELD NOTES

FIELD NOTES

FIELD NOTES

FIELD NOTES

FIELD NOTES

A BOONE AND CROCKETT CLUB FIELD GUIDE TO MEASURING AND JUDGING BIG GAME

FIELD NOTES

Acknowledgments for
A Boone and Crockett Club Field Guide to Measuring and Judging Big Game

Chapters and data compiled with the able assistance of:
Boone and Crockett Club Records Committee, 1997

C. Randall Byers, Chair	John P. Poston
George A. Bettas	Joe W. Bishop
Eldon L. Buckner	Frank Cook
John O. Cook III	H. Hudson DeCray
Robert H. Hanson	Frederick J. King
Legrand C. Kirby III	William C. MacCarty III
Thomas A. McIntyre	William E. Moss
Jack S. Parker	Daniel A. Pedrotti
Arthur C. Popham, Jr.	Richard D. Reeve
Jack Reneau	Norman C. Roettger
Glenn A. St. Charles	Paul D. Webster
Walter H. White	Philip L. Wright, Ph.D.

Field Judging Comparisons:
Keith Balfourd, Marketing Coordinator and Official Measurer

Design and Production:
Julie T. Houk, Director of Publications

Photo Contributors:
Mike Duplan – Mule deer on cover
Michael Francis – Black bear for field judging
Dick Hancock – Black bear inset for field judging
Brad Garfield – Grizzly bear for field judging
Milo Burcham – Grizzly bear inset for field judging

Pen and ink illustrations by:
Larry Jensen – Lewistown, Montana
DeWayne Williams – Missoula, Montana

Printed by:
Walsworth Publishing Company
Marceline, Missouri